NEW STUDIES

With the clouds of heaven

Titles in this series:

An index of Scripture references for all the volumes may be found at
http://www.thegospelcoalition.org/resources/nsbt

NEW STUDIES IN BIBLICAL THEOLOGY 32

Series editor: D. A. Carson

With the clouds of heaven

THE BOOK OF DANIEL IN BIBLICAL THEOLOGY

James M. Hamilton Jr.

APOLLOS

INTERVARSITY PRESS
DOWNERS GROVE, ILLINOIS 60515

APOLLOS
An imprint of Inter-Varsity Press, England
Norton Street
Nottingham NG7 3HR, England
ivpbooks.com
ivp@ivpbooks.com

InterVarsity Press, USA
P.O. Box 1400
Downers Grove, IL 60515-1426, USA
ivpress.com
email@ivpress.com

© James M. Hamilton Jr. 2014

James M. Hamilton Jr. has asserted his right under the Copyright, Designs and Patents Act, 1988, to be identified as Author of this work.

InterVarsity Press® is the book-publishing division of InterVarsity Christian Fellowship/USA®, a movement of students and faculty active on campus at hundreds of universities, colleges, and schools of nursing in the United States of America, and a member movement of the International Fellowship of Evangelical Students. For information about local and regional activities, visit intervarsity.org.

Inter-Varsity Press, England, is closely linked with the Universities and Colleges Christian Fellowship, a student movement connecting Christian Unions throughout Great Britain, and a member movement of the International Fellowship of Evangelical Students. Website: www.uccf.org.uk

Unless stated otherwise, all Scripture quotations are from The Holy Bible, English Standard Version, published by HarperCollins Publishers © 2001 by Crossway Bibles, a division of Good News Publishers. Used by permission. All rights reserved.

Scripture quotations marked TNIV are taken from the HOLY BIBLE, TODAY'S NEW INTERNATIONAL VERSION® TNIV® Copyright © 2001, 2005 by Biblica www.biblica.com, and used by permission.

First published 2014.

Set in Monotype Times New Roman

Typeset in Great Britain by CRB Associates, Lincolnshire

USA ISBN 978-0-8308-2633-9
UK ISBN 978-1-78359-137-4

Printed in the United States of America ♾

InterVarsity Press is committed to ecological stewardship and to the conservation of natural resources in all our operations. This book was printed using sustainably sourced paper.

British Library Cataloguing in Publication Data
A catalogue record for this book is available from the British Library.

Library of Congress Cataloging-in-Publication Data
A catalog record for this book is available from the Library of Congress. Library of Congress Control Number: 2014951767

P	21	20	19	18	17	16	15	14	13	12	11	10
Y	34	33	32	31	30	29	28	27	26	25	24	

For
Tom Schreiner

teacher, mentor,
pastor, friend

Contents

CONTENTS

Tables

Series preface

New Studies in Biblical Theology is a series of monographs that address key issues in the discipline of biblical theology. Contributions to the series focus on one or more of three areas: (1) the nature and status of biblical theology, including its relations with other disciplines (e.g. historical theology, exegesis, systematic theology, historical criticism, narrative theology); (2) the articulation and exposition of the structure of thought of a particular biblical writer or corpus; and (3) the delineation of a biblical theme across all or part of the biblical corpora.

Above all, these monographs are creative attempts to help thinking Christians understand their Bibles better. The series aims simultaneously to instruct and to edify, to interact with the current literature, and to point the way ahead. In God's universe, mind and heart should not be divorced: in this series we will try not to separate what God has joined together. While the notes interact with the best of scholarly literature, the text is uncluttered with untransliterated Greek and Hebrew, and tries to avoid too much technical jargon. The volumes are written within the framework of confessional evangelicalism, but there is always an attempt at thoughtful engagement with the sweep of the relevant literature.

Volumes in this series have often used the expression 'biblical theology' in several ways. For example, it may refer to the carefully worked out theology of a particular biblical book or corpus (think of the volume by Gary Millar on Deuteronomy in this series); it may refer to a theme or trajectory carefully traced through all the Bible (think of the volume by G. K. Beale on the temple). Focusing on the book of Daniel, Dr Hamilton melds both of these usages. He studies Daniel while maintaining two perspectives: he wants to know what antecedent biblical sources have been taken up by Daniel as he writes his book (which of course raises a nest of complicated questions about the dating of sources), and he traces out how Daniel has been used by later biblical writers. Doubtless some will disagree with Dr Hamilton over this or that detail, for the book is rich in details, but most readers will also find it wonderfully stimulating. In addition to providing his readers with this biblical theology of Daniel, with its thought-provoking trajectories running both backward and forward, Dr Hamilton's work is also an implicit call to engage in similar work on other biblical books, in self-conscious determination to reverse two centuries or more of atomistic approaches to Scripture.

D. A. Carson
Trinity Evangelical Divinity School

Author's preface

I don't deserve to read the Bible, much less write about it. What a privilege to have God reveal himself to us in his word. What a great God, keeping covenant and steadfast love, forgiving iniquity, transgression and sin, and everywhere manifesting his power and love. The voice of the Lord breaks the cedars, and yet he also speaks so tenderly that the bruised reed doesn't break. I join the ranks of the heavenly hosts, the saints across space and time, and everything in this cosmic temple to ascribe to the Lord the glory due his name. Would that I could do so in a way worthy of him. I thank God the Father through Christ the Son by the power of the Spirit for his merciful salvation, full and complete revelation, and gracious provision.

I also gladly recite my gratitude for the support of my family as I worked on this project. My sweet wife is a wonder beyond words. She manages her household well. Let me rise to bless her. What a joy to write at home, in the context of our family. I praise God for the way my wife and our children provided blessed distractions from this Ecclesiastes 12:12 labour. Unexpected refreshment came from unplanned breaks (some would call them 'interruptions'!) that took the form of opportunities to converse with sweet Jill, to read books to our two-year-old daughter, to throw the football to the boys as they jumped on the trampoline, or to hold the newborn. The support of our parents, too, has been a strengthening encouragement. God has been unaccountably merciful to us.

My fellow elders at Kenwood Baptist Church prayed for me and helped me finish by taking on more of the preaching load as the deadline approached. Thanks to Denny Burk, Owen Strachan, John Watson, Matt Damico and Mike Frantz, and special thanks to Randall Breland and Mike Thompson for the ways they serve and lead at Kenwood. I must also thank the body of believers gathered weekly at the table of the Lord to be sustained by bread and cup, word and worship. Hallelujah! So many servants. So much Christlikeness. Such a joy to know the unity of the Spirit in the bond of peace. Praise God.

I am also glad to thank my PhD students for their help on this project: Mitch Chase, David 'Gunner' Gundersen and Colin Smothers read the book and offered helpful feedback, and they were joined by Casey Croy, Matt Emadi, Sam Emadi, Wyatt Graham, Nick Moore, Johnson Pang and Dieudonne Tamfu, all of whom helped to compile author and Scripture indexes. We at Southern are thankful to be led by Dr Albert Mohler, whose conviction is as strong as his breadth of knowledge is inspiring. I am grateful that Dan Dumas makes sure the lights come on when I show up to teach, that Randy Stinson shepherds all things academic like a wise father and that Greg Wills sets such an example as a scholar-teacher. The privilege to stand with my colleagues in this faculty is past my power to tell, and I am thankful for each of them.

I first preached through Daniel at Baptist Church of the Redeemer in Houston, Texas, in the spring and summer of 2008. I then joined the faculty of Southern Seminary, and, receiving the opportunity to lead a PhD seminar in the autumn of 2009, chose to focus that course on Daniel. Unable to find a suitable evangelical, biblical-theological study of Daniel to assign for that course, I proposed this book to D. A. Carson, and I thank him for accepting the proposal and welcoming this volume into the New Studies in Biblical Theology, a series I have long admired.

The Lord's kindnesses to me are more numerous than I can tell, as are the people whom I would like to thank. I will limit this litany of gratitude, however, to one man more: I dedicate this book to my PhD mentor at the Southern Baptist Theological Seminary, Dr Thomas R. Schreiner. The combination of competent scholarship and commitment to the glory of God that I saw in Dr Schreiner's writings was part of what first attracted me to Southern, and that only got stronger when I met him in person. I am thankful that he took me under his wing as a student. He is a scholar who serves the Lord Jesus and his church, who preaches like a believer, and lives like one too. His wisdom and example, counsel and friendship have meant so much to me. Recently my wife and I were discussing a knotty problem and I told her I wanted to seek counsel on it. She knew at once that I planned to talk to Tom. The dedication of this book to you, Tom, is an attempt to communicate my gratitude, esteem and affection. Thank you for joyfully following Christ. What a blessing to follow you as you follow him.

James M. Hamilton Jr.
1 January 2014

Abbreviations

1QS	*Community Rule/Manual of Discipline* (Dead Sea Scrolls)
4Q397 (4QMMT^d)	*4QHalakhic Letter*^d (Dead Sea Scrolls)
4QDan^c	*Daniel Manuscript C* (Dead Sea Scrolls)
4QDan^e	*Daniel Manuscript E* (Dead Sea Scrolls)
4 QMMT	*Halakhic Letter / Sectarian Manifesto* (Dead Sea Scrolls)
AB	Anchor Bible
AGAJU	Arbeiten zur Geschichte des antiken Judentums und des Urchristentums
AOTC	Apollos Old Testament Commentary
Aram.	Aramaic
Aram	*Aramaic Studies*
AV	Authorized (King James) Version
BBR	*Bulletin for Biblical Research*
BDAG	W. Bauer, F. W. Danker, W. F. Arndt and W. F. Gingrich, *A Greek-English Lexicon of the New Testament and Other Early Christian Literature*, 3rd ed., Chicago: University of Chicago Press, 2000
BETL	Bibliotheca ephemeridum theologicarum lovaniensium
Bib	*Biblica*
BSac	*Bibliotheca sacra*
CC	Concordia Commentary
CEB	Common English Bible
Col.	column
ConBOT	Coniectanea biblica
CRINT	Compendia rerum iudaicarum ad Novum Testamentum
CSB	Christian Standard Bible
ESV	English Standard Version
ET	English translation

Frags.	fragments
HCSB	Holman Christian Standard Bible
HDR	Harvard Dissertations in Religion
Hebr.	Hebrew
HUCA	*Hebrew Union College Annual*
JATS	*Journal of the Adventist Theological Society*
JDFM	*Journal of Discipleship and Family Ministry*
JPS	Jewish Publication Society translation
JSNTSup	Journal for the Study of the New Testament, Supplement Series
JTI	*Journal of Theological Interpretation*
LCL	Loeb Classical Library
masc.	masculine
LXX	Septuagint
MT	Masoretic Text
NA27	Nestle-Aland *Novum Testamentum Graece*, ed. Barbara and Kurt Aland, Johannes Karavidopoulos, Carlo M. Martini and Bruce M. Metzger, 27th rev. ed., Stuttgart: Deutsche Bibelgesellschaft, 1993
NA28	Nestle-Aland *Novum Testamentum Graece*, ed. Barbara and Kurt Aland, Johannes Karavidopoulos, Carlo M. Martini and Bruce M. Metzger, 28th rev. ed., Stuttgart: Deutsche Bibelgesellschaft, 2012
NACSBT	NAC Studies in Bible and Theology
NASB	New American Standard Bible
NET	New English Translation
NETS	New English Translation of the Septuagint
NIGTC	New International Greek Testament Commentary
NIV	New International Version
NKJV	New King James Version
NLT	New Living Translation
NSBT	New Studies in Biblical Theology
NT	New Testament
NTT	New Testament Theology
OG	Old Greek
OT	Old Testament
pl.	plural
RevQ	*Revue de Qumran*

RSV	Revised Standard Version
SBJT	*Southern Baptist Journal of Theology*
SCHT	Studies in Christian History and Thought
sing.	singular
s.v.	(sub verbo) under the heading or word given
Th	Theodotion
TNIV	Today's New International Version
TOTC	Tyndale Old Testament Commentaries
tr.	translation, translated by
TynB	*Tyndale Bulletin*
VTSup	Supplements to Vetus Testamentum
WBC	Word Biblical Commentary
WUNT	Wissenschaftliche Untersuchungen zum Neuen Testament

Chapter One

Preliminaries

If you're wondering what kind of book this will be, this opening chapter sets forth the parameters within which I will pursue the contribution the book of Daniel makes to biblical theology. I am here attempting an evangelical and canonical biblical theology of Daniel. This introductory chapter seeks to define biblical theology, provide an orientation to the canonical framework in which I will work and draw out the implications of the word 'evangelical', implications that impinge upon how we think about the historicity of the events described in the book of Daniel, the date of its composition and who wrote it. This chapter will provide neither an exhaustive treatment nor the final word on these issues; it will set forth my perspective on them. The discussion that follows addresses each word in the phrase 'evangelical and canonical biblical theology of Daniel'. This chapter on preliminaries will end with a preview of those to follow.

Biblical theology

Biblical theology is the attempt to understand and embrace the interpretative perspective of the biblical authors. Rather than repeat what I have tried to say in other places,[1] this section will focus on how we access the interpretative perspective of the biblical authors, the relationship between this definition of biblical theology and authorial intent, and the difference between other approaches to biblical theology and the one pursued here.

The only access we have to *the interpretative perspective of the biblical authors* is what they wrote. Rather than try to go behind the text to get at what really happened, as though the text is mere propaganda, we are trying to understand what the biblical authors have written.

When we seek to understand *what they wrote*, however, we also have inspired indications of *what they meant* in the interpretations of earlier Scripture found in the writings of later biblical authors. These are not

---

[1] I have pursued this definition in *What Is Biblical Theology?* (Hamilton 2014c), employed it in an attempt at whole-Bible biblical theology (2010b) and operated on the basis of it in shorter biblical-theological studies (see 2010a; 2012a).

limited to the interpretations of the Old Testament in the New but include the interpretations of the Old Testament in the Old. To reiterate for clarity, we have *both* what earlier biblical authors wrote *and* how later biblical authors interpreted them.

Anticipating the section below on my evangelical approach, one of my assumptions is that later biblical authors correctly understood what earlier biblical authors meant. At the human level, there is exegetical warrant for the interpretations of earlier Scripture we find in the writings of later biblical authors: these later authors were good exegetes. At the theological level, the inspiration of the Spirit ensured that they correctly understood earlier Scripture.[2] So for instance, if Psalm 78:69 likens the temple to the heavens and the earth, the psalmist has correctly understood what Moses intended to communicate in his Pentateuchal depiction of the relationship between the created world and the tabernacle.[3] We thus have insight into the interpretative perspective of Moses both from what he wrote (Gen. 2 and Exod. 25 – 40) and from the way later inspired authors interpreted his writings.

Pursuing biblical theology in this way will be profoundly intertextual.[4] How did Daniel engage earlier Scripture to summarize, interpret and build on what the biblical authors who preceded him had accomplished? Answering these questions about Daniel requires attending not only to the way that he engaged earlier authors but also to the way that later authors engaged him. Later biblical authors, inspired by the Holy Spirit, have correctly understood Daniel, and we who believe the Bible to be inspired should allow the inspired interpreters to guide our interpretation of what Daniel wrote (see Hamilton 2010b: 46–47).

In addition to a significant focus on intertextuality (which constitutes the whole-Bible dimension of any biblical-theological endeavour),

---

[2] This is against the perspective of Longenecker (1999), with Schreiner (2008), Silva (1996), Beale (1994) and others.

[3] For further discussion see Hamilton (2010b: 73–74), which relies on Wenham (1994), Beale (2004), Alexander (2008) and others.

[4] Careful attention to the biblical texts in their original languages and in more literal English translations, many conversations with Tom Schreiner (who should not be blamed for my views!) and the writings of Hays (2005) and Beale (2008: 22–35) have shaped my thinking on intertextuality. Beale (2012: 39–40) now thinks it may be better to use phrases such as 'inner-biblical exegesis' or 'inner-biblical allusion' instead of 'intertextuality', but I am not ready to surrender this handy term. In using it I am focused on authorial intent, and I employ it as an umbrella term for the ways later biblical authors engage earlier Scripture. Cf. Scheetz's discussion of 'Intertextuality, Canon Criticism, and Biblical Studies' (2011: 1–35).

understanding what the biblical authors wrote demands an understanding of how literature functions. Among other things, being
sensitive to the literary dimensions of biblical texts requires us to
discern how the authors structured their work, what kinds of things
they assumed their audience would know,[5] and the perspective from
which they intended their work to be interpreted. The insight we can
gain on some topics will be limited by the amount of evidence we
have, but evangelical assumptions enable more confidence than is
possible from other perspectives. For instance, once Deuteronomy
was in place,[6] later authors expected their writings to be interpreted
against the backdrop of Deuteronomy.

Thus the author of Ruth did not feel the need to quote Deuteronomy
23:3 but simply assumed that his readers would know that it excludes
Moabites. He intended his book to be interpreted in the light of
Deuteronomy 23:3, but he took for granted the fact that his audience
would know that text. In the opening words of his book, the author
of Ruth also assumed that his audience would know the book of
Judges: 'And it came about in the days of the judging of the judges'
(Ruth 1:1, my tr.). Similarly, the author of Kings assumed that his
audience would interpret 1 Kings 11 in the light of Deuteronomy 17.
Validating these assertions about what the biblical authors assumed is
exactly what the work of tracing the interpretative perspective of the
biblical authors entails. In part, this means understanding how later
authors quote and allude to earlier Scripture, which is a literary
endeavour. Hays (2005: 34–45) has outlined helpful criteria, on which
Beale (2008: 15–35) has built, and the ensuing paragraphs stand on
the shoulders of their useful discussions.

What follows may at first seem unconventional, but those who
understand what authors are doing *constantly* make these kinds of
interpretative moves. The previous paragraph contained the assertion
that the author of Ruth invoked the book of Judges and engaged
Deuteronomy 23:3, even though he neither used a quotation formula
nor overtly alluded to those texts in ways that are typically acknowledged in academic discussions of intertextuality. The author of Ruth
did not need to allude to, echo or quote Deuteronomy 23:3 in order
to engage it. How can such a suggestion be made? The validity of the
suggestion depends on how we understand the culture in which

---

[5] Moses, for instance, assumed in Leviticus that his audience would understand
quite a lot about sacrifice.
[6] The evangelical assumption here is that the true story is the one the Bible itself
tells, with Deuteronomy coming from Moses (cf. Deut. 31:9, 24, 30; 33:1).

the biblical authors wrote. For this suggestion to stand, that culture would have to have been saturated in the Scripture that was available when the author of Ruth wrote. This takes us right to the question of the interpretative perspective of the biblical authors.

A contemporary example will illustrate the way authors and audiences share unstated information. I wrote the first draft of these thoughts on Tuesday 5 February 2013. The previous Sunday, 3 February 2013, was 'Super Bowl Sunday'. The Baltimore Ravens beat the San Francisco 49ers in the NFL Championship Game. Consider for a moment everything assumed about readers of this book in the use of the abbreviation 'NFL', the mention of the 'Baltimore Ravens', and the reference to the game that was played as both 'the NFL Championship' and 'the Super Bowl'. No flock of birds comes to mind at the mention of the Ravens, no one (in the USA) needs the explanation that the Super Bowl *is* the National Football League Championship game, and everyone knows that Baltimore and San Francisco are both cities.

These things are so much a part of US shared culture that they require no explanation. In fact, they are so much a part of our culture that we can talk to others about the events – and write about them – without overtly mentioning them. Consider the way that I referenced the game during the announcements before the worship service of Kenwood Baptist, the church I serve as pastor, on the morning under discussion. One of our elders was hosting a Super Bowl party at his home (we do not have a Sunday evening service). I did not have to use the words 'Super Bowl party' to make that announcement. Overt mention of the event was unnecessary. The announcement went something like this:

> Warren and Jody are opening their home this evening to all and sundry. Evidently there's something happening on television tonight, maybe you know the details, apparently some commercials are going to be aired. If you'd like to watch the proceedings with others from our congregation, you're welcome to bring a bag of chips, a jar of salsa or a two-litre to Warren and Jody's house.

At the words 'Evidently there's something happening on television tonight, maybe you know the details' there were smirks and sniggers in the congregation, and there was a wry look on my face. Everyone knew what was referenced, even though the words 'Super Bowl' and the phrase 'football game' were never used. Nor did anyone need an explanation of the connection between the Super Bowl and the commercials that have become part of the cultural phenomenon.

The fact that authors can do this sort of thing in writing – make allusions that are not overt – is what Peter Leithart discusses in his chapter 'The Text Is a Joke' (2009: 109–139). The chapter exposits the way that jokes assume cultural information that comedians need neither articulate nor explain. Comedians assume shared information, and this information is crucial for anyone to 'get' their jokes. The biblical authors make similar assumptions, and the task of biblical theology is to identify and demonstrate such assumptions.

From the way the biblical authors have written, it appears that awareness of earlier biblical texts could be taken for granted in their culture the way awareness of the Super Bowl can be in ours. The evidence of rampant disobedience in ancient Israel does not prove the biblical writings were unknown but that the Bible's teaching about sin is true. A strong indication of widespread awareness of the Scriptures can be found in the clipped, compressed, evocative references to the Torah that pervade the Old Testament Prophets and Writings. The conclusion that David, Isaiah, Hosea and the others were writing for people who would have understood their elided utterances is hard to deny. Authors intend to be understood. If they have not explained themselves, they probably thought no explanation necessary.

The pursuit of *the interpretative perspective of the biblical authors* will thus be a literary and intertextual enterprise, and both of these factors inform our pursuit of the backstory against which the biblical authors intended their writings to be read. This backstory is not always presented on the surface of the biblical writings. There is a plot that continues when Genesis ends and Exodus begins, but that plot is not on the surface, where Charles Dickens puts it at the end of 'Book the First: Recalled to Life' in *A Tale of Two Cities*, with readers continuing into 'Book the Second: The Golden Thread'. Instead, the unfolding plot of the Pentateuch must be discerned from the accumulation of the statements and stories, and developments often come in dialogue between the characters or in speeches or prayers.[7]

The Bible's plot is like what we find in James Joyce's *Ulysses*, which on the surface bears little resemblance to Homer's *Odyssey* but was intended by Joyce to be something like an instalment in an Odyssean

---

[7] For a book focused 'on the story line as it unfolds', see Schreiner 2013: xii.

25

typological pattern (cf. Gilbert 1959: 34–37).[8] If Joyce intended Leopold Bloom as an instalment in a typological pattern, and if there is even a character that represents Joyce himself in Stephen Dedalus, I would suggest that Joyce has imitated biblical authors such as David and Daniel, who presented themselves and others as instalments in typological patterns.[9] The point here is that the Bible's backstory plot informed the book of Daniel, as Daniel plugged into that wider narrative, and in the revelations his book describes the story was carried forward.

Everything said here about biblical theology is based squarely on the pursuit of the meaning that the biblical authors intended to communicate. Focusing biblical theology on the *interpretative perspective of the biblical authors* moors it to authorial intent. This has massive implications for how we approach both salvation history and thematic questions in biblical theology.

For thematic studies, the question of what the biblical authors intended trains our gaze on themes they themselves develop. If we are pursuing this method, we do not bring themes to the Bible but examine the texts to see how later biblical authors have developed thematic issues set forth in earlier biblical texts.

Similar things can be said about our examination of the salvation-historical unfolding of the Bible's story. If we are looking for the interpretative perspective of the biblical authors, we will only be interested in a transition from one so-called dispensation to another if we can demonstrate that it was the intention of Moses or Paul or John to communicate a change in dispensations. If we think that Moses has indicated a change from one dispensation to another, our claims will be significantly strengthened if we can show that Isaiah or Peter

[8] Note that Gilbert read his commentary on Joyce's *Ulysses* aloud to Joyce himself, and that Joyce both affirmed and corrected Gilbert's interpretation. Gilbert writes, 'in the course of writing this Study I read it out to Joyce, chapter by chapter, and that, though he allowed me the greatest latitude in the presentation of the facts and indeed encouraged me to treat the subject on whatever lines were most congenial to me, it contains nothing . . . to which he did not give his full approbation; indeed, there are several passages which I owe directly to him' (1959: viii; cf. v–ix).

[9] Earle Ellis rightly wrote, 'a typological understanding of Scripture governed the interpretation of NT writers', and explained that 'typology views the relationship of OT events to those in the new dispensation not as a "one-to-one" equation or correspondence, in which the old is repeated or continued, but rather in terms of two principles, historical correspondence and escalation. . . . the OT type not only corresponds to the NT antitype but also is complemented and transcended by it' (1982: 1–2). I have largely followed Ellis in my efforts to exposit the typological patterns in the Bible (2008a; 2008b; 2010c; 2012c; 2014d). Cf. the proposal from Ribbens that typology be defined as iconic *mimēsis* (2011).

or some other biblical author interpreted Moses that way. The question for dispensationalists and covenant theologians alike is this: Did the biblical authors intend to communicate the contours of these systems? Similar questions can be asked of those who argue for one schematic understanding of the Bible's storyline over another (as does Goldsworthy [2012]). Did the biblical authors intend to communicate this schema rather than another?[10] If someone proposes a schematic outline of Israel's history (as do covenant theologians, dispensationalists, and biblical theologians such as Goldsworthy), the question they must answer is: Where did the biblical authors themselves indicate that this was their own schematic perspective on the Bible's big story?

If we are looking for the interpretative perspective of the biblical authors, an outline that biblical authors have used to summarize and interpret the Bible's big story, along the lines of what we find in Nehemiah 9 or Acts 7, will be more convincing than one that modern scholars have discerned from the text. We should seek to show that our schemas and outlines are ways of bringing into sharper focus those that the biblical authors themselves have employed. Our aim is to explain how and why they saw things the way they did.

In this study of the theology of the book of Daniel, the goal is to understand and explain Daniel's interpretative perspective. We thus seek to understand both how Daniel has engaged earlier Scripture to present his message and how later Scripture engaged Daniel to exposit what he wrote. This approach to biblical theology moves us towards greater understanding of what Daniel intended to communicate. As indicated above, examining how Daniel engaged earlier Scripture and how later writers of Scripture engaged Daniel makes certain assumptions about the canon of Scripture.

The canon of Scripture

I am convinced that the sixty-six books of the Protestant canon have been inspired by the Holy Spirit and are therefore inerrant (see further Hamilton 2010d). Roger Beckwith's (1985) masterful treatment of the question of the Old Testament canon provides a thorough, logical, convincing discussion of the issues. Michael Kruger (2012) has recently 'revisited' the question of the New Testament canon. There are two main ways that canonical issues will influence this study of

[10] I am referring here to Graeme Goldsworthy's book *Christ-Centered Biblical Theology*, a good portion of which is devoted to arguing that the Robinson–Hebert schema is superior to that of Vos–Clowney (Goldsworthy 2012).

the theology of the book of Daniel. The first has to do with the boundaries the word 'canonical' provides for 'biblical' theology, and the second has to do with the tripartite (i.e. three-part: Law, Prophets, Writings) order of the Old Testament books.

There may be redundancy in the assertion that this is an exercise in 'canonical biblical theology', because for me the words 'biblical' and 'canonical' both refer to the sixty-six books of the Protestant canon. The redundancy is necessitated, however, by the confusion of biblical theology with the study of the history of religions. A history of religions approach to biblical theology focuses on the historical development of ideas and concepts, with an evolutionary undercurrent at work, as though the theology reflected in the texts mutated in more sophisticated directions as humanity evolved upward, becoming ever more refined. This problematic approach does not distinguish between the books of the Old Testament and non-canonical early Jewish literature, and liberal scholarship typically associates the book of Daniel with those inter-testamental books. Evangelical persuasion and canonical methodology intersect in the following two conclusions: (1) that Daniel was written prior to the events the book prophesies, and (2) that the Old Testament canon was closed before the Maccabean crisis. These conclusions have tremendous interpretative implications.

The fact that this is a 'canonical' biblical theology does not mean I will ignore early Jewish literature (see chapter 7), but I do not think the authors of that body of literature were inspired by the Spirit of God the way the author of Daniel was. At points these authors of non-biblical literature distinguish their writings from the books they view as having been inspired by the Spirit (e.g. 1 Macc. 4:46; 9:27; 12:9; 14:41; 2 Macc. 2:13; Prologue to Sirach; *4 Ezra* 14:45–46; 2 Bar. 85:1–3; for discussion see Hamilton 2010d: 240–244), nor were apocryphal books either recognized as authoritative Scripture by the synagogue or quoted as Scripture in the New Testament (on which see esp. Beckwith 1985; and more briefly Hamilton 2010d: 245–247). So the phrase 'biblical theology' distinguishes this project from an attempt to describe the history of religions, and the word 'canonical' connotes the sixty-six books of the Protestant canon.

The word 'canonical' also points to the tripartite arrangement of the books of the Old Testament aiding our attempt to understand the interpretative perspective of the biblical authors. There are both historical and theological reasons for embracing the tripartite arrangement of the books of the Old Testament in Hebrew Bibles and, for instance, in JPS Torah printings of the Old Testament in English.

The historical reasons for embracing the tripartite order include the most significant fact that *this is the only order of the Old Testament books that has come down to us from antiquity*. There simply is no such thing as a Septuagintal or ancient Christian order of the Old Testament books. The orders of the Old Testament books in Greek translations of the whole Bible differ from one another and include apocryphal books. The order of Old Testament books we now find in our English translations is nothing more than a modern printing convention (Seitz 2008: 27–30). By contrast, we have attestation to the tripartite order from intertestamental literature (Prologue to Sirach, lines 8–10), Qumran (4QMMT[11]), the New Testament (Luke 24:44) and rabbinic writings (*Baba Bathra* 14b). Beckwith (1985) has answered virtually every question that could be imagined on this topic, and I have followed Stephen Dempster's lead (1997; 2003) in building on work that David Noel Freedman has done (1991) on the symmetry of the tripartite arrangement of the Old Testament (Hamilton 2010b).

When we turn from historical to theological considerations for embracing the tripartite order of the books of the Old Testament, the simple fact is that Luke presents Jesus as speaking of the Old Testament in these terms (Luke 24:44). Why wouldn't followers of Jesus want to follow him in their mental organization of the books of the Old Testament? Should we replace with human tradition the way Jesus thought about the Old Testament? Should we shrink from the difficulty of rearranging our thoughts to match the thoughts of Jesus? Should we decline opportunities to conform our thinking to the way Jesus thought because our way of thinking seems simpler to us? In addition to the way the tripartite arrangement is validated by and sheds light on Luke 24:44, embracing the tripartite order puts us in a position to understand other statements that Jesus made. The most natural understanding of what Matthew and Luke present Jesus as saying about the blood of all the martyrs from Abel to Zechariah (Matt. 23:35; Luke 11:51) is that Jesus has in mind the first and last martyrs described in the Old Testament (Gen. 4:4; 2 Chr. 24:20–21). We can see this, however, only if we think of Chronicles as the last book in the Old Testament, which seems to be the way Jesus thought about it. Why would followers of Jesus arrange the books of the Old Testament in such a way that it is more difficult for

---

[11] 4Q397, Frags. 14–21 (= 4Q398 14–17 I; 4QMMT C 1–17), line 10 (García Martínez and Tigchelaar 2000: 801).

people to understand something Matthew and Luke present Jesus as having said?

To the historical evidence for the tripartite order and the interpretative traction it gives us on Matthew 23:35 and Luke 11:51 we can add that there are biblical-theological advantages for approaching the Old Testament from this perspective. Broad generalities here briefly present what I have explored in greater detail elsewhere (Hamilton 2010b: 59–64, 139–140, 187–190, 267, 271–275, 350–352): the Torah tells the true story of the world, and the ramshackle narrative rumbles forward in the Former Prophets. The Latter Prophets provide poetic commentary on the narrative. The Writings continue the poetic commentary, summarizing and interpreting the narrative that began in Genesis and continued through Kings; then the latter books of the Writings return to narrative storyline, beginning with Esther, continuing through Daniel, Ezra–Nehemiah, and concluding with Chronicles.

This way of conceptualizing the arrangement of the books of the Old Testament canon fosters a dynamic interaction in our thinking between the narrative in the Torah and Former Prophets, the interpretative proclamation based thereon in the Latter Prophets and early Writings, and the continuation of the narrative in the later books of the Writings, among which we find Daniel. Beckwith (1985: 138–139) has suggested, persuasively, that Daniel and Chronicles have been put where they are because of their narrative character.

In conjunction with this canonical approach to the books of the Old Testament, I accept the claims of the books as they stand. This means that I will accept at face value the evidence in the texts that points to the conclusion that Daniel would have had access to most of what we now recognize as the Old Testament. He would not, of course, have had access to those books written after his time. Anticipating what follows in the next section regarding an evangelical approach to Scripture, those who go behind what is on the surface of the text to create an alternative narrative that explains what really happened, as though the story the texts tell is propaganda, are at best engaging in hazardous speculation, which at worst serves projects of subversive revisionism that cannot be regarded as historical or critical.

An evangelical approach

One catalyst of the desire to write this book was the lack of a robust canonical biblical-theological treatment of Daniel that took an

evangelical perspective on the date of the book of Daniel.[12] Since work
on this project began, some studies have appeared (e.g. Davis 2013;
Greidanus 2012), but we will never exhaust the Bible's riches. The
evidence favours evangelical conclusions on questions of date and
authorship. This discussion focuses mainly on date. On authorship,
the fact that Jesus is presented as referring to Daniel as having said
what we find in the book of Daniel settles the matter (Matt. 24:15).[13]
It is possible that a later author or editor may have put Daniel's
first-person accounts into a wider narrative. It is more probable,
however, that the biblical authors often referred to themselves in both
first and third person, and that works of genius and inspiration were
written by inspired prophets who were themselves geniuses who needed
no editor(s) to shape their material for distribution.

The Maccabean date of Daniel is a foregone conclusion for many
scholars. The view that the book of Daniel was written after the events
it purports to predict has become so ensconced as to be assumed –
surprisingly – even by more evangelical interpreters.[14] In the Daniel
volume of the Apollos Old Testament Commentary, Ernest C. Lucas
posits that where one lands on these questions does not affect the
interpretation of the book. Having referenced the introductory issues
of 'the unity of the book, its authorship, the date of its composition and issues of historicity', Lucas asserts that 'the theological
meaning of the stories and visions in Daniel is not closely tied up with
decisions about the issues traditionally dealt with in the Introduction'
(2002: 18).

On the contrary, such issues *do* result in a significantly different
theological meaning. There is a massive difference between the theological meaning of a wish-fantasy and that of a historically reliable
account of God miraculously preserving someone alive in a fiery
furnace. Dismissing a false fable as irrelevant to my conduct reflects
my view of the theological meaning and value of fairy tales. Risk-
ing my life because I believe the stories results from convictions about

[12] This is not to say that evangelicals have not written on Daniel. It is to say that
many evangelical treatments advocate either dispensational or covenantal perspectives
and are not endeavours in canonical biblical theology.

[13] See also the recent discussions defending Danielic authorship in Steinmann
(2008: 1–19) and Greidanus (2012: 14–15).

[14] For instance, in a discussion of 'The "Most High" God and the Nature of Early
Jewish Monotheism', Richard Bauckham writes, 'I exclude Daniel from this count [of
instances of the phrase 'the Most High' in the Hebrew Bible] and include it in early
Jewish literature simply because it so clearly belongs chronologically with the latter'
(2007: 378, n. 11; cf. 41). N. T. Wright also seems to assume, without discussion, a
'second century BC' date for Daniel (2003, 3: 109).

theological meaning that cannot be separated from historicity. The narratives portray God as preserving his people and promising to raise them from the dead, and this material will influence my conduct only if I believe that God has done and will do those things. The author of Daniel encouraged people to be faithful to Yahweh even unto death (e.g. Dan. 11:32–35). The book of Daniel inspires faithfulness to Yahweh because it teaches that God and his kingdom matter more than the preservation of one's own life. Undergirding this is the fact that Yahweh can deliver people from death (Dan. 3, 6) and predict the future (Dan. 11), including the future resurrection and reward of the faithful (Dan. 12:2–3).

If some Maccabean-era author is making fraudulent claims, if these are fictional deliverances and not future predictions but recitals of what has already happened presented *as though* being predicted by Daniel, then there is no real proof that Yahweh can either deliver from death or predict the future. This means that there is no proof that he is any better than the false gods who can neither reveal the future nor deliver their worshippers, which is exactly what the book of Daniel claims Yahweh can do, especially by means of the revelations in Daniel 2 and 7 – 12 and the deliverances in Daniel 3 and 6.

If the deliverances of Daniel 3 and 6 are not historical, no one should be encouraged by these stories to trust that Yahweh can also deliver them if they are faithful like Daniel and his friends, nor should anyone think that Yahweh might raise the dead and reward them for their faithfulness. That man who risks his own life or the safety of his children for a God who cannot predict the future or raise the dead is a fool. The whole theological meaning of the book depends upon Yahweh's ability to deliver his people and declare the future before it takes place. If he cannot do these things, no one should 'stand firm and take action' and risk his life for Yahweh (Dan. 11:32).

We should not be shallow in our thinking about these issues and their implications: if the stories of deliverance are not historical, and if the predictions are not actual declarations of events yet to take place, the book of Daniel is nothing more than a curious piece of fiction from the ancient world retaining no right to bind the conscience in any authoritative way. It may entertain us. It may even ennoble us the way Shakespeare and Dickens do. But if not historical and predictive, Daniel is no better than a mythological account, on a level with the *Iliad*, the *Prayer of Nabonidus* or *Bel and the Dragon*. If, on the other hand, the deliverances described in Daniel actually took place in history, and if the future really has been predicted in the book of Daniel, then Daniel

demands to be regarded as the very word of God, speaking authori-
tatively to how people should live, binding their conscience to obey.

As Greidanus (2012: 5–15) has recently argued, the stronger position
is the historic one: that Daniel wrote the book attributed to him before
the events the book predicts took place. There are good historical
reasons for these conclusions, and going away from them creates
massive theological problems. The following historical and theological
considerations inform the evangelical starting points, or presuppositions, within which I operate.

Historical evidence for an early date

In his *Jewish Antiquities*, Josephus describes an event he presents as
having taken place in 332 BC:[15]

> he [Alexander the Great] gave his hand to the high priest and, with
> the Jews running beside him, entered the city. Then he went up
> to the temple, where he sacrificed to God under the direction of
> the high priest, and showed due honour to the priests and to the
> high priest himself. And, when the book of Daniel was shown to
> him, in which he had declared that one of the Greeks would destroy
> the empire of the Persians, he believed himself to be the one
> indicated; and in his joy he dismissed the multitude for the time
> being, but on the following day he summoned them again and told
> them to ask for any gifts which they might desire . . .

Two things to note here: first, Josephus clearly regarded Daniel to be
the author of the book: 'the book of Daniel . . . in which he had
declared . . .' Secondly, Josephus placed this event in 332 BC, so
Josephus believed that the book of Daniel had been written by then.
This is historical testimony that can be taken to reflect general opinion
among Jews in the first century AD. Josephus gives no indication
that the book of Daniel might have been written *after* rather than
before the events it purports to predict.

Along with what we see in Josephus, some observations on the state
of Judaism at the time many believe Daniel was written are in order. As
is well known, by the time of the Maccabean crisis Judaism had frag-
mented into sects and parties. Those who had entered into a covenant
with one another at Qumran appear to have concluded that the Jerusalem

---

[15] For the date and the text, see the LCL ed. of *Jewish Antiquities* 11.317, p. 467,
notes c and e (Josephus 2001).

establishment was so corrupt the only hope was to go out to the wilderness to prepare the way of the Lord (cf. the quotation of Isa. 40:3 in 1QS VIII, 14[16]). The literature produced by these various groups is recognized as *sectarian* precisely because it reflects the agendas, emphases and concerns of particular groups within Judaism. The book of Daniel was accepted not by a particular sect or set of groups within Judaism but by *all Judaism*,[17] and this strongly indicates that it was written before the fragmentation of Judaism, as Beckwith (1985: 357–358) argues:

> both the Essenes and the rest of the Jews accepted Daniel into the canon. This extraordinary difference of treatment strongly suggests that Daniel cannot have been either of sectarian or of recent origin. Well before the emergence of the three contending religious parties in the Maccabean period, two of the books of 1 Enoch had already been written, yet even so they had only achieved acceptance in narrow circles, as the later books of 1 Enoch were also to do. The book of Daniel, on the contrary, though related in a particularly distinct manner to one of the former two books of 1 Enoch, the Book of Watchers (1 En. 1–36), was to achieve nationwide acceptance, as nothing less than Holy Scripture. The simplest explanation of this phenomenon would be that Daniel is the oldest of the apocalypses; that it did not, like the rest, have a secretive (much less a sectarian) origin; and that the production of other apocalypses, in imitation of it, was due not only to its impressive character as literature, but to the fact that, when they began to be written, it was already a contender for a place in the canon.[18]

[16] García Martínez and Tigchelaar 2000: 89.

[17] Ulrich writes, 'The book of Daniel exercised greater influence in the late second temple period than would be expected of one of the smaller books of the Bible . . . Various groups within Judaism appear to have found the person of Daniel . . . important for their developing religious reflections. While this is true for broader Judaism in general, it is likewise true for the covenanters at Qumran' (2001: 573).

[18] Ulrich writes, 'A final observation on the text of Daniel as illumined by the scrolls found at Qumran is that there are no textual variants due to "sectarian" motivation' (2001: 583). Ulrich basically acknowledges the point Beckwith makes – that all sects embraced Daniel – but Ulrich maintains his a priori commitment to a Maccabean era date for Daniel in spite of this evidence: 'Despite the fact that the twelve-chapter edition of the book was composed in the troubled period that gave rise to several of the Jewish parties, including the Pharisees and the Essenes, none of the variants betrays any clue that a scribe altered the prophet's text in favor of one party's theology or beliefs as opposed to another's. Sectarian or denominational polemics were not uncommon, of course, but the evidence for Daniel, in line with other books of Scripture, indicates that all parties apparently agreed to argue their points of difference elsewhere and to keep the text of the Scriptures free of such' (583).

At least eight manuscripts of Daniel have been found at Qumran. Gerhard Hasel (1990) has summarized the impact these findings ought to have on the discussion of the date of Daniel. Hasel quotes Frank Moore Cross on the point that 'one copy of Daniel is inscribed in the script of the late second century B.C'. Hasel identifies this text as 4QDan^c, for which he posits a date of 'around 125 B.C.' (1990: 38–39).[19] Regarding the proposed Maccabean date for Daniel, with Daniel originating at the time of the crisis brought about by Antiochus Epiphanes between 168 and 164 BC, Hasel observes, 'It seems difficult to believe that such a significant number of Daniel manuscripts would have been preserved in a single desert community, if the book had really been produced at so late a date' (40). Hasel also points out that those who adhere to the late date 'will now have to demonstrate that a mere forty or fifty years was sufficient time for all the editorial and other processes needed – according to their tradition-historical and redaction-critical theories – for the book to be developed into its present form *and* become canonical' (41; similarly, Waltke 1976: 321–322).

4Q Florilegium (4Q174, Frags. 1 Col. II, 3, 24, 5) quotes Daniel as Scripture, using the phrase 'as is written in the book of Daniel, the prophet' (García Martínez and Tigchelaar 2000: 355). The reference here to 'the book of Daniel, the prophet' constitutes another indication that Daniel was viewed as the author of the book. VanderKam and Flint observe, 'The last surviving parts of the text cite Ps. 2:1 (persecution in the last days, with survival of a remnant who will perform the law), which is clarified by Dan. 12:10, and Ps. 5:2–3, which relate to the last days and are elaborated through the promise in Isa. 65:22–23' (2002: 224). 11Q *Rule of Melchizedek* (11Q13, Col. II, 18) also quotes Daniel as Scripture, apparently interpreting the anointed one predicted in Daniel 9:25 as the fulfilment of Isaiah 52:7.[20]

---

[19] Ulrich lists both 4QDan^c and 4QDan^e as 'late 2nd or early 1st c. BCE' (2001: 574). In the same volume, Peter Flint lists 4QDan^c as 'late 2nd c. BCE' and 4QDan^e as '2nd c. BCE' (2001: 330). Flint also holds to a '2nd century BCE' date for Daniel (2001: 365). On the earliest translation of Daniel into Greek, Alexander A. Di Lella writes, 'The date of OG-Dan. has generally been assigned to the late second or early first century BCE. What is beyond question is that OG-Dan. is prior to Th-Dan' (2001: 590–591). Theodotion-Daniel (Th-Dan) is the translation typically cited in the NT (Wesselius 2001: 593).

[20] The text is as follows: 'This [. . .] is the day of [peace about whi]ch he said [. . . through Isa]iah the prophet, who said: [*Isa. 52:7* <<How] beautiful upon the mountains are the feet [of] the messen[ger who] announces peace, the mess[enger of good who announces salvati]on, [sa]ying to Zion: your God [reigns.>>] Its interpretation: The mountains [are] the prophet[s . . .] . . . [. . .] for all . . . [. . .] And the

The manuscript evidence – the copies of Daniel found at Qumran – is in itself a strong argument for an early date for Daniel. When we combine the hard evidence of the manuscripts with the *treatment* of Daniel at Qumran – the book of Daniel being interpreted *as Scripture* in non-biblical Qumran texts – the argument for an early date for Daniel from the evidence at Qumran grows stronger still.

Another weighty indication of an early date for Daniel is the influence of Daniel on books such as *1 Enoch*, Tobit and Ecclesiasticus (Beckwith 2002). In addition to these books we should add Baruch, which makes heavy use of Daniel (cf. esp Bar. 1:15–22 and Dan. 9:7–14). Moore writes of Baruch, 'The place and time of the final compilation seem to be Palestine in the early part of the second century B.C., i.e. prior to the defiant Jewish mood of 168 B.C. . . .' (1977: 260). Harrington writes of Tobit, 'It was probably composed by a Jewish author in the third or second century' (1999: 11). Given the obvious influence of Daniel on Baruch and Tobit,[21] with these books reflecting a situation *prior* to the Maccabean crisis,[22] it would seem very difficult to date Daniel *after* the Maccabean crisis. Against the notion that the direction of influence goes the other way (Tobit influencing Daniel) stands the fact that Daniel, not Tobit or Baruch, is quoted as Scripture and used to interpret other Scripture at Qumran and in the New Testament. The evidence that Qumran, the synagogue and the early church recognized Daniel as Scripture indicates that Daniel influenced *1 Enoch*, Baruch and Tobit rather than the other way around. *1 Enoch* in particular looks like a development of Daniel,

---

messenger i[s] the anointed of the spir[it] as Dan[iel] said [about him: *Dan. 9:25* <<Until an anointed one, a prince, it is seven weeks.>>' (García Martínez and Tigchelaar 2000: 1209). Waltke observes that Dan. 11:40–45 is taken by modern liberal scholars to be an actual attempt at prediction that failed and points out that were that the case 'it seems incredible' that Daniel's 'alleged contemporaries' from the Maccabean era would have regarded him as a prophet (Waltke 1976: 322).

[21] The influence of Daniel on Tobit will be discussed in chapter 7.

[22] Nickelsburg on Tobit: 'It surely antedates the persecution of Antiochus' (1984: 45). Moore: 'most scholars of the past two centuries have dated [Tobit] to somewhere between 250 and 175 B.C.E., that is, after the canonization of the Prophets as Scripture (cf. Tob. 14:4) but before the Maccabean period (167–135 B.C.E.). . . . The book's *terminus ad quem* is unquestionably pre-Maccabean' (1996: 40–41). DeSilva: 'It seems reasonable to set the earliest date of composition as sometime during the third century B.C.E. The book reflects the same ethos as in Ben Sira and Judith with regard to dietary laws, burial of the dead, endogamy, and piety . . . based on the discovery of the fragments of Tobit at Qumran, the earliest of which dates from 100 B.C.E. Tobit's failure to reflect any knowledge of the issues surrounding the Hellenization crisis and Maccabean Revolt suggests that the book was written sometime between 250 and 175 B.C.E.' (2002: 69).

with Daniel being the more restrained in its description of heavenly beings.[23]

There are other factors that point to an early date for Daniel and an early recognition of it as Scripture, such as the fact that while we have Daniel in Hebrew/Aramaic and translated into Greek, neither Origen nor Jerome knew of a Hebrew text for Tobit (Moore 1996: 52), nor do Hebrew texts survive for Baruch, 1 Maccabees or *1 Enoch*.

In addition to these historical considerations, there are also relevant theological issues.

Theological considerations for an early date

The theological issue in view here is not the one mentioned earlier, that Jesus referred to the content of the book of Daniel as having been spoken by the prophet Daniel, though for me that is a decisive consideration. The issue now under consideration is the moral and ethical problem created by the suggestion of a late date for Daniel. Some more evangelical interpreters seem to regard questions of date and historicity as matters of indifference, but these issues are not morally neutral. Put bluntly, a late date for Daniel demands an author who was a scoundrel of a high order. A late date for Daniel requires some later author setting out to deceive his audience, creating in them the impression that things *he knew* had already taken place were actually being predicted. His purpose in creating this impression was to give himself the moral standing with his audience necessary for him to call them to suffer and die for the cause he advocated – when he knew all along that his claims were false.[24]

Imagine the level of cynicism involved in such a project. The author knew he was not giving actual predictions. He knew he was being deceptive. He knew he was calling people to lose their lives, *and he knew he was calling them to take on impossible odds in a campaign whose foundation he knew to be false.* This cannot be compared to a

---

[23] Beckwith writes, 'Though the angelology and eschatology of Daniel are more highly developed than those of the Prophets and Psalms . . . , they are less highly developed than those of even the earliest books of 1 Enoch' (1985: 415, n. 75).

[24] Beckwith writes, 'there was no convention which allowed writers to make such claims without danger of their being taken literally. It is sometimes suggested that writers conscious of being inspired were not doing anything seriously misleading by attributing their works to other inspired writers, but this is open to two objections: (*i*) they did not simply attribute their writings to other inspired writers, but to *ancient* inspired writers, and this involved them in the use of deceitful devices like *vaticinia post eventum*, which *were* seriously misleading. (*ii*) If they were conscious of being inspired, why did they not have the confidence to use their own names' (1985: 359). And again, 'God does not need men's lies to support his truth' (362).

situation where authors engage in fictional projects in which they intend to tell the truth and inspire readers, along the lines of what J. R. R. Tolkien or J. K. Rowling have accomplished. No one reading those books thinks that this world is Middle-earth or that there really is a Hogwarts out there somewhere. By contrast, the book of Daniel is set in the world as we know it. The author gives no indication that his intention is to teach by means of a fictional presentation. He claims to represent the real world, the world as the Bible describes it.

Faithfulness to Yahweh was the foundation of the Maccabean resistance (cf. 1 Macc. 1:54–63). Old man Maccabee and his sons were willing to die rather than be defiled with the pig flesh of Antiochus (2:15–38, 50). The author of 1 Maccabees presents father Mattathias on his deathbed exhorting his sons to remember what God had done for previous generations of Israelites: Abraham, Joseph, Phineas, Joshua, Caleb, David, Elijah (2:51–58), and then appealing to the examples found in the book of Daniel: 'Hananias, Azarias and Misael, because of their faith, were saved from fire. Daniel, by his simplicity, was rescued from the mouth of lions' (2:59–60, NETS). The author of 1 Maccabees presents Mattathias as exhorting his sons to risk their lives the same way that Daniel and his friends did, and for the same reasons: because Yahweh is more important than life, because Yahweh's power trumps death.[25] For this argument to work, Mattathias, the author of 1 Maccabees, and the audience of 1 Maccabees had to believe that Daniel and his friends *belonged with biblical heroes* of the faith and that the book of Daniel described *what really happened*. No one risks his life for fables, legends and myths, and cruel would be the father who exhorted his sons to do so.

Was it a deception? Did some pseudonymous author successfully deceive everyone from Mattathias, father of Judas Maccabeus, to Jesus of Nazareth? I find it historically implausible, yea impossible, to imagine that someone could so successfully sell such a despicable deception. The proposed pseudonymous author of the supposedly forged and false book of Daniel could never have hoped to have been so wildly successful that not until Porphyry (third century AD) would anyone suspect what he had done, and then not until the modern age

---

[25] Early Christians came to similar conclusions and were encouraged to do so by the book of Daniel. Shelton's study of Hippolytus' *Commentary on Daniel* shows that 'about 204 CE during a time of severe Roman persecution against the church, the commentary applies the text of Daniel in a way that offered encouragement and theological credibility to the martyrs witnessed by the church' (2008: 1).

would it be widely recognized that he had duped the vast majority of those exposed to his fabrications.[26]

This moral issue has implications that go beyond what we should think of the author who would attempt such a scam to what we should do with his book. Those who conclude that the book of Daniel is a forgery should not print it in the Protestant canon, esteeming and treasuring it, but should rather repudiate it as repugnant.

If it is a forgery, a fraud used to compel people to risk their lives for the sake of falsehood, even to the point of having their babies hanged and whole families put to death (1 Macc. 1:61), then we should regard this book the way we would respond to a book by some Second World War era propagandist who encouraged Japanese soldiers that the honour of the emperor mattered more than their lives, so they should fight to the death for the emperor, crying out, 'may you [the emperor] live ten thousand years!' (the meaning of *banzai*!). We would not venerate such literature but scorn it for its narrow, benighted, devastating perspective. Its only value would in such a case derive from the limited, slanted, ultimately false historical information to be found in it. Issues of authorship and historicity, however Ernest C. Lucas may protest, very much affect the theological meaning of the book of Daniel.[27]

Evangelical presuppositions

The book of Daniel should not be rejected as a forged piece of unfortunate resistance literature produced in the lost cause of a false god. Rather, the God described in the book of Daniel is the only living and true God, who did and can deliver from death, and he revealed the future to his prophets. He inspired Daniel to write this book, the supernatural deliverances recorded in the book really happened, the book really did, and does, predict the future. The book of Daniel is the word of God, and God so worked through the inspiration of its author, whom the evidence indicates was Daniel himself, that error did not

[26] Even as he endorses the Maccabean date for Daniel, Spangenberg describes what a new idea it is: 'The theory of the Maccabean origin of the Book of Daniel . . . was introduced at German universities towards the end of the nineteenth century. The theory only became acceptable in Protestant scholarly circles outside Germany after the First World War (1914–1918) and in Catholic scholarly circles after the Second World War (1939–1945). In South Africa, however, scholars in the departments of Biblical Studies and the Old Testament only introduced the theory to students during the seventies of the previous century' (2006: 440).
[27] Gerald Bray (2012: 87) comes to similar conclusions regarding the Pastoral Epistles.

enter into the book. As the word of God, the book of Daniel binds the conscience and demands obedience.

Chapter by chapter preview

Believing that Daniel is the word of God and that it records both true events and future prophecies neither closes down interpretative possibilities nor answers all questions. The questions multiply, and this study will not answer all of them.

This book explores Daniel's theology by seeking answers to the following queries. Chapter 2: How does the Old Testament present the history and future of the world, and what does Daniel contribute to that presentation? Chapter 3: How has Daniel structured his presentation, and what does that structure contribute to the meaning of the book? Chapter 4: What do the visions of Daniel 2, 4, 7–8 and 10 – 12 mean? How are we to understand the depiction of the four kingdoms that are followed by the kingdom that will never be destroyed? Chapter 5: What does Gabriel reveal to Daniel when he tells him about the seventy weeks of years in Daniel 9? Chapter 6: How are we to understand the various heavenly beings in the book of Daniel? Is the fourth man in the fire to be identified with the one like a son of man?

The next three chapters move from the book of Daniel itself to how later writers interpreted Daniel. Chapter 7: How was Daniel understood in non-canonical early Jewish literature? Chapter 8: How was Daniel understood in the New Testament outside the book of Revelation? Chapter 9: How has the book of Daniel influenced the book of Revelation?

The final chapter of this project takes up the question of the patterns in Daniel seen against the context of the whole canon. Chapter 10: What can we say about the patterns of events in Daniel and the similarities between Daniel and other characters in the big story of the Bible, that is, what does Daniel contribute to biblical typology?

This book will not be an exhaustive or final word on these matters. 'Of making of many books there is no end' (Eccl. 12:12). My hope is to pay close attention to the text of Daniel, in both the original languages in which it was written and in Greek and English translations, to set what Daniel wrote in the broader context of biblical theology, and to move readers towards a clearer understanding of how we should live today in response to the message of Daniel.

Chapter Two

From Eden to the end: Daniel in Old Testament salvation history

This chapter sets out what the book of Daniel reveals against the wider storyline of canonical biblical theology. If we think of the Bible's story as it unfolds in the tripartite arrangement of the books of the Old Testament, we see the following: the primary history in the Torah and the Former Prophets (Genesis–Kings) begins at creation and ends with exile. The poetic commentary, the Latter Prophets and the first sections of the Writings (Isaiah–Ecclesiastes), explore the significance of these events, also pointing beyond them to a new exodus and return from exile. In the final section of the Writings (Esther–Chronicles) there is a return to historical narrative, and at many points this historical narrative is forward looking.

The book of Daniel makes historical, prophetic and apocalyptic contributions to this forward-looking historical narrative. The image seen by Nebuchadnezzar and interpreted by Daniel (Dan. 2), the four beasts of Daniel's dream vision (Dan. 7), the seventy sevens revealed to Daniel by Gabriel (Dan. 9), and the history of the future in the Book of Truth (Dan. 10 – 12) all point to what will take place between Daniel's own time and the consummation of God's purposes.[1] Thus Daniel reaches back to grab the thread of the story by opening with the exile of Daniel and other sons of Israel to Shinar (Dan. 1); then carries it forward to 'the end of the days' (Dan. 12:13).

The Old Testament sketches in the contours of the history and future of the world. The treatment is not exhaustive, but this literature answers major world view questions: Who made us? Who are we? How did we get here? What has gone wrong? What is the maker doing to set things right? How will things turn out in the end?

---

[1] Chapter 4 will demonstrate this for Dan. 2, 7, 8 and 10 – 12, and chapter 5 shows that the same holds in Dan. 9.

The Old Testament's answers to these questions are the intellectual matrix in which Daniel writes. In order to understand the particular contribution of the book of Daniel, we begin with an attempt to map the highway of God's purposes in salvation history, the causeway that begins at creation and continues to new creation. This exercise in the cartography of salvation history, charting God's plan for the ages of the world, will begin with what Moses prophesies about the future of the history of Israel. From this starting point in the Torah we will survey the contribution of the Former and Latter Prophets,[2] before focusing on the way that Daniel latches on to the Law and the Prophets and points forward to the end of the exile and the consummation of all things. We will see that Daniel intends to connect his story to the Law and the Prophets, and then that he makes significant contributions to the future of salvation history, taking his readers all the way to the grand consummation of all things.

The history of Israel's future in the Torah

God built a cosmic temple in which he placed his image, giving him a suitable helper and commanding him to exercise dominion. The man was charged to subdue all the dry lands so they would be part of the garden of God's glory (Gen. 1:26–28; 2:15, 18; see Beale 2004: 81–82). When God's image transgressed, God exiled man and woman from the land of life (Dempster 2003: 67). Banished from God's presence to the cursed and barren ground east of Eden, Adam named his wife Eve as an act of faith in response to the word of judgment promising that the serpent would meet his fate at the feet of the skull-crushing seed of the woman (Gen. 3:15, 20; Hamilton 2006; 2010b: 79). Genesis then carefully traces the line of descent through a ten-member genealogy from Adam to Noah (Gen. 5); then through another ten-member genealogy from Noah's son Shem to Abram (Gen. 11; Dempster 2003: 71, 75). To Abram God promised blessings, blessings that correspond to and promise to overcome the curses (cf. Gen. 3:14–19 and 12:1–3; see Hamilton 2007).

From Abraham to the curses of the covenant

The promises made to Abraham (Gen. 12:1–3) were passed to his son Isaac (26:2–4), who then passed them to his son Jacob (27:27–29; 28:3–4). Jacob blessed the sons of Joseph with the birthright (Gen.

---

[2] The parameters of this study permit only the barest summary. For fuller discussion of the Law and the Prophets, see Hamilton 2010b.

48:15–16; 1 Chr. 5:1), 'yet Judah became great among his brothers, and the prince came from him' (1 Chr. 5:2, my tr.; cf. Gen. 49:8–12). God declared the sojourn in Egypt to Abram before it came to pass (Gen. 15:13); then as promised he brought Israel out of Egypt through mighty acts of judgment (15:14; cf. Exod. 6:6). Yahweh glorified himself over Pharaoh (Exod. 14), entered into covenant with Israel at Sinai (19 – 24), gave them instructions for the tabernacle (25 – 31), renewed the covenant and revealed himself to Moses after the golden calf outrage (32 – 34); then took up residence in the tabernacle, previewing the way his glory would fill the cosmos (35 – 40).

At Sinai, Moses instructed Israel in Leviticus 1 – 25 on how to live with a holy God, and, significantly for our purposes, this included instructions about sabbatical years and the year of jubilee. Both the sabbatical year cycles and the jubilee are relevant for understanding Daniel 9 and what the seventy weeks indicate about the consummation of history. Moses taught Israel to work the land for six years; then to let it rest in the seventh (Lev. 25:1–7). He went on to tell them that they should count 'seven Sabbaths of years', totalling forty-nine years, the fiftieth year being the jubilee (25:8–17). On the Day of Atonement in the forty-ninth year they were to sound the trumpet (25:9), proclaiming liberty, everyone returning to their clans and lands (25:10).

After these instructions, Moses began to lay out the blessings and curses of the covenant in Leviticus 26, prophesying the history of Israel's future as he did so. Both Leviticus 25 and 26 are vital for understanding the exile, the kingdom of God described in Daniel, and the revelation made in Daniel 9.

The curses of the covenant in Leviticus 26: significant sevens and sets of sevens

Moses presented the blessings of obedience to the covenant in Leviticus 26:1–13. These culminate in a promise of the renewal of the experience of Eden, Yahweh walking among his people (Wenham 1994). Moses followed these promised blessings of Yahweh's presence with ominous curses. If they obey, Yahweh will walk among them; if they disobey, he will 'walk contrary' to them (Lev. 26:24).

Several times in these curses Yahweh declared through Moses that he would discipline Israel 'sevenfold'[3] for their sins (Lev. 26:18, 21,

---

[3] The Hebrew in these instances is simply the numeral 'seven' (שֶׁבַע, šeba'). There is another Hebrew term used at points for 'sevenfold' (שִׁבְעָתַיִם, šib'ātayim), but though that term is not used in these instances in Leviticus, 'sevenfold' seems to be what the numeral 'seven' communicates (so ESV, RSV; cf. AV: 'seven times more'; similarly, HCSB, JPS, NASB, NIV).

24, 28). After these four statements that Yahweh would discipline Israel 'sevenfold for your sins', Moses announced to them that when Yahweh exiled them from the land, scattering them among the nations (26:33), the land would enjoy the sabbatical years that Israel disobediently refused to give it (26:34–35). Later in this chapter we will examine the relationship between Jeremiah 25 and 29, Daniel 9 and 2 Chronicles 36, and those texts build on the Leviticus 26 declarations that the land would enjoy its Sabbaths and that Yahweh would punish Israel sevenfold for her sins. Moses went on to prophesy that after the land had its rest, after the people were punished sevenfold for their sins, when they confessed their sin, humbled their hearts and made amends for their sin, Yahweh would remember his covenant (Lev. 26:40–45).

Restoration in the latter days

A similar schema regarding the history of Israel's future – without the specifics of the sevenfold punishment and the land being repaid the denied sabbaticals – is announced by Moses in Deuteronomy 4:26–31, and then elaborated upon in Deuteronomy 28 – 32. The sequence of broken covenant, discipline culminating in exile, followed by repentance and eschatological restoration is then narrated in the Former and Latter Prophets and sung in the Writings (see Ciampa 2007).

Having prophesied the exile after Israel breaks the covenant in Deuteronomy 4:25–28, Moses makes a significant reference to 'the latter days' in 4:29–30, 'But from there you will seek Yahweh your God and you will find him, if you search for him with all your heart and with all your soul. When you are in tribulation, and all these words find you in the latter days, you will return to Yahweh your God and hear his voice' (my tr.).[4]

The fulfilment of Mosaic prophecy in the Prophets and the Writings

Having highlighted the way that Leviticus and Deuteronomy point forward to Israel's exile, during which the land will enjoy its Sabbaths and the people will be punished sevenfold before being restored in the

---

[4] Cf. also the prophecies of what will take place 'in the latter days' in Gen. 49:1; Num. 24:14; and Deut. 31:29.

latter days, in this section we turn our attention briefly to the fulfilment of what Moses prophesied in the Prophets and the Writings.

The Former Prophets

The Mosaic proclamations regarding the future of Israel's history play out just as he said they would in the narrative of Joshua–Kings. The authors of these narratives have clearly studied Moses, Deuteronomy in particular, and they narrate Israel's history such that their audience cannot fail to miss the way that the words of Moses have come to pass. They are so successful, in fact, that many scholars have concluded that Deuteronomy must have been written after rather than before the events took place. The roots of such deceptions thrive in some soils, but wither where the words 'you shall not bear false witness' hold sway (Deut. 5:20).

Israel enters the land, breaks the covenant and Yahweh patiently disciplines them. Eventually they fill up the full measure of their transgressions and Yahweh exiles them from the land (cf. 2 Kgs 24:20). As Adam was exiled from Eden, Israel was driven from the land of promise. In the centuries leading up to exile, significant biblical-theological summaries of Israel's history are added to the Mosaic prophecies. These come from the likes of Joshua (Josh. 23 – 24), Samuel (1 Sam. 12) and Solomon (1 Kgs 8).

The Latter Prophets

Isaiah, Jeremiah, Ezekiel and the Twelve prophesy on the basis of what Moses announced in the Torah, and the Former Prophets narrate in Joshua–Kings. The Latter Prophets, Isaiah to the Twelve, announce that Israel has broken the covenant, that Yahweh has patiently disciplined them, and that if Israel refuses to repent, Yahweh will keep his word and drive them into exile. After exile, the prophets promise a glorious eschatological restoration: new exodus, return from exile, new David, new covenant, new Eden, new creation.[5] The best part of all this will be the renewed experience of God's presence and the renewed relationship with him.

Jeremiah made significant biblical-theological connections between what Moses prophesied in Leviticus and Deuteronomy. When Jeremiah prophesies that Yahweh has decreed seventy years for Babylon

---

[5] See table 3.11 in Hamilton 2010b: 232, 'Key Words, Thematic Links, and Similar Phrases and Concepts in the Twelve', which tracks the linguistic and conceptual repetition of statements of warning, judgment and promised salvation in the Twelve Minor Prophets.

(Jer. 25:11–12), he appears to have been interpreting the number of years the land would keep the Sabbath. This, at any rate, seems to be the way the chronicler understood Jeremiah: 'He took into exile in Babylon those who had escaped from the sword . . . to fulfil the word of Yahweh by the mouth of Jeremiah, until the land had enjoyed its Sabbaths. All the days that it lay desolate it kept Sabbath, to fulfil seventy years' (2 Chr. 36:20–21, adapted ESV).[6]

In the letter that Jeremiah wrote to the exiles in Babylon we find a connection Jeremiah forged between Leviticus and Deuteronomy. Reiterating Yahweh's promise to bring Israel back to the land when the seventy years are completed for Babylon (29:10), Jeremiah then affirms that this will be in keeping with the plans that Yahweh has for his people (29:11), which Moses prophesied. Assuming that the chronicler is correct and Jeremiah is interpreting Leviticus when he announces seventy years for Babylon, when Jeremiah then quotes Deuteronomy 4:29 (Jer. 29:12–13), we see that he is bringing together two related passages from the writings of Moses. Jeremiah thus synthesizes Leviticus 26:34 and Deuteronomy 4:29, fusing them and pointing to the fulfilment of the different statements Moses made about the future of Israel's history.

To summarize, the points of contact between Leviticus, Deuteronomy and Jeremiah include the following:

1. When Israel is exiled, the land will enjoy its Sabbaths (Lev. 26:34).
2. In exile, Israel will seek Yahweh and find him when they search for him with all their heart and all their soul (Deut. 4:29).
3. These things will come upon Israel in the latter days (Deut. 4:30), and, following Moses, Jeremiah also addresses the latter days (Jer. 23:20; 30:24; 48:47; 49:39).
4. Jeremiah prophesies seventy years for Babylon (Jer. 25:11–12; 29:10), and a later biblical author, the chronicler, interprets these seventy years as the years the land kept Sabbath (2 Chr. 36:20–21; cf. Lev. 26:34).
5. Jeremiah promises those in exile that, as Moses said, they would seek Yahweh and find him when they searched for him with all their heart and all their soul (Jer. 29:13; cf. Deut. 4:29).

---

[6] This way of construing the relationships is superior to that of Ben Zion Wacholder, who holds that Daniel uses Chronicles but dissents from the interpretation of Jeremiah's seventy years found in 2 Chr. 36:20–21 (Wacholder 1975: 202, with n. 6).

The Writings

This section elaborates on the fulfilment of the Law and the Prophets in the Writings, focusing on one of the books in the Writings, Daniel. I have alluded to 2 Chronicles 36:20–21 above, but this text from the Writings is so significant that I risk belabouring the point. The chronicler explains (2 Chr. 36:20–21, adapted ESV) that Nebuchadnezzar

> took into exile in Babylon those who had escaped from the sword, and they became servants to him and to his sons until the establishment of the kingdom of Persia, to fulfil the word of Yahweh by the mouth of Jeremiah, until the land had enjoyed its Sabbaths. All the days that it lay desolate it kept Sabbath, to fulfil seventy years.

This interpretative comment makes an explicit connection between the sabbatical years that Moses prophesied the land would enjoy (Lev. 26:34–35) and the seventy years for Babylon prophesied by Jeremiah (Jer. 25.11–12; 29:10). The chronicler asserts that Jeremiah's prophecy was fulfilled. The land enjoyed its seventy sabbatical years (2 Chr. 36:21). Since the chronicler goes on to describe the decree issued by Cyrus that the people could return to the land, he seems to see the seventy years fulfilled between the earliest deportation in 605 BC and the first wave of returnees to the land in 538 BC.

From Daniel to the end of days

The fulfilment of the Law and the Prophets in Daniel

Daniel presents himself as being among that first group of exiles taken to Babylon by Nebuchadnezzar in 605 BC (Dan. 1:1–7). He thus experienced the visitation of the curse of exile prophesied by Moses in Leviticus 26, Deuteronomy 4 and Deuteronomy 28 – 32. He lived out the warnings announced by the Former Prophets in passages such as Joshua 24 and 1 Kings 8, as well as those of the Latter Prophets seen in texts such as Isaiah 39:6–7, Hosea 11:5 and Amos 5:27.

Daniel ties his narrative to the broader biblical storyline by asserting that 'the Lord gave Jehoiakim king of Judah into [Nebuchadnezzar's] hand' (1:2), a statement that applies the perspective on the events taught by Moses and the Prophets. Daniel also uses the theologically loaded place name of 'Shinar' to describe Babylon – Nebuchadnezzar is identified in Daniel 1:1 as 'king of Babylon', but in Daniel 1:2 took his plunder not to Babylon but to 'Shinar'. This place name evokes memories of Nimrod, the beginning of whose kingdom was 'Babel' (in Hebrew Babel and Babylon are spelled the same: בבל, *bbl*) 'in the land of Shinar', from which he went on to build Nineveh in Assyria (Gen. 10:8–11). Genesis 11 also presents the attempt to build a tower into heaven 'in the land of Shinar' (Gen. 11:2). Shinar thus comes to be associated with rebellion against God: it is the land of the seed of the serpent, where God's enemies dwell.

Daniel 9 relates how, studying Jeremiah in the first year of Darius, 539–538 BC, Daniel perceived that with the passing of roughly seventy years since 605 BC, the prophesied time had come (Dan. 9:1–2). Daniel then relates how he began to do exactly what Moses (Lev. 26:40) and Solomon (1 Kgs 8:46–53) had said the people would do: confess sin (Dan. 9:3–19). As Daniel in 9:3–19 prayed and confessed sin, he lived out what Moses in Leviticus 26:40 and Deuteronomy 4:30–31 said Israel would do. The confession of sin is introduced in Daniel 9:2 by the words 'I, Daniel, perceived in the books the number of years that, according to the word of Yahweh to Jeremiah the prophet, must pass before the end of the desolations of Jerusalem, namely, seventy years' (adapted ESV). The first part of Daniel 9 thus builds an interpretive bridge between the Law and the Prophets. Jeremiah had connected Leviticus 26, Deuteronomy 4 and 1 Kings 8 (cf. Jer. 25:11–12; 29:10–14). Daniel built on these connections by adding to Jeremiah's prophecy his own perception that Jeremiah's prophecy was being fulfilled. He then received a revelation[7] that, like other revelatory material in Daniel, points forward to the consummation of all things (Dan. 9:20–27; cf. Dan. 2, 4, 7, 10 – 12; see chapter 4 below).

Interestingly, it seems that the new revelation given to Daniel is but a nuancing clarification of what Moses had stated in Leviticus 26 regarding Israel's sevenfold punishment (similarly, Goldingay 1989: 232). Daniel perceives that Jeremiah's seventy years are drawing to completion (Dan. 9:2), and when Gabriel comes to Daniel (9:20–23) he informs him that the seventy years will be visited sevenfold, saying in Daniel 9:24 (adapted ESV):

---

[7] Wacholder writes, 'the author of Daniel goes on in 9:24–27 to present his own chronological exegesis of Jeremiah's 70-year prophecy' (1975: 202). There is undoubtedly interpretation happening as Daniel describes what happened to him. Nevertheless, in first-person statements, Daniel claimed that Gabriel made these things known to him.

> Seventy weeks are decreed about your people and
>   your holy city,
> to finish the transgression,
> to put an end to sin,
> and to atone for iniquity
> to bring in everlasting righteousness,
> to seal both vision and prophet,
> and to anoint a most holy place.

We will return to Daniel 9:24–27 in chapter 5 below. Here we consider the way this prophecy links backward and forward, reaching back to take up what had been made known earlier; then adding to the progress of revelation by sketching in an outline of the future. These seventy weeks appear to be a sevenfold visitation of Jeremiah's seventy years (Lev. 26:28, 34; Jer. 25:10–11; 29:10). A sevenfold seventy is 490 (70 × 7), and this number 490 also happens to be a tenfold jubilee. Wacholder observes, 'Daniel never uses the term jubilee directly, but his numbers can be only understood in the light of Lev. 25:1–23, which gives seven sabbaticals as the maximum time of sanctioned bondage' (1975: 204). The sevenfold punishment during which the land would enjoy its Sabbaths described in Leviticus 26 immediately follows the instructions for the sabbatical years and the year of jubilee in Leviticus 25. Whereas Daniel seems to think the time for the end of the exile has come, he is pointed forward to the fulfilment of a sevenfold punishment for the sabbatical years, when God's purposes in history will culminate in a tenfold jubilee.

Can Daniel's forecast of the future be synthesized?

The book of Daniel is a carefully constructed chiasm.[8] The book opens with exile (Dan. 1) and ends with a vision culminating in the return from exile (Dan. 10 – 12). Between these outer bookends are dreams and visions that relate to the fourfold kingdoms of the world that will precede the coming of a kingdom that will not pass away (Dan. 2, 7 – 9).[9] Within the brackets of these chapters on the four-kingdom schema are two deliverances: of the three young men from the fiery furnace (Dan. 3) and of Daniel from the lions' den (Dan. 6). At the centre of this chiastic structure (see below) are the matching stories of the humbling of Nebuchadnezzar (Dan. 4) and Belshazzar (Dan. 5).

---

[8] For discussion and a defence of this literary structure, see chapter 3.
[9] For further discussion of the four kingdoms and the everlasting dominion that follows, see chapter 4.

In itself this chiastic structure tells a story: between the exile and the return from exile there will be a series of human kingdoms, and in spite of their attempts to destroy God's people he will preserve his own. Pompous rulers of rebel kingdoms will be humbled, through which judgment God achieves salvation for his people and gives them the kingdom that belongs to the son of man, who exercises everlasting dominion. See below for the chiastic structure of Daniel.

Daniel 1, exile
    Daniel 2, statue: four kingdoms, everlasting dominion
        Daniel 3, delivered from the fiery furnace
            Daniel 4, Nebuchadnezzar humbled
            Daniel 5, Belshazzar humbled
        Daniel 6, delivered from the lions' den
    Daniel 7 – 9, visions: four kingdoms, everlasting dominion
Daniel 10 – 12, return from exile

There are remarkable instances of overlapping vocabulary and imagery in these matching sections and in the various depictions of the future in Daniel. The similarities in language and imagery invite Daniel's audience to make connections between the discrete units. When these connections are considered in the light of each other, a composite forecast emerges that can be summarized as follows: in the latter days, transgression will be fulfilled as a little horn makes great boasts and persecutes God's people until the appointed time of the end, when the little horn will be unexpectedly broken, at which point the son of man will receive everlasting dominion in a kingdom the saints will possess for ever.

The rest of this chapter will exposit this composite forecast as it is unfolded in the book of Daniel, highlighting the connections between discreet units that join and blend together to portray the fulfilment of Scripture.

In the latter days

We saw above that Moses spoke of the 'tribulation' that would 'come upon' God's people 'in the latter days' (Deut. 4:30). Both Isaiah and Micah described the 'mountain of the house of Yahweh' being 'established as the highest of the mountains' 'in the latter days' (Isa. 2:2; Mic. 4:1). These and other earlier scriptural statements were evoked when Daniel declared to Nebuchadnezzar that God was revealing to him 'what will be in the latter days' (Dan. 2:28). The revelation portrayed a great image whose feet were struck by a stone 'cut out by no human hand', as a result of which the whole statue crumbled, while the stone 'became a great mountain and filled the whole earth' (2:31–35). Daniel seems to interpret Nebuchadnezzar's vision through the conceptual framework given to him by Deuteronomy 4 with help from Isaiah 2 and Micah 4.

We see another reference to the 'latter days' in Daniel 10:14. Daniel 10 – 12 is one revelation. Daniel 10 introduces this section of the book with Daniel recounting his encounter with at least one heavenly being (Dan. 10:5–15) and perhaps a second (10:16–19).[10] The heavenly being Daniel encountered in chapter 10 then revealed to him 'what is inscribed in the book of truth' (10:21), and the revelation is recounted in Daniel 11 – 12. The heavenly being speaking with Daniel told him that he 'came to make [him] understand what is to happen to [his] people in the latter days. For the vision is for days yet to come' (10:14).

The vision recounted in Daniel 10 – 12 treks through nation rising against nation until, as in the 'latter day' revelation made to Nebuchadnezzar, the ruler of the evil empire 'shall come to his end' (Dan. 11:45) and God's people will be delivered (12:1). In Daniel 2 the crushing of the statue is followed by the little stone becoming a great mountain that fills the whole earth. This fits naturally, too, with the latter-day vision of Isaiah 2:1–4 and Micah 4:1–5, where Yahweh's eschatological kingdom radiates out from the mountain of the house of the Lord, the highest of the mountains.

When the transgressors have reached their limit

Israel's past is the paradigm for Israel's future. Genesis depicted God telling Abraham that his descendants would 'come back here in the fourth generation, for the iniquity of the Amorites is not yet complete' (Gen. 15:16). What God told Abraham in Genesis 15 was enacted when Israel came out of Egypt to conquer Canaan. The paradigm in view, then, entails an appointed measure of sin being completed prior to the purging judgment Israel would visit when they put the Canaanites under the ban. This paradigm parallels two explanations that Gabriel gives to Daniel. As Daniel considers the vision given to him regarding the second and third kingdoms in Daniel 8, Gabriel refers to 'the latter end of their kingdom, when the transgressors have reached their limit' (Dan. 8:23). The phrasing of Genesis 15:16 and Daniel 8:23 does not match at the lexical level, but at the conceptual

---

[10] For discussion of the heavenly beings in the book of Daniel, see chapter 6.

level the ideas communicated are synonymous.[11] The same can be said about the second such statement Gabriel makes to Daniel in Daniel 9:24, when he says, 'Seventy weeks are decreed . . . to finish the transgression'. The idea that transgression has a full measure that will be fulfilled before the end will come seems to have informed the thinking of both Jesus, who told the brood of vipers (i.e. seed of the serpent) to 'fill up . . . the measure of your fathers' (Matt. 23:32), and Paul, who said that the enemies of the gospel 'always . . . fill up the measure of their sins' (1 Thess. 2:16).

The little horn(s)

The vision in Daniel 7 is of four beasts that symbolize four successive kingdoms (Dan. 7:1–8, 17, 23). The fourth beast has ten horns, and among them appears a little horn that plucks up three horns before it (7:8). These horns symbolize rulers (7:24a), and the fact that they are all horns seems to point to a certain (military) similarity between them. They culminate in a small horn who destroys three of those who came before it (7:24b).

Daniel 8 presents something similar happening during the third kingdom rather than the fourth. The goat, which is identified later in the chapter as the king of Greece (Dan. 8:21), has a great horn that is broken off and replaced by four smaller horns (8:8). From one of these comes a small horn (8:9). Here again there is not an exact terminological match between Daniel 7:8 and 8:9 – in part because chapter 7 is Aramaic and chapter 8 Hebrew – but at the conceptual level we are dealing with the same image of a small horn.

The small horn of Daniel 8 does things that are similar to what the small horn of Daniel 7 did. The little horn in Daniel 7:8 is 'speaking great things', and the little horn in Daniel 8:23 is 'a king of bold countenance'. In both cases the defeat of the arrogant little horn results in the deliverance of God's people (Dan. 7:11, 21–22, 25–27; 8:9–14, 23–26).

Why is there such similarity between the little horn of the third kingdom and the little horn of the fourth? It would appear that a pattern is being repeated. In this pattern the kings of the earth exalt themselves against God and his people, persecuting the saints; then, through the defeat of the arch-enemy, God's people are delivered. The repetition indicates that Daniel means to depict this 'type' of thing

---

[11] The reference to 'the transgression that makes desolate' in Dan. 8:13 may be relevant here as well.

as happening through the course of history until the pattern culminates and is fulfilled in the final instance of the typological pattern.[12] This way of looking at the matter matches both Paul's description of the 'lawless one' in 2 Thessalonians 2:12 and John's words about the antichrists and the Antichrist in 1 John 2:18.

How long?

Twice in Daniel the question 'how long?' is posed. In Daniel 8:13 'a holy one' asks the question, and in Daniel 12:6 'someone' asks it. The questions are linked not only by the fact that they are lexically identical but also by the fact that in both cases Daniel hears someone else ask the question. Further connecting these texts are statements that the visions are for 'many days from now' (Dan. 8:26) and 'for days yet to come' (10:14). Daniel 10 introduces the vision made known in Daniel 11 – 12, which like the vision in Daniel 8 carries history down to the end of the third kingdom.

These connections would support the idea, too, that the answers given to the question 'How long?' are related to one another. The answer given in Daniel 8:14 is '2,300 evenings and mornings'. The answer given in Daniel 12:7 is 'time, times, and half a time', and this seems to be exposited by the references to 1,290 days in 12:11 and 1,335 days in 12:12. These answers in Daniel 12 seem to pertain to the third kingdom, but here we have another point of connection between the third and fourth kingdoms, for in Daniel 7:25 the little horn from the fourth kingdom will prevail against the saints 'for a time, times, and half a time'.

The various time references all pertain to a period of roughly three-and-a-half years. There are 42 months in three-and-a-half years, and if we assume 30 days in a month, 42 times 30 amounts to 1,260. Thus, the 1,290 days in Daniel 12:11 would refer to a period of three-and-a-half years plus one month. Similarly, the 1,335 days in 12:12 adds another month and a half.[13] These references to just over three-and-a-half years in Daniel 12:11–12 inform the reference to 'time, times, and half a time' in 12:7, giving warrant for understanding this as a reference to one year, two years and half a year – three-and-a-half years.

---

[12] I am grateful for a stimulating conversation with Peter Gentry, who first drew my attention to this typological reading of the similarity between the third kingdom in Dan. 8 and the fourth in Dan. 7.

[13] J. van Goudoever (1993: 538) seeks to explain these numbers by appealing to the Zadokite Calendar.

The connections between Daniel 8 and Daniel 12 noted above prompt us to approach these chapters as mutually interpretative of one another, which also supports the notion that the '2,300 evenings and mornings' of Daniel 8:14 should be understood as a roughly three-and-a-half-year period. Davis writes of the 2,300 evening-mornings, 'They are commonly taken in one of two ways. Since the regular offering was offered up twice daily, some take the figure as denoting 2,300 sacrifices on 1,150 days. Others hold that verse 14 is referring to 2,300 evening-morning units and so do not halve the number' (2013: 109). Because of the similarity between these time references in Daniel, I am inclined to think that the 2,300 evenings and mornings refer to 1,150 days, which is approximately three years and three months of days.

Why all these references to three-and-a-half years? The answer seems to lie in the halving of the seventieth week in Daniel 9:27, 'And he shall make a strong covenant with many for one week, and for half of the week . . .'

How does this help us understand these time references? One half of one 'week' of years would be three-and-a-half years. It seems that Daniel portrays both the third (Dan. 8:13; 12:7–12) and fourth (Dan. 7:25) kingdoms as prevailing against the saints for a period of roughly three-and-a-half years. It also appears that the kingdom at the end of the sequence, the fourth, has its time of dominance described in the reference to the halving of the seventieth week in Daniel 9:27, as that period seems to inform the reference to time, times and half a time in 7:25.

War on the saints

Another point of contact between the third and fourth kingdoms is the war on the saints that both pursue. In Daniel 7:21 the little horn of the fourth kingdom 'made war with the saints and prevailed over them'. Verse 25 adds that he

> shall wear out the saints of the Most High . . .
> and they shall be given into his hand.

In Daniel 8:9–14 the little horn of the third kingdom overthrows the sanctuary (8:11), and verse 12 explains, 'a host will be given over to it'. Both sanctuary and host are 'trampled underfoot' in 8:13.

Here again the third kingdom is described in similar terms in both Daniel 8 and 10 – 12. The little horn from the third kingdom

perpetrates 'the transgression that makes desolate' (הפשע שמם, *hapeša'
šōmēm*) in Daniel 8:13, and he likewise appears to be responsible for
'the abomination that makes desolate' (שקוץ שמם, *šiqqûṣ šōmēm*) in
12:11. In Daniel 8:13 this affects 'the regular burnt offering' (התמיד,
hatāmîd), and the same holds for 12:11 (התמיד, *hatāmîd*). The little
horn from the third kingdom apparently stops the regular burnt
offering and replaces it with 'the abomination that makes desolate'
(esp. 12:11; cf. 8:13).[14]

Once again there seems to be an analogue for this in the final, fourth
kingdom. Daniel 9:27 states, 'he shall put an end to sacrifice and
offering [ישבת זבח ומנחה], *yašbît zebaḥ ûminḥâ*]. And on the wing of
abominations shall come one who makes desolate [ועל כנף שקוצים משמם,
wě'al kěnap šiqqûṣîm měšōmēm], until the decreed end is poured out
on the desolator [שמם, *šōmēm*].' Only in Daniel 9:27 does 'the desolator'
seem to be a person; the 'one who makes desolate' appears to be the
'prince who is to come' mentioned in 9:26.[15] The time link between
the two texts – 7:25's 'time, times, and half a time' being informed
by the 'half of the week' in 9:27 – argues that 'the prince who is to
come' of 9:26, the 'one who makes desolate' of 9:27, should be identified with the little horn from the fourth kingdom whose activities are
described in 7:24–25.

As we saw when comparing the little horn of the third kingdom
(Dan. 8:9) with the little horn of the fourth (7:8), it appears that the
activities of the third portend the activities of the fourth. If the ruler
of the final, fourth kingdom is described in Daniel 9:27, then like the
ruler of the third kingdom, he is depicted putting an end to sacrifice
in the temple, stopping the worship of the people of God, and
replacing it with desecrating sacrileges. If he himself is the desolating
sacrilege, there is another match with the way that in Daniel 11:36–37
the wicked king exalts and magnifies himself above every god. The
self-exaltation and programme of persecution pursued by the antichrist of kingdom three seems to point forward to what the Antichrist
of kingdom four – *the* Antichrist – will do.

[14] Johan Lust writes, 'An investigation of the relevant texts shows that the abomination of desolation often replaces the "Tamid" or its altar' (2001: 681).
[15] Lust again: 'The conclusion for the Danielic passages is that there the participles
must refer to Antiochus – he is the "appaller." This interpretation fits very well in
context, especially in 9:27, where the participle שמם is repeated at the end of the
verse. . . . This encourages us to recognize a reference to Antiochus as the desolator or
appaller on whom God's final wrath is going to be poured out' (2001: 686–687). Lust
is correct that the desolator is personal, but incorrect that it is Antiochus.

The appointed time of the end

The war on the saints appears to continue until the appointed time of the end. Thus Daniel 12:6–7, 'How long shall it be till the end of these wonders? . . . it would be for a time, times, and half a time, and that when the shattering of the power of the holy people comes to an end all these things would be finished.' Daniel 12:9 then states that 'the words are shut up and sealed until the time of the end' (cf. 12:4). In keeping with this, having seen the vision about the third kingdom in Daniel 8:5–14, Daniel is told in 8:17, 'Understand, O son of man, that the vision is for the time of the end.' Again in 8:19 Gabriel tells Daniel 'it refers to the appointed time of the end'. As the third kingdom is then described in more detail in Daniel 11, we find in 11:27 that 'the end is yet to be at the time appointed', and this is an exact match of the language of Habakkuk 2:3. Daniel 11:29 also describes what will happen 'at the time appointed', 11:35 clarifying, 'it still awaits the appointed time'. Then 11:40 comes to the moment 'at the time of the end'.

All these descriptions of the time of the end appear to pertain to the third kingdom. After the self-exalting king of the third kingdom comes to his end (Dan. 11:45), however, Daniel's people are delivered (12:1), the dead are raised (12:2) and the wise 'shine like the brightness of the sky above; and those who turn many to righteousness, like the stars for ever and ever' (12:3). Since the book of Daniel presents a fourth kingdom after the third, and since we have seen parallels between the third and fourth kingdoms, it would seem that here again the destruction of the third kingdom, which simultaneously results in deliverance for God's people, is pointing forward to the fulfilment of these patterns in the final, fourth, kingdom, as described in Daniel 7 and 9.

There came one like a son of man

Daniel sees the fourth beast destroyed (Dan. 7:11), while dominion is taken from the other beasts but their lives are prolonged (7:12). Then came one like a son of man with the clouds of heaven to be presented before the Ancient of Days (7:13). He received dominion and a kingdom (7:14). This one like a son of man deserves consideration in his own right (see chapter 6), but at this point we can observe that the combination of 'son of man' and 'dominion' and 'kingdom' in the context of the Old Testament canon immediately calls to mind Psalm 8, where David (see the superscription to Ps. 8) styles himself as a new Adam (cf. Ps. 8:6–9 and Gen. 1:28), a son of man (Ps. 8:4) exercising dominion (8:6) over the beasts (8:7–8) in the kingdom God has promised to him and his seed (cf. Ps. 2:5–12; 2 Sam. 7:9–16). Daniel 7 goes on to depict the little horn from the fourth kingdom as making war on the saints (Dan. 7:21) 'until the Ancient of Days came, and judgment was given for the saints of the Most High, and the time came when the saints possessed the kingdom' (7:22). It appears that the persecution of God's people ends with the destruction of the little horn (7:11, 21, 25–26), at which point the son of man receives the kingdom (7:13–14), which the saints possess (7:22). Daniel 7:27 states that this kingdom of the Most High 'shall be an everlasting kingdom'.

Everlasting dominion

The book of Daniel describes only one kingdom as lasting for ever, never to be destroyed. Daniel declares to Nebuchadnezzar that the God of heaven will set up this kingdom (Dan. 2:44–45). Nebuchadnezzar then confesses that the Most High God's 'kingdom is an everlasting kingdom, / and his dominion endures from generation to generation' (3:33 [ET 4:3]). After his sanity is restored, Nebuchadnezzar again confesses:

> his dominion is an everlasting dominion,
> and his kingdom endures from generation to generation.
> (4:31 [ET 4:34])

Darius likewise declares regarding Daniel's God:

> his kingdom shall never be destroyed,
> and his dominion shall be to the end.
> (6:27 [ET 6:26])

The same language is used to describe the kingdom given to the son of man:

> his dominion is an everlasting dominion
> which shall not pass away
> and his kingdom one that shall not be destroyed.
> (7:14)

Daniel 7:27 reiterates this again regarding the kingdom of the Most High, indicating that the kingdom of the Most High is the one given to the son of man, and the saints will possess it for ever under his reign (7:18, 22; cf. 12:1).

God's kingdom will be realized when the arch-enemy of God's people is destroyed, through which the Davidic son of man receives dominion, and the saints will reign with him for ever.

Conclusion

Many questions remain to be explored, many mysteries to be examined. We have seen, however, that Daniel followed Jeremiah's lead in connecting key eschatological passages from the Torah. Building on Jeremiah's interpretation of Leviticus and Deuteronomy, Daniel was given a more developed and nuanced revelation of how Mosaic prophecy would be fulfilled. The visions of Daniel reveal a series of four stylized kingdoms. The activities of the wicked ruler of the third kingdom will be typologically fulfilled in the activities of the wicked ruler of the fourth kingdom. Given the way that Nebuchadnezzar plundered the temple and exiled God's people (Dan. 1:1–4), we can say that his activities also typify those of the little horns of kingdoms three and four. The pattern of activity of the arch-enemy of God's people includes vicious persecution, self-exaltation (and cf. Dan. 4:30), an attempt to stamp out the worship of God, and the unexpected demise of the wicked king, through which God's people are saved.

These stylized four kingdoms are allotted a period of time that will fulfil a sevenfold punishment of Jeremiah's seventy sabbatical years for the land. When their time is up, when transgression has been fulfilled, the people of Israel will experience a tenfold jubilee. A Davidic Son of Man will be presented before the Ancient of Days to receive dominion and a kingdom, and the saints will possess that kingdom for ever.

With the opening statements of his book, Daniel has plugged his narrative into the broader biblical story, and in what the visions of his book reveal, that story is continued all the way to consummation. In the Old Testament's story, the placing of Israel in the land parallels the placement of Adam in the garden of Eden, as the exile of Israel from the land parallels the exile of Adam from the garden. The latter-day restoration to which Israel's prophets point is a return from exile that is nothing less than a return to Eden. The events that take place around the first year of Darius, where Daniel 9 is set, inaugurate that return from exile, but the revelatory visions of Daniel show that much suffering will be endured before the four kingdoms have had their day and the one like the son of man receives everlasting dominion.

Daniel presented his book as an instalment in the larger story, a story that began in Eden, and his book carries that story all the way to its consummation at the end of days. Having considered this broad storyline and Daniel's contribution to it, we turn our attention to the literary structure of the book of Daniel.

Chapter Three

The literary structure of Daniel

The book of Daniel is like a series of individual snapshots, so arranged that intriguing connections between the photographs join together to produce a larger picture. Therefore this discussion of the literary structure of Daniel will explore the structure of the book at three levels. First, we will address the division of the book into its discrete units, which broadly follows the chapter divisions in English translations. Secondly, we will investigate the structural relationships between these discrete chapters/units. Thirdly, based on the structural relationships between the book's units, we will overview the literary structure of the book as a whole.[1]

Modern books are typically divided into chapters with clear headings and subheadings, varying font sizes and strategic spacing to show divisions in the text. Modern Bible publishers print chapter and verse numbers, and sometimes subheadings, which were not put there by the biblical authors but by later students of the texts.

Ancient authors, such as those who wrote the books now in the Bible, employed other more intra-textual ways of demarcating sections within their writings. These methods of marking out divisions or shifts in thought range from changes in topic to repetitions of key words that can serve to form an *inclusio* around a unit of text or establish a chiastic structure. David Dorsey identifies 'symmetry, parallelism, and structured repetition' as key structuring devices employed by the biblical authors (1999: 16). How do these considerations apply to the book of Daniel?

Daniel's discrete units

The discrete units in the book of Daniel are marked off in two major ways. First, the units are introduced by similar opening statements

---

[1] I wish to thank David 'Gunner' Gundersen for his excellent suggestions that improved this paragraph.

that typically state the name of the reigning king, the year of his reign and something about the setting (listed below). Secondly, these units are largely self-contained accounts of something that happened to Daniel or his friends, or self-contained accounts of visions or dreams that were revealed to Daniel.[2]

There is not an exact correspondence between the discrete units in the book of Daniel and the chapter divisions in printed texts of the book, nor do all printed texts divide the chapters at the same places. The self-contained accounts within the book, however, are clearly discernible, even if it is not immediately clear whether some words at the transition from chapters 3 to 4 and from 5 to 6 are to be grouped with what goes before or what comes after.

In terms of content, the self-contained units of the book of Daniel are as follows:

1. *Daniel 1*: The account of Daniel and his friends being taken into exile in Babylon, the four youths refusing to be defiled by what they eat, and God giving them wisdom.
2. *Daniel 2*: The account of Nebuchadnezzar's dream, which the magicians can neither reveal nor explain, but Daniel doing both as God reveals the dream and its interpretation to him; in response Nebuchadnezzar confesses God's greatness and exalts Daniel and his friends.
3. *Daniel 3*: The account of Nebuchadnezzar's golden image, around which the officials gather and bow down, while Daniel's three friends refuse to bow; God delivers the three Jewish men who refused to bow; then the officials gather around the image of God; Nebuchadnezzar confesses God's greatness and exalts Daniel's three friends.
4. *Daniel 4*: The account of Nebuchadnezzar's dream, again interpreted by Daniel: God humbling Nebuchadnezzar for seven periods of time, after which Nebuchadnezzar is restored to sanity and regains his kingdom.
5. *Daniel 5*: The account of Belshazzar's feast, God humbling Belshazzar by sending the message through the handwriting on the wall, which Daniel interprets.

---

[2] Wesselius speaks of 'a nearly complete absence of continuity between the various episodes' (2001: 291). He later writes, 'In view of these discontinuities, it is amazing that, as noted above, unambiguous signs of linguistic and stylistic continuity and homogeneity exist within the chapters of the book, both in the Hebrew and the Aramaic parts' (2001: 295).

6. *Daniel 6*: The account of Darius' decree prohibiting prayer except to Darius under threat of the lions' den, God delivering Daniel from the lions' den after Daniel continues to pray in defiance of the decree.

7. *Daniel 7*: The account of Daniel's dream vision of the four beasts from the sea, the throne of the Ancient of Days, and the son of man who receives the kingdom, with a member of the heavenly court interpreting the vision for Daniel.

8. *Daniel 8*: The account of Daniel's vision of the ram and the goat, which Gabriel explains to him.

9. *Daniel 9*: The account of Daniel studying Jeremiah, realizing the prophesied seventy years have nearly passed, and responding with a Scripture-saturated, repentant prayer seeking God to act for his own sake, followed by Gabriel coming and revealing to him the appointed seventy weeks.

10. *Daniel 10 – 12*: The account of Daniel encountering several heavenly beings, and the revelation of what is inscribed in the book of truth, culminating in the resurrection of some to life and some to everlasting contempt.

Whereas there are twelve chapters in printed texts of Daniel, we see only ten discrete units because all of Daniel 10 12 deals with one episode.[3] These units are introduced by the following similarly worded opening statements (my tr.):

1:1, ‏בשנת שלוש למלכות יהויקם מלך־יהודה . . . ירושלם‎
bišnat šālôš lĕmalkût yĕhôyāqîm melek-yĕhûdâ . . . yĕrûšālaim
1:1, 'In year three of the kingdom of Jehoiakim king of Judah . . . Jerusalem'

2:1, ‏ובשנת שתים למלכות נבכדנצר‎
ûbišnat šĕtayim lĕmalkût nĕbukadneṣṣar
2:1, 'And in year two of the kingdom of Nebuchadnezzar'

3:1, ‏נבוכדנצר מלכא עבד‎
nĕbûkadneṣṣar malkā' 'ăbad
3:1, 'Nebuchadnezzar the king made . . .'

---

[3] Gooding states, 'All are agreed that there are ten major elements in the book, corresponding roughly to the traditional chapter divisions in each case, except that chapters 10–12 record one single vision and not three' (1981: 52).

MT 3:31, נבוכדנצר מלכא
něbûkadneṣṣar malkā'
ET 4:1, 'Nebuchadnezzar the king'

MT 4:1, אנה נבוכדנצר
'ănâ něbûkadneṣṣar
ET 4:4, 'I, Nebuchadnezzar'

5:1, בלשאצר מלכא עבד
bēlša'ṣṣar malkā' 'ăbad
5:1, 'Belshazzar the king made . . .'

MT 6:1, ודריוש מדיא קבל מלכותא
wědāryāweš mādāy'a qabēl malkûtā'
ET 5:31, 'And Darius the Mede received the kingdom'

MT 6:2, שפר קדם דריוש והקים על־מלכותא
šěpar qodām dāryaweš wahăqîm 'al-malkûtā'
ET 6:1, 'It seemed good before Darius, and he established over the kingdom . . .'

7:1, בשנת חדה לבלאשצר מלך בבל
bišnat ḥădâ lěbēl'šaṣṣar melek bābel
7:1, 'In year one of Belshazzar king of Babel [Babylon]'

8:1, בשנת שלוש למלכות בלאשצר המלך
bišnat šālôš lěmalkût bēl'šaṣṣar hammelek
8:1, 'In year three of the kingdom of Belshazzar the king'

9:1, בשנת אחת לדריוש בן־אחשורוש מזרע מדי אשר המלך על מלכות כשדים
bišnat 'aḥat lědāryaweš ben-'āḥašwērôš mizzera' mādāy 'ăšer homlak 'al malkût kaśdîm
9:1, 'In year one of Darius, son of Ahasuerus, from the seed of the Medes, who was made king over the kingdom of the Chaldeans'

10:1, בשנת שלוש לכורש מלך פרס
bišnat šālôš lěkôreš melek pāras
10:1, 'In year three of Cyrus king of Persia'

11:1, ואני בשנת אחת לדריוש המדי עמדי
wă'anî bišnat 'aḥat lědāryāweš hammādî 'omdî
11:1, 'And I, in year one of Darius the Mede, I stood'

12:1, וּבָעֵת הַהִיא יַעֲמֹד מִיכָאֵל הַשַּׂר הַגָּדוֹל
ûbā'ēt hahî' ya'ămōd mîkā'ēl haśśar hagādôl
12:1, 'And at that time he shall stand, Michael the great prince . . .'

This review of the chapter openings shows that chapters 1 and 2 begin the same way; then after the Aramaic openings of chapters 3–7, the return to Hebrew in chapter 8 begins with an opening that matches chapters 1–2. The elements of these openings (chs. 1, 2, 8) are as follows:

in year → number → of the kingdom → to [king's name] → king of [place]

Chapters 9 and 10 match this formula almost exactly, lacking only 'of the kingdom' (לְמַלְכוּת, *lĕmalkût*).

In the Aramaic section of Daniel (2:4 – 7:28), only chapter 7 begins with a formula like the ones that open Daniel 1, 2, 8, 9 and 10. The Daniel 7 formula is most like the one in chapters 9 and 10, lacking 'of the kingdom'.[4]

In the Aramaic section, the openings of chapters 3 and 5 match one another precisely, but there is not an exact match at the transition from chapters 3 to 4 or from 5 to 6. The closest things to matches at these transitions are the statements that begin with the respective king's name where English versions begin chapter 4 (ET Dan. 4:1; MT 3:31), and where printings of the Old Testament in Hebrew/Aramaic begin chapter 6 (MT Dan. 6:1; ET 5:31). Because of this, as reflected in the list of chapter openings above, I think that the English translations are correct in their designation of Daniel 4:1, whereas the enumeration of the verses followed in Hebrew/Aramaic texts are incorrect to enumerate that verse as 3:31, enumerating what is marked as 4:4 in English translations as 4:1. The same pattern that has me convinced that English translations rightly designate the opening of chapter 4 has me convinced that Hebrew/Aramaic texts rightly designate the opening of chapter 6, whereas English translations enumerate 6:1 (MT) as 5:31.

---

[4] Perhaps Ezra consciously modelled the opening statement of his book on the Danielic formula, as Ezra 1:1 follows the same pattern seen in the opening words of Dan. 7, 9 and 10 (against Wesselius 2001: 300, who suggests that 'Daniel is dependent on Ezra instead of the other way round'). In combination with numerous other literary parallels between Daniel and Ezra (on which see Wesselius 2005), with Ezra following Daniel in the Hebrew order of the books, Ezra takes on the feel of a continuation of the book of Daniel.

As for chapters 11 and 12, their openings are similar to one another, with indications that an angelic being has stood up to help someone, but these two chapters continue what was introduced at the beginning of chapter 10. The openings of chapters 11 and 12 do not match the openings of the other discrete units in Daniel, and the content related in Daniel 11 and 12 continues what was introduced in chapter 10.

The book of Daniel can be divided up into these ten episodes, but similar words, phrases and concepts recur from one episode to the next. Moreover, a consistency of theme runs throughout. These features indicate that the book's parts are contributing to a greater whole. What can we say about the relationships between these ten discrete units of the book of Daniel?

Relationships between Daniel's discrete units

As just noted, while the book of Daniel contains ten discrete episodes, these episodes are bound together by a dense repetition of words, phrases and concepts, forging a material similarity among the discrete episodes, as though the whole structure is built of the same metal. To demonstrate this unifying element of the book of Daniel, and to gain leverage on the book's structure, let us consider the repeated words, phrases and concepts that appear in the parts and in the whole of the book.

One aspect of the book's unity has already been set forth above: the consistency of the opening statements of the discrete episodes. While not uniform, there is an overwhelming similarity in all the statements, with each statement following one of two formulas (see above, the single exception being the opening statement at Dan. 5:31 [MT 6:1]). Another feature of the book's unity is the consistent reference to time.

Time references in Daniel

The book of Daniel refers both to historical times that are to be taken literally and to symbolic ways of considering the end of history, the end times. The historical time markers may be seen in the opening statements of the discrete units detailed above. Other references to literal time within history in the book of Daniel include the following:

- 'for three years' (1:5; cf. 'at the end of the time', 1:18)
- 'At the end of ten days' (1:15; cf. 1:12)
- 'until the first year of Cyrus' (1:21)
- 'He changes times and seasons' (2:21; cf. 2:9, 'till the times change'; cf. 7:25)

- 'let seven periods of time pass over him' (4:16)
- 'till seven periods of time pass over him' (4:23)
- 'seven periods of time shall pass over you, till you know' (4:25, 32)
- 'from the time that you know that Heaven rules' (4:26)
- 'At the end of twelve months' (4:29)
- 'At the end of the days' (4:34)
- 'At the same time my reason returned to me' (4:36)
- 'until he knew' (5:21)
- 'That very night' (5:30)
- 'for thirty days' (6:7)
- 'the number of years that . . . must pass . . . , namely, seventy years' (9:2)
- 'for three weeks' (10:2)
- 'twenty-one days' (10:13)

In addition to these literal references to historical time, there are also what seem to be symbolic references to time that point to the consummation of all things. These symbolic references at points build on and develop references to literal, historical time:

- 'what will be in the latter days' (2:28)
- 'what would be after this' (2:29)
- 'what is to be' (2:29)
- 'in the days of those kings' (2:44)
- 'what shall be after this' (2:45)
- 'for a season and a time' (7:12)
- 'until the ancient of days came' (7:22)
- 'the time came when the saints possessed the kingdom' (7:22)
- 'think to change the times and the law' (7:25; cf. 2:21)
- 'For how long . . . For 2,300 evenings and mornings. Then . . .' (8:13–14)
- 'the vision is for the time of the end' (8:17)
- 'at the latter end of the indignation, for it refers to the appointed time of the end' (8:19)
- 'at the latter end of their kingdom' (8:23)
- 'it refers to many days from now' (8:26)
- 'Seventy weeks are decreed' (9:24)
- 'there shall be seven weeks. Then for sixty-two weeks' (9:25)
- 'after the sixty-two weeks' (9:26)
- 'for one week' (9:27)
- 'for half of the week' (9:27; cf. 7:25; 8:14; 12:7, 11–12)

- 'in the latter days. For the vision is for days yet to come' (10:14)
- 'the end is yet to be at the time appointed' (11:27)
- 'At the time appointed' (11:29)
- 'until the time of the end, for it still awaits the appointed time' (11:35)
- 'till the indignation is accomplished' (11:36)
- 'At the time of the end' (11:40)
- 'At that time . . . a time of trouble . . . But at that time' (12:1)
- 'until the time of the end' (12:4)
- 'How long shall it be till the end of these wonders?' (12:6)
- 'when the shattering of the power of the holy people comes to an end all these things would be finished' (12:7)
- 'until the time of the end' (12:9)
- 'Blessed is he who waits and arrives at the 1,335 days' (12:12)
- 'till the end . . . at the end of the days' (12:13)

Some of these symbolic eschatological references could be taken literally, such as the reference in Daniel 2:44 to 'the days of those kings'. These kings appear to follow Nebuchadnezzar, who is identified in 2:38 as the head of gold; then told in 2:39–40 that the various kings follow him. The reference in 2:28 to the 'latter days', however, adds a symbolic layer of significance to the days of these historical kings (cf. Gladd 2008: 31–32).

A similar dynamic appears to be at work in the 'seven periods of time' that pass over Nebuchadnezzar in Daniel 4 (Dan. 4:16, 23, 25, 32). The statement in Daniel 4:34, 'At the end of the days I, Nebuchadnezzar, lifted my eyes to heaven', is similar to other references to the 'end of days' in Daniel (e.g. 12:13, and see other references to the 'end' of periods of time bulleted above). When we recognize that we are dealing with the end of a 'sevenfold' period of time in Daniel 4, we begin to wonder whether the historical story of Nebuchadnezzar's insanity and restoration might point to something beyond itself – something like the restoration of Israel after its own sevenfold period of wandering insanity (cf. Dan. 9:1–2, 24–27).

The same kind of thing might also be at work in the reference to 'the end of the time' in Daniel 1:18. There is a repeated pattern in the historical narratives that involves Jews being afflicted and then exalted:

- Daniel and his friends are exiled (1:6); then exalted (1:17–20).
- They face death with the other wise men of Babylon (2:14, 18), are delivered and given authority (2:46–49).

- Daniel's friends are cast into the fiery furnace (3:21); then promoted (3:30).
- Nebuchadnezzar (4:8–9) and Belshazzar (5:13–16; cf. 5:11–12) acknowledge Daniel's unique wisdom and ability to interpret, because 'the spirit of the gods is in you' (4:9; 5:14; cf. 4:8; 5:11, 29).
- Daniel is cast into the lions' den (6:16), yet prospers (6:28).

These historical deliverances correspond to the apocalyptic indications that the people of God will suffer and then be vindicated and receive the kingdom (cf. Dan. 7:25–27; 8:25; 9:27; 12:7). Such considerations indicate that the 'end of the time' (1:18) in which Daniel suffers before his exaltation (1:17–20) is a kind of enacted parable typifying the 'end of the time' in which the people of God will suffer before receiving the kingdom.[5] As can be seen from the pattern of suffering followed by exaltation, there are strong thematic connections between the historical narratives in Daniel 1 – 6 and the apocalyptic visions in Daniel 7 – 12.[6]

The terminology seen in Daniel 2:9 about the magicians stalling 'till the times change' and in Daniel's words about the Lord in 2:21, 'He changes times and seasons', recurs in 7:25, 'He . . . shall think to change the times'. The reuse of this Daniel 2 terminology in Daniel 7 works the same way the reference to 'the end of the days' did in Daniel 4:34, suggesting that the historical narrative of Daniel 2 might present a pattern of eschatological significance. Daniel 2:21 states that the God of heaven 'changes times and seasons', so when the little horn (Dan. 7:8) from the fourth beast (7:23), which symbolizes a king (7:17) from the fourth kingdom, attempts to 'change the times' (7:25), the references work together to suggest that this king is trying to do what only God can do. Daniel confessed that only God can change the times (Dan. 2:21), and just as God marked the days of

---

[5] Supporting this idea is the fact that in Rev. 2:10 John alludes to the ten-day test in Dan. 1:12. This ten-day test the church in Smyrna faces is a symbolic reference to the period of time they will suffer before those who overcome are rewarded (cf. Rev. 2:11). John seems to take his cue from the way historical periods of time are transposed into symbolic periods of time in Daniel.

[6] Thus it is inaccurate and misleading to suggest that differences in language and genre warrant a conclusion like the following: 'The disjunctive nature of this and other internal evidence suggests that MT Daniel is a composite work, the result of a complicated process of composition and redaction that incorporated what for its author/ redactor were both contemporary and older materials' (DiTommaso 2005: 3). On the contrary, the similarity between what the historical narratives *depict* and the apocalyptic visions *predict* points to an author who is both showing and telling what he wants his audience to learn.

Nebuchadnezzar's kingdom, he has also marked the days of the little horn from the fourth beast, try as he might to change the times.

Another instance of literal times providing the foundation for symbolic meaning can be seen in the way that the 'seventy years' prophesied by Jeremiah (Dan. 9:2) modulate into the 'seventy weeks' revealed to Daniel by Gabriel (9:24). The reference to 'half of the [seventieth] week' in Daniel 9:27 informs several other references to three-and-a-half-year periods in Daniel: 'a time, times, and half a time' (7:25), '2,300 evenings and mornings' (8:14), 'a time, times, and half a time' (12:7), '1,290 days' (12:11), and '1,335 days' (12:12). That the halving of the seventieth week informs these other three-and-a-half-year periods indicates, again, that these visions are meant to be mutually interpretative.

How are these references to three-and-a-half-year periods of time? As seen in chapter 2 above, if we assume thirty days in a month, then multiply that number, 30, by three-and-a-half years of months, 42, the total is 1,260 (42 × 30 = 1,260), a number that appears several times in the book of Revelation, apparently as John's interpretation of half of Daniel's seventieth week (cf. Rev. 11:2–3; 12:6, 14).[7] The '2,300 evenings and mornings' probably refers to 1,150 days of evening and morning sacrifices (see Steinmann 2008: 405–406), a period of time just three months and twenty days short of 1,260 days, that is, just under three-and-a-half years (three years, two months, twenty days). The 'time, times, and half a time' of Daniel 7:25 appears again in 12:7, and there it is closely followed by a reference to 1,290 days, indicating that the 'time, times, and half a time' refers to a three-and-a-half-year period. The same formula is interpreted as three-and-a-half years by John in Revelation 12:6 and 14. In Revelation 12:6 John references 1,260 days; then in 12:14 he calls the same period of time 'time, and times, and half a time'.

The 1,290 days of Daniel 12:11 is one month more than three years six months. Similarly, the 1,335 days of 12:12 is a period of time two months and fifteen days longer than three years and six months. Given that we are here considering the way that the reuse of phrases and concepts inform our understanding of the structure of the book of Daniel, we should not pass on without observing that all these references to half of a seven-year period occur in Daniel 7 – 12.[8]

---

[7] For further discussion, see chapter 10 below and my work on Revelation (Hamilton 2012b, esp. table 21.2).

[8] A possible historical foundation for this is the three-year period of training Daniel and his friends are put through in Dan. 1.

Before drawing together these observations on time in Daniel, let me also note that there are multiple references to time in every chapter of Daniel *except* chapters 3 and 6. This lack of time focus points to a connection between the narratives of Daniel 3 and 6. The nearest things to time references in Daniel 3 are the observations on the immediate response of worship Nebuchadnezzar demands when the music plays, the immediate consequence that will follow if they do not obey (Dan. 3:5, 6, 15) and the observation that 'at that time' the Jews were accused (3:8). Unlike other chapters in the book, Daniel 3 lacks any designation of a particular year or a certain period of time. Daniel 6 is similar, lacking any designation of a particular year when the events of the chapter took place, and the only time references noted are the 'thirty days' in which prayer may be made to Darius alone in 6:7 and 12, the observation that Daniel prays thrice daily in 6:10 and 13, and the statements that the king laboured 'till the sun went down' in 6:14, spent the night fasting in 6:18, and returned at daybreak in 6:19. Compared with the time references from the other chapters in the bullet points above, Daniel 3 and 6 stand out. These chapters have nothing to say about the years in which their events took place, nothing about a particular period of time (whether that be a three-year period as in 1:5, a sevenfold period as in 4:16 [cf. 5:21] or a three-week period as in 10:2, 13), and nothing in the way of an eschatological reference (as in e.g. 2:28–29; 7:25; 8:14, 17, 23; 9:24–27; 10:14; 11:27; 12:9).

 These observations on time references in Daniel point to a significant relationship between the historical narratives and the apocalyptic visions: the time periods and patterns of events seen in the historical narratives lay the foundation for the time periods and patterns of events seen in the apocalyptic revelations. Similar conclusions can be drawn about the repetition of the idea that God is sovereign over human kings across the book of Daniel.

God's sovereignty over human kings

The book of Daniel opens in 1:2 with a statement about God's sovereignty over human rulers, 'the Lord gave Jehoiakim king of Judah into [Nebuchadnezzar's] hand'. This idea is reiterated in Daniel's paean of praise after God has revealed Nebuchadnezzar's dream to him in 2:21, 'he removes kings and sets up kings', which is then illustrated in the revelation of the successive kingdoms in 2:36–40. Just as Daniel 3 and 6 lacked time references, Daniel 3 and 6 also lack statements pointing to God's sovereignty over kings. Just as Daniel 4 and 5 both refer to the spirit of the holy gods being in Daniel, Daniel 4 and 5 both state that 'the Most High rules the kingdom of men and gives it to whom he will and sets over it the lowliest of men' (Dan. 4:17, 25, 32; 5:21).

Just as we have seen historical time indicators point beyond themselves to apocalyptic patterns, so also the statements in the historical narratives about God's sovereignty over human kings point beyond themselves to the demonstration of the same reality in the apocalyptic visions. The idea is not overtly stated in the visions, but again and again kings are removed, again and again the final king is brought down in an unexpected way, and the kingdoms of the world give way to a kingdom that shall not be destroyed. There is a four-kingdom sequence followed by the kingdom of God in Daniel 2 and 7, while Daniel 8 and Daniel 10 – 12 focus more directly on the second and third kingdoms.

How do the apocalyptic visions in Daniel depict the demise of proud human kings? The little horn from the fourth kingdom is killed and burned in 7:11, the little horn from the third kingdom is broken 'by no human hand' in 8:25, 'the decreed end is poured out on the desolator' in 9:27, and the king of the north 'shall come to his end, with none to help him' in 11:45.

The actions of these kings proclaim their pride: the little horn from the fourth kingdom was 'speaking great things' in 7:8, 'great words' in 7:11, 'against the Most High' in 7:25. The little horn from the third kingdom became 'as great as the Prince of the host' in 8:11 and 'shall even rise up against the Prince of princes' in 8:25. The people of 'the prince who is to come' destroy city and sanctuary in 9:26, and then he puts 'an end to sacrifice and offering' in 9:27. And the king of the north 'shall exalt himself and magnify himself above every god, and shall speak astonishing things against the God of gods' in 11:36. This pride is reminiscent of Nebuchadnezzar's boastful failure to honour God (Dan. 4:28–32) and Belshazzar's proud misuse of the vessels of the Jerusalem temple (5:2–4).

The historical attack on the temple and the plundering of its vessels in Daniel 1:1–2 also provide the historical pattern for the apocalyptic attacks on the temple pursued by proud pagan kings in Daniel 7 – 12. These attacks threaten the temple and put an end to sacrifice:

- 'a host will be given over to it together with the regular burnt offering . . . the regular burnt offering . . . and the giving over of the sanctuary and host to be trampled underfoot' (8:12–13)

- 'the people of the prince who is to come shall destroy the city and the sanctuary. . . . for half of the week he shall put an end to sacrifice and offering' (9:26–27)
- 'Forces from him shall appear and profane the temple . . . , and shall take away the regular burnt offering' (11:31)
- and 'from the time that the regular burnt offering is taken away' (12:11)

The kings of the earth exalt themselves against the Lord, attack his temple, seek to stamp out sacrifice to him and set up the abomination of desolation:

- 'the transgression that makes desolate' (8:13)
- 'on the wing of abominations shall come one who makes desolate' (9:27)
- 'And they shall set up the abomination that makes desolate' (11:31)
- 'and the abomination that makes desolate is set up' (12:11)

As surely as God humbled Nebuchadnezzar and Belshazzar, as surely as the kingdoms of Babylon, Medo-Persia and Greece fell before the hand of the Sovereign, so the fourth beast will meet its end and the one like a son of man will receive everlasting dominion (Dan. 7:13–14). The references to the kingdom that will have no end are yet another feature of Daniel that ties the book together.

Never-ending kingdom

God is sovereign over the kings of the earth, so at the appointed time he will establish his kingdom. This idea is stated and restated across the book of Daniel; and as the statements recur, the relevant phrases are introduced, broken apart and put back together in ways that vary stylistically but do not alter meaning: the one like the son of man will reign for ever and his people will enjoy his kingdom with him.

In order to draw attention to the use and reuse of key phrases, short lines, ALL CAPS, *ALL CAPS ITALIC*, **bold**, ***bold italic***, SMALL CAPS and *SMALL CAPS ITALIC* will be employed to make the reuse of relevant words and phrases easier to track in what follows.

Daniel 2:44
And in the days of those kings the God of heaven will set up a
kingdom

that **shall never be destroyed,**
nor shall the *kingdom* be left to another people.
It shall break in pieces all these kingdoms and bring them to an end,
and it shall stand FOR EVER . . .

Daniel 4:3
> How great are his signs,
>   how mighty are his wonders!
> His *kingdom* is an *EVERLASTING kingdom*,
>   And his DOMINION ENDURES FROM GENERATION
>   TO GENERATION.

Daniel 4:34
> for his DOMINION is an *EVERLASTING* DOMINION,
>   and his *kingdom* ENDURES FROM GENERATION
>   TO GENERATION

Daniel 6:26–27
> for he is the living God,
>   enduring FOR EVER;
> his *kingdom* **shall never be destroyed,**
>   and his DOMINION shall be to the end.
> He delivers and rescues;
>   he works signs and wonders . . .

Daniel 7:14
his DOMINION is an *EVERLASTING* DOMINION,
which shall not pass away,
and his *kingdom* one that **shall not be destroyed.**

Daniel 7:18
possess the *kingdom* FOR EVER, for ever and ever.

Daniel 7:27
> their *kingdom* shall be an *EVERLASTING kingdom*,
>   and all dominions shall serve and obey them.

To contribute to these themes of God's sovereignty over human kings and his ability to establish an everlasting kingdom, the confessions of God's greatness from pagan kings (Dan. 2:47; 4:2–3; 34–35) join with

74

the decrees from the pagan kings that the god of the Jews should be honoured (3:29; 6:26–27).

Summary of relationships between units

From what we have seen we can say that there are strong connections between Daniel 3 and 6:

- Both involve a death threat for those who will not comply with a pagan decree (Dan. 3:6; 6:7).
- Both show faithful Jews refusing to comply with the pagan decree, recognizing that it is better to die nobly than live ignobly[9] (3:12, 16–18; 6:10).
- Both present the pagan king questioning God's ability to deliver his people (3:15; 6:20).
- Both mention God's angel helping God's servants (3:28; 6:22).
- Both show God's faithful being supernaturally preserved while the wicked who oppose them die (3:22, 27; 6:22, 24).
- Both accounts explicitly state that God's servants *trusted* in him (3:28; 6:23).
- Both present the pagan king responding to God delivering his servants by praising God and decreeing that he should be respected (3:28–29; 6:26–27).
- Both accounts resolve with a statement of how the faithful Jews were promoted or prospered (3:30; 6:28).

These correspondences between Daniel 3 and 6 indicate that Daniel intentionally included these details and framed these accounts to draw attention to their similarity. We can say similar things about how Daniel linked other chapters, such as 4 and 5:

- Both are concerned with a revelation made to the king (Dan. 4:5; 5:5).
- Unlike Daniel 2, in neither Daniel 4 nor 5 does the king hide what has been revealed from those he hopes will interpret the revelation (2:5–11; 4:7–8; 5:8).
- In both Daniel 4 and 5 the king calls for the wise men, enchanters, Chaldeans and astrologers, in the hope that they will be able to interpret the revelation (4:6–7; 5:7–8).

---

[9] I owe this phrase to my friend Ray Van Neste, who used it on his blog *Oversight of Souls*, in a post entitled 'Once to Every Man and Nation', 13 May 2013 <http://rayvanneste.com/?p=2463>, accessed 30 Jan. 2014.

- In both cases, after the charlatans have failed, Daniel is brought in to interpret the revelation (4:8; 5:10–13).
- In both accounts Daniel is described as a man 'in whom is the spirit of the holy gods' (4:8–9, 18; 5:11, 14).
- Both accounts deal with kings coming to know that 'the Most High God rules in the kingdom of mankind and sets over it whom he will' (4:17 [my tr.], 25–26, 32; 5:21).
- Both accounts deal with the humbling of proud kings (4:30; 5:22).
- Both accounts show Daniel's interpretation coming to pass (4:28; 5:30).

In addition to the strong connections between chapters 4 and 5, 3 and 6, there are obvious correspondences between chapters 2 and 7:

- Both Daniel 2 and 7 deal with dreams and their interpretations (Dan. 2:1–7, 24–26, 36; 7:1, 16).
- Both present dreams that symbolize a succession of four kingdoms followed by the kingdom of God (2:36–45; 7:11–14, 17, 23–27).
- Both accounts speak of the changing of the times (2:9, 21; 7:25).
- Both accounts are concerned with the end times (2:28–29; 7:22).
- Both accounts link the kingdom of God to David – the stone cut from no human hand that brings down the statue (2:45; cf. David's stone that slew Goliath[10] and the stone laid in Zion in Isa. 28:16 and Ps. 118:22), and the 'one like a son of man' (Dan. 7:13) is reminiscent of the Davidic 'son of man' in Ps. 8:4.
- Both accounts say the kingdom of God 'shall never be destroyed' (Dan. 2:44; 7:14).

We are yet to consider how chapters 1, 8, 9 and 10–12 might relate to other units in the book. How do they fit? Daniel 2 and 7 are concerned with a schematic revelation of what will take place between Daniel's own day and the coming of God's kingdom. The same can be said about Daniel 8 and 9: these two chapters are concerned with what will take place between Daniel's own day and the coming of God's kingdom. For that reason, I would suggest that chapters 7–9 should be thought of as a unit that balances chapter 2.

---

[10] I owe this insight to Dempster (2003: 214).

That leaves us with chapters 1 and 10–12. Like chapters 2 and 7–9, Daniel 10 – 12 reveal what will take place between Daniel's own day and the coming of God's kingdom. There are a number of indications, however, that the author intended to forge connections between chapters 1 and 10–12:

- Only in Daniel 1:21 and 10:1 do we read of a 'year' of Cyrus.
- In both units
  - the 'wise' (1:4, 17, 20; 11:33, 35; 12:3, 10);
  - endure for 'three years' (1:5; 12:7, 11–12);
  - and because they 'understand' (1:17; 11:33; 12:10);
  - they will 'stand' (1:4–5, 19; 12:13) before the king/King.

In addition to these overt points of contact there are also more thematic connections between Daniel 1 and 10 – 12. Daniel 1 depicts the culmination of the curses of the covenant as Yahweh's people and implements of temple worship are exiled to Shinar (Dan. 1:1–4). Daniel 10 – 12 depicts the promised salvation that will come through and after the Pentateuchal predictions of covenant cursing (see Lev. 26; Deut. 4:25–31; Deut. 28 – 32). Both Ezekiel 37 and Hosea 5:14–15 treat exile from the land, departure from the realm of life, as death. Ezekiel 37 and Hosea 6:1–3 also point to return from exile amounting to resurrection from the dead. So it is in Daniel. With the resurrection in Daniel 12:2–3, we find the answer to the departure from the land of life in Daniel 1. The dying in Daniel 1 is answered by the rising in Daniel 12:2–3.

The literary structure of the book of Daniel

The observations above on the discrete units of the book of Daniel and the interconnectedness of those discrete units put us in a position to evaluate proposals that have been made regarding the structure of Daniel. The discrete units of Daniel are not arranged in chronological order: Daniel 5:30 relates the death of Belshazzar, and then Daniel 8:1 presents a vision Daniel saw in the third year of Belshazzar's reign. The recognition that chronology is not the book's organizing principle invites us to consider what literary designs guided the arrangement of the book's discrete units.

Perhaps the two most basic ways of grouping the discrete units in Daniel are according to (1) language and (2) genre. The book of Daniel opens in Hebrew, 1:1 – 2:4; then halfway through Daniel 2:4

there is a switch to Aramaic, and the book stays in Aramaic to the end of chapter 7, switching back to Hebrew for chapters 8–12. Joyce Baldwin observed that 'the change of language from Hebrew to Aramaic and back to Hebrew is deliberate on the part of the author', creating 'an ABA pattern in the over-all structure' (1978: 59).

With Baldwin's observation, I would add that the change from and back to Hebrew also matches the pattern of the exile from the land and the promised return from exile. The entrance into the land, exile from it and restoration thereto is prophesied in the Torah, narrated and proclaimed in the Prophets, and woven through the songs and sayings of the psalmists and sages in the Writings.[11] The languages of Daniel enact the big story of the Old Testament.

The contents of Daniel are often also described as historical narrative in chapters 1–6 followed by apocalyptic visions in chapters 7–12 (see e.g. Gentry 2003: 60; Steinmann 2008: 20–21). As we have seen above, the historical narratives are paradigmatic adumbrations in history of what the apocalyptic revelations declare will happen in the future.

Are considerations of language and genre to be considered the decisive factors in the structure of the book? While important, they are not decisive. There is visionary material in both Aramaic (e.g. Dan. 7) and Hebrew (e.g. Dan. 8), and there is historical narrative in both Hebrew (e.g. Dan. 1) and Aramaic (e.g. Dan. 2 – 6), so the questions of language and genre should not be seen as determinative for the structuring of the book.

Andrew Steinmann (2008: 21–25), however, has proposed a structure for the book of Daniel that accounts for the two languages and two genres of the book. He argues (24) that Daniel 1 – 7 is an Aramaic chiasm with a Hebrew introduction, chapter 1 being in Hebrew, chapters 2–7 in Aramaic. He also observes that whereas chapters 1–6 are historical narrative and chapter 7 is a vision, the visionary material serves as a hinge, connecting the two parts of the book, highlighting Daniel 7 'as the pivotal chapter of the entire book' (23). Steinmann (25) then presents Daniel 7 – 12 as a Hebrew chiasm with an Aramaic introduction, chapter 7 being in Aramaic, and chapters 8–12 in Hebrew. All of chapters 7–12 are visionary.

Steinmann refers to this as an 'Interlocked Chiastic Structure' (2008: 22) that can be visualized as follows:

---

[11] See, for instance, my summary of the way the psalter sings this story (2010b: 275–290).

1 Prologue
2 Nebuchadnezzar dreams of four kingdoms and the kingdom
   of God
3 Nebuchadnezzar sees God's servants rescued
4 Nebuchadnezzar is judged
5 Belshazzar is judged
6 Darius sees Daniel rescued
7 Introduction 2: Daniel has a vision of four kingdoms and the
   kingdom of God
8 Details on the post-Babylonian kingdoms
9 Jerusalem restored
10 – 12 More details on the post-Babylonian kingdoms

This approach is attractive because it accounts for issues of genre and language and rightly sees the correspondences between chapters 2 and 7, 3 and 6, and 4 and 5 – picking up on the chiasm in the Aramaic section apparently first seen by Lenglet (1972). Lenglet's convincing chiasm matches what Steinman and others see in Daniel 2 – 7. What Steinmann does with Daniel 7 – 12 rightly recognizes the new departure in chapter 7, capturing both the clear relationship between chapters 8 and 10–12 and the climactic nature of the end of chapter 9. As we consider other proposals, I will compare them with this one and offer my evaluations.

In several places Peter Gentry (2003: 65; 2010: 27; Gentry and Wellum 2012: 533) has adapted the structure proposed by David Gooding (1981: 52). See table 3.1 below.

Table 3.1 David Gooding's adapted structure

Daniel's faithfulness	*Daniel's faithfulness*
Ch 1 refusal to eat the king's food, vindication	Ch 6 refusal to obey king's command, vindication
Two images	*Two visions of beasts*
Ch 2 Nebuchadnezzar's dream image	Ch 7 the four beasts
Ch 3 Nebuchadnezzar's golden image	Ch 8 the two beasts
Two kings disciplined	*Two writings explained*
Ch 4 discipline of Nebuchadnezzar	Ch 9 Jeremiah's prophecy
Ch 5 writing on the wall and destruction of Belshazzar	Ch 10–12 the writing of truth and the destruction of the king

Because of the strong parallels between chapters 2 and 7 and 3 and 6, I agree with Goldingay: 'Gooding's tracing of a structure balancing chaps. 1–5 and 6–12 . . . is less convincing' (1989: 325). Gooding's proposal overemphasizes the move from chapter 5 to 6; it would seem more natural to make a divide of this sort between chapters 6 and 7.

The narrative component of Daniel 1 – 6 is strongly discernible, with dialogue between various human characters and descriptions of the actions of men. The visions of chapters 7–12, by contrast, have only minimal narratival comments on time and setting, the actions described take place in visions, and the only dialogue takes place between Daniel and heavenly beings – no conversations between humans, as occurs in chapters 1–6.

Lenglet's chiasm for chapters 2–7 is very convincing, and Steinmann's proposal above is more compelling than Gooding's because it sees a new departure in chapter 7 rather than chapter 6. Proposals that capture the strong parallels between the deliverances from fiery furnace and lions' den in chapters 3 and 6 will be more convincing than what Gooding suggests.

Gentry also adapts the chiastic structure of the book set forth by Daniel I. Block (Gentry 2010: 27; Gentry and Wellum 2012: 532–533):

1 Prologue
    2 Image of four metals: triumph of God's kingdom
        3 Persecution of Daniel's friends
            4 Humbling of Nebuchadnezzar before God
            5 Humbling of Belshazzar before God
        6 Persecution of Daniel
    7 Vision of four beasts: triumph of God's kingdom
    8 Vision of future history
        9 Daniel's prayer and God's response
        10 Daniel's grief and God's response
    11:1 – 12:4 Vision of future history
12:5–13 Epilogue

What Gentry proposes here for Daniel 2 – 7 matches what Lenglet, Steinmann and others recognize about these chapters, while the proposal for chapters 8–12 differs slightly from Steinmann's. This Block-Gentry proposal has the advantage of noting the way that chapter 12 brings the book to its resolution, though the resurrection described in Daniel 12:1–3 belongs to that resolution. There is not a new departure at Daniel 12:5 but a continuation of what began in 10:1, nor is it convincing to separate chapter 10 from chapters

11–12.[12] While Daniel 11:1 mentions a king's name and year, the statement is made in the continuation of what was begun in chapter 10 rather than serving as an introduction to a new account. Daniel 12:1 continues the narrative begun in Daniel 11, which in turn was begun in Daniel 10. These considerations make the chiastic structure for Daniel 8 – 12 put forward by Steinmann preferable to this one proposed by Block–Gentry.

I noted above that considerations of genre and language are significant but not determinative. While chapters 1–6 clearly have a narrative feel that chapters 7–12 lack, it is also worth observing that chapters 2 and 4 are largely concerned with visions that point to the end of all things, both given to Nebuchadnezzar, with Daniel interpreting those visions.

Interestingly, in chapters 2 and 4, the pagan king Nebuchadnezzar has dream-visions interpreted by Daniel, whereas in chapters 7–12 Daniel has dream-visions interpreted by heavenly beings. Chapter 5 is similar to chapters 2 and 4, in that Daniel interprets the mysterious handwriting on the wall. This means that while there are differences between chapters 1–6 and 7–12 (e.g. the presence or absence of narratival features noted above), the break between these chapters should not be seen as a radically new departure.

Though the book of Daniel stands as ten discrete accounts, these accounts are interlocked with one another and achieve a profound level of interrelated connectedness. The author has achieved this through the reuse of terminology and a similarity in the structure of the individual episodes that has been noted throughout this discussion.

Before presenting my own proposed understanding of the literary structure of the whole book of Daniel, let us briefly consider one suggested by John Goldingay (1989: 325):

1 Exile and the questions it raises: story
  2 A vision of four empires
    3 A trial of faithfulness and a marvelous deliverance
      4 An omen interpreted and a king challenged and chastised
        5 An omen interpreted and a king challenged and chastised

---

[12] Gentry does note that Alfred Kuen has proposed an A, B, A structure for chapters 8–12 that would match Steinmann's proposal, with chapter 9 in the middle (Gentry and Wellum 2012: 533, n. 4).

6 A trial of faithfulness and a marvelous
deliverance
7 A vision of four empires
8 Aspects of this vision developed
9 Exile and the questions it raises: vision
10 – 12 Aspects of this vision developed

Those who have read the foregoing discussion will be able to predict my objections to this arrangement: it fails to capture the points of contact between chapters 2 and 7, 3 and 6, and 4 and 5. We can appreciate the way that Goldingay juxtaposes the book's opening and closing units, but his summary of chapters 10–12, 'Aspects of this vision developed', does not articulate the best reasons for linking chapters 1 and 10–12.

Of the proposals reviewed here, Steinmann's has the most to commend it. The strengths of his proposal include the way it accounts for the shifts in language and genre: seeing chapters 1–6 as an Aramaic chiasm of historical narrative with a Hebrew introduction, followed by chapters 7–12 as a Hebrew chiasm of apocalyptic visions with an Aramaic introduction. The pivotal role of chapter 7 and the placement of chapter 9 at the centre of the book's second chiasm are also attractive.

Could Daniel have intended multiple chiastic structures – one covering the whole book and another in which the book breaks in half with a chiasm on each side? Though possible, it may also be too complex to be convincing. The structure Steinmann has proposed may be the one Daniel intended. Ultimately, I am not convinced by it, because, as indicated above, there are important ways in which the end of the book of Daniel matches its beginning.

Daniel 1 recounts the beginnings of the exile, and Daniel 10 – 12 presents a visionary depiction of the end of exile. The exile in Daniel 1 is a departure from the realm of life into the unclean realm of the dead, and Daniel 12 depicts the resurrection from the dead. Both chapters show how the faithful are given wisdom and understanding.

With these considerations, if there is a way to account for the whole book in one chiasm that is simpler, easier to remember and more directly accounts for the details and message, such a chiasm would take us closer to what Daniel intended in the structure of his material. I have proposed a chiasm that I am convinced has these virtues, and it can be set forth as follows:

1, Exile to the unclean realm of the dead
   2, Four kingdoms followed by the kingdom of God
      3, Deliverance of the trusting from the fiery furnace
         4, Humbling of proud King Nebuchadnezzar
         5, Humbling of proud King Belshazzar
      6, Deliverance of the trusting from the lions' den
   7 – 9, Four kingdoms followed by the kingdom of God
10 – 12, Return from exile and resurrection from the dead

This chiastic structure enables us to put the message of Daniel into one sentence: 'Daniel encourages the faithful by showing them that though Israel was exiled from the land of promise, they will be restored to the realm of life at the resurrection of the dead, when the four kingdoms are followed by the kingdom of God, so the people of God can trust him and persevere through persecution until God humbles proud human kings, gives everlasting dominion to the son of man, and the saints reign with him.'

At the centre of the chiasm, Daniel 4 and 5 assure the persecuted people of God that however powerful human rulers may appear, God is sovereign over who reigns for how long, and he is able to humble those who walk in pride. The two narratives of the humbled kings in Daniel 4 and 5 are bracketed by the two narratives of deliverance – from fiery furnace and lions' den. God will humble the proud and deliver the faithful.

In addition to the way that God's ability to humble the proud and deliver his people encourages the persecuted to be faithful, the schematic revelations in Daniel 2 and 7 – 9 assure God's people that he has a plan, that he is the one who 'changes times and seasons; he removes kings and sets up kings; he gives wisdom to the wise and knowledge to those who have understanding' (Dan. 2:21).

God humbles the proud. God saves his people. God has a plan.

Daniel 1 and 10 – 12 link the book to the broader biblical storyline. The opening reference to Shinar (Dan. 1:2) denominates a biblical setting for the Danielic drama, and the resurrection of the dead (12:2) articulates a hope implicit since the curse of death and the promise of a blessing that would overcome the curse (cf. Gen. 2:17; 3:15; 5:21). We turn now to a closer examination of Daniel's treatment of the four-kingdom schema.

Chapter Four

Four kingdoms; then everlasting dominion: the history of the future

The phrase 'apocalyptic literature' intimidates many because it sounds mysterious, hints at something potentially frightening and promises to be complicated. The authors of this material probably intended to frighten rebels into repentance, but I suspect that their contemporaries would not have found the apocalyptic genre as difficult as later generations have.[1] Such difficulty would have defeated the authors' purpose in communicating.[2]

What is the best way to deal with the difficulties of this foreign genre? Roger Beckwith has proposed a way forward: 'probably the only way to redeem [the word 'apocalyptic'] is to define it by characteristics which the Revelation of John has in common with early examples of the genre like Daniel and 1 Enoch' (1985: 344). In other words, make a careful study of the books themselves and seek to understand their unique characteristics. Beckwith himself (345) proposes the following definition:

---

[1] Gerald Bray writes, 'One of the real advances in twentieth-century biblical scholarship was its rediscovery of the genre of apocalyptic literature, which has made it easier to interpret the last book of the Bible and to justify its place in the canon. For many centuries, Revelation was either ignored or misunderstood because no one really knew what to do with its rich symbolism. Many made the mistake of treating it as a literal prophecy, which led to fantastic predictions of the imminent end of time, and so on. Invariably, readings of that kind would turn out to be wrong, and that discredited the book in the eyes of many serious scholars. Now, however, it is possible to appreciate the text of Revelation for what it is and to realize that it is one of the most profoundly theological books in the entire Bible. It may take some time for awareness of this to percolate down to the average churchgoer, who is still liable to be misled by sensational interpretations, but there is a new scholarly consensus on the subject that promises to enhance, not diminish, the book's reputation and usefulness in the life of the church' (2012: 51–52).

[2] There were in the ancient world those who authored esoteric treatises meant to hide knowledge from all but the privileged few. Still, ancient audiences would have been familiar with apocalyptic literature, and the biblical authors did not intend to hide their real message but communicate it.

apocalyptic is literature akin to prophecy, concentrating on one aspect of prophecy, the revealing of secrets, and setting forth great secrets revealed by God to a favoured saint or prophet, whether about his purpose for the future, about the constitution of nature or about the unseen world, the mode of the revelation being sometimes highly symbolical but sometimes literal and unusually detailed.

This is not the only way to describe apocalyptic literature,[3] but it will serve as a working definition for this investigation. The key point I want to emphasize is that we should persist in close reading of the text itself. If we keep reading, keep asking questions and keep revising our conclusions in accordance with the text's own contents, we will make progress on the meaning of apocalyptic literature. Persistence in close study of the text will also keep us from using our definition of apocalyptic literature the way Procrustes used his iron bed.

The following elements in Beckwith's definition are richly represented in Daniel:

- the revealing of secrets
- setting forth great secrets revealed by God to a favoured saint or prophet
- God's purpose for the future
- the mode of revelation is highly symbolical
- the mode of revelation is sometimes literal and unusually detailed

The contention of this chapter is that while some aspects of the symbolism in Daniel may remain opaque, the main thrust of the apocalyptic material is clear. The various visions are united in the revelation of a single basic message: a schematic sequence of four kingdoms will be followed by the kingdom of God.

Each of these four kingdoms will control the land of promise, three of the four are named, and though the fourth kingdom is not overtly identified as Rome, Rome is the kingdom in control in the land of promise between the third kingdom, identified as Greece, and the inauguration of God's kingdom through Jesus of Nazareth.[4] We will

---

[3] Collins (1993: 54) has put forward an oft-cited and relied-on definition, but the above seems to match more closely the features of Daniel. Cf. also Beale (1999: 37, 40, 41), Carson and Moo (2005: 714) and Goldingay (1989: 320).

[4] Those who date Daniel to the Maccabean era typically identify the four kingdoms as Babylon, Media, Persia and Greece (see e.g. Collins 1993: 166–170). Steinmann has provided a thorough response, showing that the four kingdoms are Babylon, Medo-Persia, Greece and Rome (2008: 144–157).

also see that there are features of the visions that extend what is prophesied about these four kingdoms beyond their application to the
named kingdoms, creating a typological sort of pattern of what can
be expected from human governments. The features indicating a typological pattern are particularly evident in the statements made about
the third and fourth kingdoms.

We will examine the seventy weeks of Daniel 9 in the next chapter.
This chapter's examination of the four-kingdom sequence in Daniel
2, 7, 8 and 10 – 12 will establish the framework within which the
seventy weeks of Daniel 9 must be understood. As we saw in the
previous chapter, the structure of the book reflects intentional literary
design. That design includes preparing the reader for Daniel 9 with
what is revealed in Daniel 2, 7 and 8, encompassing also the setting
of Daniel 2 across from Daniel 7 – 9 in the chiastic arrangement of
the book.

We turn to the revelations of Daniel 2, 7, 8 and 10 – 12, and will
examine them in order of appearance.

The image in Daniel 2

The secret revealed in Daniel 2 is *both* the dream Nebuchadnezzar
refuses to describe to his magicians *and* its meaning (Dan. 2:1–11).
God reveals the dream to Daniel (2:12–24), and Daniel tells the king
that in the dream God has made known 'what will be in the latter
days' (2:28), 'what would be after this' and 'what is to be' (2:29). The
symbol seen is 'a great image' with head of gold, chest and arms of
silver, middle and thighs of bronze, and feet of iron and clay. God
reveals to Daniel that the sectioned materials of the image represent
different kingdoms.

The first kingdom is identified as Babylon, with Nebuchadnezzar
its royal representative: Daniel declares to Nebuchadnezzar, 'you are
the head of gold' (Dan. 2:38). Daniel then explains to Nebuchadnezzar that the 'chest and arms of silver' (2:32b) mean 'Another
kingdom inferior to you shall arise after you' (2:39a), while the 'middle
and thighs of bronze' (2:32c) are 'a third kingdom of bronze, which
shall rule over all the earth' (2:39b).

Note the fluidity between king and kingdom here: Babylon can be
identified with its *king*, Nebuchadnezzar, while the kings who follow
him are designated as other *kingdoms*. The meaning, however, is the
same. That is, those kingdoms that come after Nebuchadnezzar will
have kings (cf. 5:31; 7:17, etc.). Kings, not the people, will rule those

kingdoms – Daniel does not prophesy some ancient (inconceivable for that time and place) democratic arrangement.

This easy interchange of king and kingdom is relevant to our understanding of the statements that the saints receive the kingdom in Daniel 7 (7:18, 22, 27). That kingdom will also have a king. We should observe as well that the particular sense in which these kingdoms will reign over 'all the earth' is that they conquer one another, with the land promised to Israel coming under their dominion.

Daniel's interpretation of Nebuchadnezzar's dream culminates with his description of the fourth kingdom, symbolized by the 'legs of iron, its feet partly of iron and partly of clay' (Dan. 2:33). Having described the image from head to toe, Daniel describes its end: 'a stone was cut out by no human hand, and it struck the image on its feet of iron and clay, and broke them in pieces' (2:34).

The stone that strikes the fourth kingdom of the image was cut out 'by no human hand'. Daniel 8:25 will describe how the little horn from the third kingdom will 'be broken – but by no human hand'. That the third and fourth kingdoms are brought down 'by no human hand' comprises one of many points of contact between them.[5]

Daniel seems to have interpreted Nebuchadnezzar's dream through the categories given to him from the Hebrew Scriptures. For example, when Daniel recounts his recitation of the dream to Nebuchadnezzar, he uses language reminiscent of Psalm 1:4's description of the fate of the wicked to describe the demise of the four kingdoms: 'all together were broken in pieces, and became like the chaff of the summer threshing floors; and the wind carried them away, so that not a trace of them could be found' (Dan. 2:35).

In his comments on the interpretation of the dream, Daniel has more to say about the fourth kingdom than all the others combined (cf. Dan. 2:38–39 and 2:40–43). The details given about this fourth kingdom – its conquests (2:40), its divided nature making it at once firm, soft and brittle (2:41–42), and its doomed attempts to forge alliances by marriage (2:43) – are almost an abbreviated summary of the similar description of the third kingdom in Daniel 11. Daniel 11 is far more detailed and specific, but that chapter too concerns conquest, differences between peoples, and failed attempts to unify by marriage. The prophecy about the fourth kingdom in Daniel 2 matches the more expansive description of the third in Daniel 11.

---

[5] As Dan. 2 is in Aramaic and Dan. 8 in Hebrew, the language in these statements does not match exactly. Both do, however, speak of no 'hand' being involved.

Daniel exposits for Nebuchadnezzar the meaning of the stone cut with no human hand that causes the wicked to be 'like chaff that the wind drives away' (Ps. 1:4), saying in Daniel 2:44–45:

> And in the days of those kings the God of heaven will set up a kingdom that shall never be destroyed, nor shall the kingdom be left to another people. It shall break in pieces all these kingdoms and bring them to an end, and it shall stand for ever, just as you saw that a stone was cut from a mountain by no human hand, and that it broke in pieces the iron, the bronze, the clay, the silver, and the gold. A great God has made known to the king what shall be after this. The dream is certain, and its interpretation sure.

Earlier in the passage, Daniel had described how in the dream, 'the stone that struck the image became a great mountain and filled the whole earth' (Dan. 2:35). The little stone symbolizes the kingdom that God will set up, which will last for ever. God's kingdom destroys all human kingdoms and fills the earth, pointing to the way that his kingdom will enjoy dominion over the entire world as his glory fills the earth.

Nebuchadnezzar's response to the revelation of the dream is double-minded. On the one hand, he pays homage to Daniel (Dan. 2:46), telling him, 'Truly, your God is God of gods and Lord of kings, and a revealer of mysteries' (2:47); then exalting Daniel and his friends over Babylon (2:48–49). On the other hand, Nebuchadnezzar sets up 'an image of gold, whose height was sixty cubits and its breadth six cubits' (3:1). Having just dreamed of an 'image' (2:31) wherein he was represented by the head of gold to be followed by three other human kingdoms represented by silver, bronze and clay/iron, Nebuchadnezzar sets up an 'image' of gold from top to bottom (3:1). In view of the demand that all are to worship the image or die (3:2–6), it would appear that Nebuchadnezzar has set up this golden image to declare that his kingdom will not be replaced by those of silver, bronze and clay/iron. It will be gold all the way down.

Daniel 3 shows Nebuchadnezzar incapable of visiting the death penalty on God's servants, and chapter 4 shows him driven to insanity until seven periods of time pass over him. Interestingly, when the tree is chopped down in Nebuchadnezzar's Daniel 4 dream, the stump is left with 'its roots in the earth, bound with a band of iron and bronze' (Dan. 4:15). Nebuchadnezzar will not escape those other elements. His kingdom will not stand for ever. When these things are interpreted, Daniel explains to Nebuchadnezzar that his dehumanized condition will continue 'till you know that the Most High rules the kingdom of men and gives it to whom he will' (4:25; cf. 26, 32). Daniel 5 makes a similar point, with 5:30–31 narrating the transition from the first to the second kingdom.

The beasts in Daniel 7

In Daniel 2 and 4, Nebuchadnezzar's dreams are interpreted by Daniel. In Daniel 7 and 8, Daniel's visions are interpreted by an angel. In Daniel 2, Nebuchadnezzar dreamed of an image made of four metals. The metals represented human kingdoms. The image was crushed by a stone. The stone symbolized God's kingdom. In Daniel 7, there are four beasts that 'are four kings' (Dan. 7:17), and dominion is taken from these beasts and given to the one like a son of man who receives everlasting dominion (7:13–14). The visions of Daniel 2 and 7, then, depict four human kingdoms preceding the institution of the kingdom of God.

Daniel refers to what was revealed to him in Daniel 7 as both a 'dream' and as 'visions of his head' (Dan. 7:1). Daniel perceived the dream-vision and the angel's interpretation, which he then processed in his thinking, recorded in writing and incorporated into his book. In this sequence, he has interpreted what he saw, presented his interpreted account, and in his book he intended to give instruction to those who read his work (cf. 11:33; 12:3, 10).

Daniel seems to have recognized wider biblical resonance in the symbols of the dream he recounts in chapter 7, and he seems to have intended his audience to discern that resonance as well. The particular resonance I have in mind is the way that dominion over the beasts was given to the man in Genesis 1:26–28. The Hebrew phrase 'son of man' would have evoked that first man, whose name, Adam, is the same term rendered 'man' (אדם, 'ādām).[6]

Man enjoyed that dominion until he was tempted by a beast – the serpent – and sinned (Gen. 3:1–7). God then placed enmity between the seed of the woman and the seed of the serpent (Gen. 3:15). The serpent, a beast, usurped the dominion given to man.

[6] Dan. 7 is in Aramaic, but the term used in the Aramaic phrase 'son of man' is also used in the Aramaic Targum on Gen. 1:26 for 'man' (אנש, 'ĕnôš, though the proper name אדם, 'ādām, also appears in the Targum on Gen. 1:26). The Targumic text consulted is the one available in BibleWorks, which is 'derived from the Hebrew Union CAL (Comprehensive Aramaic Lexicon) Project'.

Identifying human kingdoms of the world with beasts contrasts them with the 'one like a son of man' (Dan. 7:13). Daniel probably filtered this dream through another biblical text that speaks of a Davidic son of man to whom dominion over the beasts was given. The superscription of Psalm 8 names it 'A Psalm of David'. In Psalm 8:4 (MT Ps. 8:5) the question is asked

> what is man that you are mindful of him,
> and the son of man that you care for him?

The verses that follow this question (8:6–8, MT 7–9) rehearse how God gave 'dominion' to 'the son of man' over 'the beasts of the field'.

When Daniel relates his dream, then, in which four human kings are symbolized as beasts, these beasts possess dominion usurped by the snake, dominion God gave to his viceregent image-bearer at creation. If the beasts have the dominion that God gave to man, it is as though the seed of the serpent rather than the seed of the woman, the son of Adam, rules the realm. Assuming that Psalm 8 originated with David, Daniel would have been aware of it. These inter-textual connections between Genesis 1 – 3 and Psalm 8 add Adamic and Davidic texture to the Daniel 7 dream-vision.[7]

The first beast in Daniel 7 is described in terms reminiscent of Nebuchadnezzar: in Daniel 4:33 Nebuchadnezzar's 'hair grew as long as eagles' feathers, and his nails were like birds' claws'. In Daniel 7:4, the first beast 'was like a lion and had eagles' wings', and then just as Nebuchadnezzar was restored to his humanity, 'as I looked its wings were plucked off, and it was lifted up from the ground and made to stand on two feet like a man, and the mind of a man was given to it' (Dan. 7:4). This beast, then, symbolizes the king of Babylon and his time of authority, his kingdom.

The second beast in Daniel 7:5 is described in a way that comports with what will be revealed in chapter 8 (cf. Dan. 8:3–4, 20) of 'the kings of Media and Persia' (8:20). Similarly, the description of the third beast (7:6) matches what chapter 8 will say about 'the king of Greece' and those who come after him (8:21–22; cf. 8:5–8).

As with Nebuchadnezzar's dream in Daniel 2, the fourth kingdom is given most space in Daniel 7 (Dan. 7:7–8, 11). Calling to mind the

---

[7] Porter suggests that 'the animal metaphors of Daniel 7 and 8 find their origin in the root metaphor of the shepherd', and argues that 'the root metaphor "shepherd," mediated by the office of the king, has generated external metaphors . . . relative to the beasts of Daniel 7 and 8' (1983: 60–61).

feet and legs of Nebuchadnezzar's Daniel 2 dream, the fourth beast of the Daniel 7 vision is characterized by iron (7:7; cf. 2:33). The iron was explained in Daniel 2:40 with the words 'there shall be a fourth kingdom, strong as iron, because iron breaks to pieces and shatters all things. And like iron that crushes, it shall break and crush all these.' Along the same lines, Daniel writes of the fourth beast in 7:7, 'and behold, a fourth beast, terrifying and dreadful and exceedingly strong. It had great iron teeth; it devoured and broke in pieces and stamped what was left with its feet.'

Daniel describes the fourth beast as having ten horns, in the midst of which arises a little horn speaking great things (Dan. 7:7–8). Later in the chapter these ten horns will be explained to Daniel as ten kings, the little horn being a king that rises after them (7:24).

Daniel 7 is unique among the dream-visions: it is the only one to include a heavenly throne-room scene. The Ancient of Days is enthroned with his servants in attendance in Daniel 7:9–10; then Daniel returns to the little horn to detail his demise in 7:11–12, before describing the one like the son of man presented before the Ancient of Days to receive everlasting dominion in 7:13–14 (on the one like a son of man, see chapter 6).

Whereas in Daniel 2 the stone cut out by no human hand strikes the feet of the statue and the whole thing crumbles and becomes like chaff blown by the wind, in Daniel 7 the little horn from the fourth beast 'was killed, and its body destroyed and given over to be burned with fire. As for the rest of the beasts, their dominion was taken away, but their lives were prolonged for a season and a time' (Dan. 7:11–12). Daniel then describes the enthronement of the 'one like a son of man' (7:13–14). The little horn is slain, the other beasts lose dominion but continue for 'a season and a time', and then the son of man is enthroned. Later texts will fill out the chronological details.[8] We turn now to the interpretation of the dream-vision given in Daniel 7:15–27.

[8] For discussion, see below in this chapter and chapters 5, 8 and 9. I do not think that the continuation of the lives of the other beasts can be definitively interpreted on the basis of what we see in the book of Daniel. Once we have the NT, however, this statement in Dan. 7:12 can be interpreted in the light of later revelation. The killing of the beast in Dan. 7:11 seems to be interpreted by Paul to refer to 'the lawless one . . . whom the Lord Jesus will kill with the breath of his mouth and bring to nothing by the appearance of his coming' (2 Thess. 2:8). If this is correct, the continuation of the lives of these other beasts goes beyond the second coming. Perhaps the continuation of their lives pertains to the subjugation of human kingdoms to King Jesus during the millennium, and perhaps they will join the rebellion described in Rev. 20:7–10. See the discussion in chapter 9 below.

When Daniel 'approached one of those who stood there and asked him the truth concerning all this' (Dan. 7:16), the one with whom he interacted was apparently among those described in attendance on the Ancient of Days in Daniel 7:10:

> a thousand thousands served him,
> and ten thousand times ten thousand stood before him;
> the court sat in judgment,
> and the books were opened.

This member of the heavenly entourage 'made known' to Daniel 'the interpretation of the things' (7:16). This kind of interaction between prophet and heavenly tour guide is a feature of apocalyptic literature seen also in Zechariah and John's Revelation.

The angel tells Daniel that the beasts 'are four kings who shall arise out of the earth. But the saints of the Most High shall receive the kingdom and possess the kingdom for ever, for ever and ever' (Dan. 7:17–18). Again we see the dynamic between the king and his kingdom that we noted above in Daniel 2. These passages portray an interchangeable relationship between the king and those he represents, between king and people. We observed earlier that this easy back and forth dynamic between king and kingdom or people can be seen in Daniel 2, when Daniel said to Nebuchadnezzar, 'You are the head of gold' (2:38); but rather than identifying the other sections of the image with *kings* to follow (as we see here in Dan. 7:17, 'These four great beasts are four kings'), the other metals in Daniel 2 are referred to as *kingdoms* (2:39–40).

The same dynamic between king and kingdom is at work in Daniel 7. The saints receive the kingdom in Daniel 7:18 and 22, but this everlasting kingdom is manifestly the same one received by the 'one like a son of man' in 7:13–14. The final statement of 7:27 refers to *his* 'kingdom', and the referent seems to be the immediately preceding 'Most High' (see further discussion in chapter 6 below). The Genesis background helps us understand this picture. God made the world and then gave dominion over it to Adam, the one in his image and likeness. When God has accomplished the restoration of his world, the 'one like a son of man [Adam]' will again exercise dominion over God's kingdom, which will be held by God's holy ones, his saints.

So the fact that Daniel 7:18 and 22 refer to 'the saints' possessing the kingdom does not mean that the 'one like a son of man' in 7:13 is a corporate symbol of the people of God. Rather, the king is the son of man who is the vicegerent of the Most High, to whom the masculine singular pronouns in 7:27 refer, and the saints are the people of his kingdom, whom he represents, who will receive the kingdom he establishes. This tension between the one and the many can be found throughout the Old and New Testaments.

Once the angel explains that there will be four kingdoms followed by the kingdom of God (Dan. 7:17–18), Daniel states his curiosity about the fourth beast, and in doing so he rehearses what he saw of the fourth beast in the vision (7:19–22). The retelling adds, however, that the little horn 'made war with the saints and prevailed over them' (7:21; cf. Rev. 11:7; 13:7). Daniel also adds a chronological note about the little horn's persecution of the people of God, noting in 7:22 that the war on the saints continued 'until the Ancient of Days came, and judgment was given for the saints of the Most High, and the time came when the saints possessed the kingdom'.

The angel explains the fourth kingdom's conquests (Dan. 7:23) and relates that the ten horns are ten kings, with the little horn a different king who comes after the ten (7:24). He then describes how the little horn speaks against the Most High, persecutes God's people, and rewrites the rules and times, noting that this will continue 'for a time, times, and half a time' (7:25). The little horn's self-aggrandizing antichrist activity will come to an end, however, when 'the court shall sit in judgement' (7:26; cf. 7:10), at which point his dominion will be removed and given to the people of the Most High, who will reign for ever (7:26–27).[9]

From the amount of space given to the kingdoms, we can say that the visions in Daniel 2, 4 and 7 focus on kingdoms one and four, while those in Daniel 8 and 10 – 12 focus on kingdoms two and three. We would be missing the point, however, if we failed to see that these kings and kingdoms will be supplanted by the true king who will enjoy everlasting dominion in his kingdom that will not be shaken.

The ram and the goat in Daniel 8

Daniel recounts in chapter 8 the vision he had in the third year of Belshazzar's reign. He writes of how he first saw a ram with two horns

[9] We will consider in chapter 6 below the two different ways Daniel refers to 'the Most High', where it will be seen that Dan. 7:27 exposits 7:13–14, as the 'Most High' referenced in 7:27 is identified with and distinguished from the Ancient of Days, and this 'Most High' in 7:27 is linked to the 'one like a son of man' in 7:13–14 by the language common to the two texts.

(Dan. 8:3). Like the second beast in chapter 7 from the vision he saw in the first year of Belshazzar (a bear 'raised up on one side' in 7:5), one of the ram's two horns is higher than the other (8:3). The conquests of the ram in 8:4 likewise correspond to the command for the bear to 'Arise, devour much flesh' in 7:5. These similarities create the impression of a pattern, fostering expectation of a certain type of behaviour – desire to conquer – from these rulers.

Also moving things in the direction of a repeated pattern, adding to the impression that typological expectation is being nourished, is the fact that in Daniel 8:4 the description of the ram (second kingdom) concludes with the words 'He did as he pleased and became great.' This is very similar to the statement regarding the goat (third kingdom) in Daniel 8:8, 'Then the goat became exceedingly great.' The goat is identified as Greece in 8:21, and again a similar statement is made about Greece in 11:3, 'Then a mighty king shall arise, who shall rule with great dominion and do as he wills.'

Just as Daniel 8:3–4 provides another look at the second kingdom, Daniel 8:5–8 provides more information on the third kingdom. We know this is the third kingdom because of its similarity to the third beast, the leopard with four heads, in Daniel 7:6. This is also confirmed by both the identification of the goat with Greece in 8:21 and the similar description of Greece in 11:2–4.

The vision indicates that the goat's conquest was swift, led by a powerful king, who is symbolized by the goat's prominent horn (Dan. 8:5; cf. 8:21). The goat, Greece, conquered the ram, Medo-Persia (8:6–7; cf. 8:20; 11:2–3). Then 'the great horn was broken, and instead of it there came up four conspicuous horns towards the four winds of heaven' (8:8; cf. 7:6; 11:4). This is exactly what happened when Alexander the Great died and his realm was divided among the four who followed him.

Daniel 8 next describes the little horn from the third kingdom, and once again there are elements of a pattern here. As noted in chapter 2 above, there are strong correspondences between the activity of the little horn from the third kingdom in chapter 8 (and 11) and the little horn from the fourth kingdom in chapter 7.

Several elements in the description of the little horn's activity show that this vision pertains to what this king from the third kingdom will do against the people of God in the land of promise: he grows great 'towards the glorious land' (Dan. 8:9), and his aggrandizement is described as 'to the host of heaven' (8:10) and to 'the Prince of the host' (8:11), whom he attacks by throwing 'some of the host and some of the stars . . . to the ground' and trampling on them (8:10; cf. the trampling to the ground in 8:7). The little horn from the fourth kingdom similarly 'stamped what was left with its feet' (7:19).

The little horn in chapter 7 from the fourth kingdom attacked the people of God (7:21, 25), and the little horn from the third kingdom does the same in chapter 8. The attack on God in chapter 8 entails the overthrow of the temple and the removal of the regular burnt offering (8:11–12).

Daniel speaks of the people of God in terms of their biblical and cosmic significance when he calls them 'the host' and 'the stars' in Daniel 8:10. It is clear from other statements in the passage (Dan. 8:13, 24–25) that this attack is on the people of God. By calling them 'the host', Joshua's encounter with 'the commander of the host of Yahweh' (Josh. 5:14, my tr.) is invoked, and referring to them as 'the stars' links them to the 'stars of heaven' promised to Abraham in Genesis 22:17 (cf. Gen. 15:5) and the 'star' that rises from Jacob in Numbers 24:17. Within the book of Daniel, referring to God's people as 'stars' in Daniel 12:3 anticipates the way those who turn many to righteousness will shine. This language also has points of contact with the *heavenly* host, along the lines of John's description of the dragon sweeping down 'stars of heaven' in Revelation 12:4 (cf. 'his angels . . . with him' in Rev. 12:9).

The heavenly overtones of the language of 'host' and 'stars' reflects Daniel speaking of the little horn from the third kingdom the same way that Isaiah and Ezekiel spoke of wicked human rulers: in satanic terms. In Isaiah 14:12–15 Isaiah spoke of the king of Babylon (Isa. 14:4) in terms that extended beyond the human king to that ancient serpent who is the devil and Satan. Isaiah spoke of the king of Babylon this way because just as Israel's king was the human representative of Yahweh on earth (cf. Isa. 7:14; 9:6), the king of Babylon was the representative of the serpent, the pre-eminent and exemplary dark champion of the seed of the serpent. In Ezekiel 28:1 Ezekiel is instructed to address the prince of Tyre, and as the lamentation continues (Ezek. 28:12), things are said of this prince of Tyre that cannot have been true of him but are true of the ancient serpent: 'You were in Eden, the garden of God' (28:13; cf. 28:13–19).

The same dynamic seems to be at work in Daniel 8:10, with the exploits of the human king, the little horn from the third kingdom, spoken of in language that reflects satanic conquests. Daniel also presents Gabriel explaining that 'his power shall be great – but not by his own power' (Dan. 8:24). This would appear to inform what Paul meant when he wrote that 'the coming of the lawless one is by the activity of Satan' (2 Thess. 2:9). Whether these wicked human kings were conscious of it or not, their activity stemmed from a power beyond what they could see, an ancient force ranged against God and his purposes (cf. Dan. 10:13, 20; 11:1).[10]

This also explains the references to Israel's leader as 'the Prince of the host' in Daniel 8:11 and as 'the Prince of princes' in 8:25. Following the precedent of earlier biblical authors, Daniel used heavenly symbolism to describe God's people and their enemies. Just as Israel's king could be addressed as the one who stood in God's place (e.g. Ps. 45:6), so wicked rulers like the king of Babylon or the prince of Tyre could be addressed as the one who stood in Satan's place.

The vision of the little horn from the third kingdom is boiled down to its essence as Daniel relates in 8:13 a conversation he heard between two holy ones. One holy one asks another, 'For how long is the vision?', and then describes the vision in three ways, saying it concerns (1) 'the regular burnt offering', (2) 'the transgression that makes desolate', and (3) 'the giving over of the sanctuary and host to be trampled underfoot' (Dan. 8:13). The little horn from the third kingdom, like the little horn from the fourth kingdom, will seek to put an end to sacrifice (8:11, 13; cf. 9:27), desolate through abominable transgression (8:13; cf. 9:27), attack the temple (8:11, 13; cf. 9:26) and persecute and kill God's people (8:12–13; cf. 7:21, 25). We will see such behaviour again when we consider the description of the king from the third kingdom in Daniel 11 (cf. 11:31–33).

One holy one in Daniel 8:13 asked another, 'For how long is the vision?', and in 8:14 Daniel writes, 'And he said to me' – so the answer to the question seems to be addressed to Daniel – 'For 2,300 evenings and mornings' (Dan. 8:14). As noted in chapters 2 and 3, this 2,300 evenings and mornings probably refers to 1,150 days of evening and morning sacrifices (Lucas 2002: 218). Steinmann observes that from the desecration of the altar of the temple on 15 Kislev in year 144 of the Seleucid era (1 Macc. 1:54, which Steinmann dates to 6 December 167 BC), to the resumption of sacrifices on 25 Kislev 148 (1 Macc. 4:52–53, which Steinmann dates to 14 December 164), 'the time of the cessation of the evening and morning sacrifices probably was

---

[10] After writing this section, I came across Goldingay's comment that Daniel 'was suggesting that he [Antiochus] – like the King of Babylon in Isa. 14 or Gog in Ezek. 38 – was the very embodiment of godless wickedness, so that the language used of him could be used of Antichrist or Satan' (1989: 317).

approximately 1,150 days' (2008: 405–406, his emphasis).[11] We also noted in chapter 3 that this 1,150-day period of time is similar to the three-and-a-half-year period of time referenced regarding the fourth kingdom in Daniel 7:25 and 9:27.

Significantly, in Daniel 9:24 just as at the end of the seventy weeks the most holy place would be anointed, so also in Daniel 8:14 at the end of the 2,300 evenings and mornings 'the sanctuary shall be restored to its rightful state'. The parallel between the little horns of the third and fourth kingdoms corresponds point for point: they exalt themselves and attack the temple, they cut off sacrifice for an approximately three-and-a-half-year period of time; then the temple is restored and sacrifice resumed. These parallels are based on actual historical realities, but they also point beyond themselves to 'the end'.

In the second half of Daniel 8, Gabriel gives Daniel understanding of the vision he beheld. Gabriel tells Daniel that 'the vision is for the time of the end' (Dan. 8:17), that 'it refers to the appointed time of the end' (8:19), and that 'the vision of the evenings and the mornings . . . refers to many days from now' (8:26). The actions of the little horn from the third kingdom bear an uncanny resemblance to the actions of the little horn from the fourth, and the pattern typified by these two rulers will find its eschatological fulfilment in one who will prevail until the coming of the Ancient of Days (cf. Dan. 7:21–22).

Kings of south and north in Daniel 10 – 12

We will return to Daniel 9 and the seventy weeks prophesied there in the next chapter. What we have seen to this point gives us footing to find our way in the perplexing detail of Daniel 10 – 12. Daniel 2 and 7 deal with the four kingdoms between Daniel's own day and the institution of the kingdom of God. Like Daniel 8, Daniel 10 – 12 zooms in on the second and third kingdoms, with most of the attention given to the third. Also like Daniel 8, this information on the third kingdom in Daniel 10 – 12 'is for days yet to come' (Dan. 10:14), that is, 'the time of the end' (11:35; cf. 11:27, 29, 36, 40; 12:4, 9, 13).

Daniel 10 describes Daniel's encounter with one or more heavenly beings, one of whom tells him 'what is inscribed in the book of truth' (Dan. 10:21). We will return to the heavenly beings in Daniel 10 in

---

[11] Steinmann notes that the dates cited above are 1,106 days, just under 1,150 days. He considers the possibility that the ban on sacrifice might have been in force prior to the desecration of the altar (cf. 1 Macc. 1:41–53), but observes that 'OT prophecies concerning time periods are usually given in round numbers' (2008: 406).

chapter 6. Our interest here is in the content of the revelation in Daniel 11 – 12.

As the angel shows Daniel the truth (Dan. 11:2), he gives less than one verse to the second kingdom, Persia (11:2), before devoting the remainder of his remarks to the third kingdom, Greece (11:2–45). The angel gives one verse to Alexander the Great (11:3), one verse to the four who followed him (11:4); then devotes considerable attention to the kings of north and south (11:5–20). The angel has discussed a few more than ten kings from the third kingdom to this point,[12] and he now devotes as much space to Antiochus Epiphanes in Daniel 11:21–35 as he gave to those who preceded the madman[13] in 11:5–20. The angel then gives not a little detail, in 11:36–45, on what appears to be a climactic set of defiant actions that lead to the downfall of this little horn from the third kingdom.

As can be seen from the previous paragraph, this eleventh chapter of Daniel has focused on the third kingdom with increasing levels of specificity. After quickly summarizing the second kingdom to set up the third (Dan. 11:2), much space is given to the kings whose reigns dig the ruts for the ruin of the madman (11:5–20), the one reigning when 'they shall set up the abomination that makes desolate' (11:31; cf. 11:21–35), and then a similar amount of space is given to the account of the great downfall of that house built on sand (11:36–45).

Goldingay suggests (1989: 311–319) that the detailed nature of this passage indicates that Daniel was presenting 'quasi-prophecy'. The modifier 'quasi' means 'as if'. Against Goldingay's suggestion that Daniel presents 'as if prophecy', the growing concentration on Antiochus Epiphanes becomes evident from the amount of space given to what is treated in this passage. The honing concentration most probably derives from the fact that Antiochus Epiphanes typifies the Antichrist. Jerome articulated this perspective long ago: 'since many of the details . . . are appropriate to the person of Antiochus, he is to be regarded as a type of the Antichrist, and those things which happened to him in a preliminary way are to be completely fulfilled in the case of the Antichrist' (1958: 129).

---

[12] Goldingay (1989: 295–296) enumerates the thirteen kings to which this passage alludes. These few more than ten rulers (horns) are followed by Antiochus Epiphanes (the little horn). The prophecy in Dan. 7:7–8 about ten horns followed by a little horn was about the fourth kingdom, so there is a loose similarity on this point between the prophesied third kingdom in Dan. 11 and the prophesied fourth kingdom in Dan. 7.

[13] Polybius, *Histories* 26.1.1, tells us that Antiochus Epiphanes was referred to by his detractors as Epimanes, 'madman'.

The descriptions of the wars and rumours of wars leading up to the rise of Antiochus can be identified with events from the period in view (see standard commentaries and resources such as the two-page chart in the ESV Study Bible, 2008: 1612–1613). For the purposes of this study we will focus our attention on the points of contact between the 'contemptible person' (Dan. 11:21 – Antiochus Epiphanes) and the little horn from the third kingdom, confirming that the little horn from Daniel 8 and the contemptible person of Daniel 11 are the same figure. We will also point to similarities between this contemptible person of Daniel 11 and the little horn of kingdom four in Daniel 7, evidencing again that these are instalments in a typological pattern.

The elements of this pattern are straightforward: (1) at the time of the end (2) a king of exaggerated wickedness arises (3) who attacks God's people and (4) tries to keep them from worshipping him, (5) setting up instead an abomination of desolation, (6) thereupon a horrible time of tribulation will continue for three-and-a-half years (7) before the wicked king meets sudden, irreversible destruction, (8) resulting in deliverance for the righteous. This is admittedly a composite of what Daniel describes, and more detail could no doubt be added to the pattern. Each aspect of this mosaic, however, is represented in Daniel 11 – 12, and below I outline its presence in Daniel 11 – 12, drawing attention to its presence also in earlier passages:

(1) *At the time of the end*:

- 'the end is yet to be at the time appointed' (11:27)
- 'At the time appointed' (11:29)
- 'until the time of the end, for it still awaits the appointed time' (11:35)
- 'At the time of the end' (11:40)
- 'At that time' (12:1)
- 'at that time' (12:1)
- 'until the time of the end' (12:4)
- 'till the end of these wonders?' (12:6)
- 'until the time of the end' (12:9)
- 'till the end . . . at the end of the days' (12:13)

This is very similar to the vision in Daniel 8 that was 'for the time of the end' (Dan. 8:17), a vision that 'refers to many days from now' (8:26). There are not overt references to the end in Daniel 7, but the little horn from the fourth beast is followed by the everlasting kingdom of God. Similarly, in Daniel 9, everything appears to be consummated in 9:24, indicating that what is revealed there also pertains to the end of all things.

Notably, there is no discernible transition to the end of all things in Daniel 11. The passage is clearly dealing with the third kingdom, and there is no indication that the focus shifts to the fourth kingdom and its little horn before the eschatological resurrection is described in Daniel 12:1–3. This would appear to indicate that what is said about this little horn from the third kingdom, this contemptible person (Dan. 11:21), pertains to the time of the end. Thus Antiochus Epiphanes typifies the end-time Antichrist, who is likewise typified by the little horn from the fourth kingdom, so the pattern depicted with reference to Antiochus Epiphanes can terminate in the final deliverance of God's people and their resurrection. The points of contact between and the interlocking nature of what is revealed in Daniel 7, 8, 9 and 10 – 12 join to lead Daniel's audience to this conclusion.

(2) *A king of exaggerated wickedness arises*:

- 'shall arise a contemptible person to whom royal majesty has not been given' (11:21)
- 'he shall act deceitfully' (11:23)
- 'they shall set up the abomination that makes desolate' (11:31)
- 'the king shall do as he wills' (11:36a)
- 'He shall exalt himself and magnify himself above every god, and shall speak astonishing things against the God of gods' (11:36b)
- 'He shall not pay attention to any other god, for he shall magnify himself above all' (11:37)

Similar wickedness is perpetrated by the little horn from the third kingdom in the Daniel 8 vision. That little horn 'will throw truth to the ground, and it will act and prosper' (Dan. 8:12), being described as 'a king of bold countenance' (8:23), who 'by his cunning . . . shall make deceit prosper' while 'in his own mind he shall become great' (8:25). This is also like the little horn from the fourth kingdom in Daniel 7 who had 'a mouth speaking great things' (7:8) and 'seemed greater than its companions' (7:20), even speaking 'words against the Most High', thinking 'to change the times and the law' (7:25).

(3) *Who attacks God's people*:

- 'and be enraged and take action against the holy covenant' (11:30)
- 'the wise . . . shall stumble by sword and flame, by captivity and plunder' (11:33)

The same kinds of attacks against God's people are advanced by the little horns from the third kingdom in Daniel 8 (Dan. 8:10, 12–13, 24) and from the fourth in Daniel 7 (7:21, 25). The prince who is to come also does violence in Daniel 9:26–27.

(4) *Tries to keep them from worshipping him*:

- 'Forces from him shall appear and profane the temple' (11:31a)
- 'and shall take away the regular burnt offering' (11:31b)
- 'the regular burnt offering is taken away' (12:11)

We have considered the activity of the little horn from the third kingdom in Daniel 8:11–13. There is nothing overt about the obstruction of worship in Daniel 7, but there is material of this nature in Daniel 9 (cf. again Dan. 9:26–27).

(5) *Setting up instead an abomination of desolation*:

- 'And they shall set up the abomination that makes desolate' (11:31c)
- 'and the abomination that makes desolate is set up' (12:11)

The phrase is not an exact parallel, but in Daniel 8:13 we read of 'the transgression that makes desolate'. Again, nothing overt is mentioned about the abomination of desolation from the little horn of the fourth beast in Daniel 7, but we do see one making desolate with abominations in Daniel 9:27.

(6) *The horrible tribulation will continue for three-and-a-half years*:

- 'a time of trouble, such as never has been . . .' (12:1)
- 'for a time, times, and half a time' (12:7)
- 'there shall be 1,290 days' (12:11)
- 'Blessed is he who waits and arrives at the 1,335 days' (12:12)

Here perhaps we have the clearest indication that these passages are interlocking and to be read in a mutually interpretative fashion. The closest the book of Daniel comes to defining what is meant by 'time, times, and half a time' – referenced in both Daniel 7:25 and 12:7 – is the halving of the seventieth week in Daniel 9:27. Through this lens we can see that the three-and-a-half-year period is also similar to the 2,300 evenings and mornings, 1,150 days, in Daniel 8:14. These conclusions are confirmed by the way that John parallels the reference to 1,260 days (three-and-a-half years of days) with the reference to 'time, and times, and half a time' in Revelation 12:6 and 14 (on the interpretation of Daniel in Revelation, see chapter 9 below).

(7) *Before the wicked king meets sudden, irreversible destruction*:

- 'Yet he shall come to his end, with none to help him' (11:45)

The little horn from the third kingdom is broken 'by no human hand' in Daniel 8:25 (cf. the stone cut out 'by no human hand' in Dan. 2:34). The little horn from the fourth kingdom 'was killed' in Daniel 7:11, and it becomes clear from 7:21–22 that he was killed *when* the Ancient of Days came, when the court sat in judgment and took away his dominion in 7:26 (cf. 7:10–11).

(8) *Resulting in deliverance for the righteous*:

- 'at that time your people shall be delivered' (12:1)
- 'those who sleep in the dust of the earth shall awake' (12:2)
- 'those who are wise shall shine like the brightness of the sky above; and those who turn many to righteousness, like the stars for ever and ever' (12:3)
- 'you shall rest and shall stand in your allotted place at the end of the days' (12:13)

Different visions in Daniel communicate the deliverance of the righteous and their reward in different ways. In Daniel 2 the stone 'became a great mountain and filled the whole earth' (Dan. 2:35). In Daniel 7 the son of man receives dominion and the saints reign with him (7:13–14, 18, 22, 27). In Daniel 8 'the sanctuary shall be restored to its rightful state' (8:14), and this is put another way in the reference to the anointing of the most holy place in Daniel 9:24.

Daniel 12:2 adds that the righteous and the wicked will be raised bodily, the righteous to be rewarded, and the wicked to be punished.

Conclusion

The visions of Daniel 2, 7, 8 and 10 – 12 are to be understood as complementary presentations of the same realities. They pattern the activities of the wicked powers that have exercised beastly dominion ever since God's vicegerent surrendered that dominion through rebellious sin against the Sovereign. These patterns are consistent – Nebuchadnezzar plunders the temple, Belshazzar uses its implements for debauched dissipation, Antiochus Epiphanes sets up the abomination of desolation, and the little horn from the fourth kingdom, who will be the final realization of this antichrist pattern, will also seek to cut off the true worship of God, replacing that with the worship of himself and the celebration of his kingdom.

The wicked will seek to stamp out the worship of God and replace it with the worship of some unworthy wreck. They will persecute those who refuse to bow, just as Daniel and his three friends were threatened with death in Daniel 3 and 6. The efforts of the wicked will come to nothing. Even if they kill the righteous, they will succeed neither in making their abominations into God nor in keeping the righteous dead. They are chaff. The wind will drive them away. Suddenly the seed of the serpent will be smashed, the one like a son of man will receive rightful dominion of everlasting duration, and the faithful will be rewarded with him as the wicked are punished.

This pattern is clear. The book of Daniel portrays this pattern in Daniel's own day, predicts that it will continue as history weaves its long tapestry (think little horn from third kingdom) and promises that it will culminate in a final king of shocking power, desolating sacrilege and unholy success. That beast will die and his body be burned when the Ancient of Days takes the throne. Then God's king will reign over God's people in God's place – all creation – and they will shine with the glory of God like stars in the heavens.

As we turn our attention to the seventy weeks Gabriel reveals in Daniel 9, we look for more insight into these patterns and their significance.

Chapter Five

Seventy weeks and seventy weeks of years: Daniel's prayer and Gabriel's revelation

The prayer in Daniel 9 radiates profound piety and biblical-theological acumen. This prayer uses statements drawn from earlier Scripture to articulate major biblical themes and summarize salvation history. As significant as Daniel's prayer is the answer to it in the revelation God sent him through the angel Gabriel. This revelation develops the summary of the biblical storyline that Daniel provided in the prayer by extending it into the future, all the way to the consummation of all things.

Daniel was prompted to pray by Jeremiah's prophecy of seventy years for Babylon (Jer. 25:11–12; 29:10), and Gabriel makes known to Daniel that the seventy years will be multiplied sevenfold in accordance with the repeated references to sevenfold punishment in Leviticus 26 (Lev. 26:18, 21, 24, 28). The sevenfold punishment of the seventy years will culminate in the consummation of all things. That consummation is succinctly summarized in the words of Daniel 9:24.

How do the prayer and the revelation contribute to biblical theology?

The prayer

In keeping with the objectives of this book, rather than pursue a line-by-line exposition of the riches of Daniel's prayer, here we will focus on Daniel's use of earlier Scripture and what it reveals of his interpretative perspective. Focusing our attention on Daniel's use of earlier Scripture brings two related concepts into sharp relief: the character of God and the history of his people. The interaction between God and his people comprises their history, and their history has a future precisely because of God's character.

We know that Jeremiah wrote to the exiles in Babylon (Jer. 29:1), and it is not difficult to imagine the whole of his prophecy being available to Daniel by 'the first year of Darius' (Dan. 9:1). In 538 BC Daniel 'perceived in the books the number of years that, according to the word of the LORD to Jeremiah the prophet, must pass before the end of the desolations of Jerusalem, namely, seventy years' (9:2). Daniel himself had been exiled in 605 BC, so whether he was counting from that time or from the destruction of the temple in 586 BC (cf. Zech. 1:12), he was looking for and praying towards the completion of that seventy-year period.

What Daniel does in his prayer grows directly out of his understanding of God's character, which he has learned from the Scriptures. In chapter 2 we reviewed the indications in Leviticus 26 and Deuteronomy 4 that Israel would enter the land, break the covenant, be exiled from the land and then experience a glorious eschatological restoration. As the judgment of exile is described in Leviticus 26, the turning point comes at verse 40, 'But if they confess their iniquity and the iniquity of their fathers . . .' This protasis ('if' clause) receives its apodosis ('then' clause) in verse 42, 'then I will remember my covenant . . .' In Daniel 9:3 and following, Daniel does exactly what Moses spoke of in the 'if clause' of the Leviticus 26 protasis by confessing iniquity.

Daniel saw the prophesied time draw nigh, and he began to act out what Moses had prophesied. When he relates the words of his prayer in 9:4, Daniel presents himself addressing God with the words of Deuteronomy 7:9, 'O Lord, the great and awesome God, who keeps covenant and steadfast love with those who love him and keep his commandments' (Dan. 9:4). This statement of God's character as one who 'keeps covenant and steadfast love' (Deut. 7:9; Dan. 9:4) appears verbatim in the two accounts of Solomon's prayer at the dedication of the temple (1 Kgs 8:23; 2 Chr. 6:14).[1] This idea is rooted in the Torah: Yahweh made this covenant with his people and will demonstrate his steadfast love to them by keeping it. And the idea is significantly restated as Solomon prays at the dedication of the temple, leading us to the intersection of temple and story, setting and plot.

Having driven them from Eden, God gave the tabernacle to his people after delivering them from Egypt; then Solomon built the temple in the land. The temple collapsed under the weight of the

---

[1] It also appears in Neh. 9:32, spelled with a holem waw instead of the mere holem in the participle. Slight variations of the phrase, or statements of these concepts, appear in other texts, reinforcing the importance of these ideas. See Ps. 89:28 (MT 29); Neh. 1:5; cf. Isa. 54:10; 55:3; Pss 25:10; 106:45.

covenant curses, engulfed in Babylonian flame and fury. In that climactic moment the curse was visited with terrible finality. But the reality that Yahweh 'keeps covenant and steadfast love' guaranteed that he would do as he had promised and restore his people. The temple was a microcosm of the world (Beale 2004), a place God made to show his glory and for his people to enjoy his presence. The plot is one of exile and return, destruction and rebuilding. God's character, keeping covenant and steadfast love, keeps even those exiled to Babylon hoping in his promises.

The scriptural invocation in Daniel 9:4 evokes the usage of the same phrase 'who keeps covenant and steadfast love' in Deuteronomy 7:9 and in 1 Kings 8:23. Deuteronomy 7:9 is immediately preceded by statements of God's electing love for Israel (Deut. 7:6–8a) and how that was shown in power at the exodus (7:8b). In 1 Kings 8, Solomon prayed an important summary of the storyline that Moses predicted and that the wider narrative of Kings portrays.

Solidifying the impact of Solomon's temple-dedication prayer on Daniel's thinking is the fact that after invoking it in 9:4, Daniel quotes it again in 9:5. As Solomon prayed in 1 Kings 8, he described the long history of sin and rebellion that would culminate in exile (1 Kgs 8:33–46). Solomon then prayed in 8:47–50:

> yet if they turn their heart in the land to which they have been carried captive, and repent and plead with you in the land of their captors, saying, 'We have sinned and have acted perversely and wickedly,' if they repent . . . then hear in heaven . . . and maintain their cause and forgive your people . . .

In Daniel 9:5, Daniel prays the very words that Solomon had placed on the lips of the exiles: 'we have sinned and done wrong and acted wickedly' (Dan. 9:5; cf. 1 Kgs 8:47).[2]

Daniel engaged what Solomon prayed at the dedication of the temple because he saw himself living out the realities with which Solomon's prayer was concerned. Solomon prayed that God would restore his people after exile; and in exile, Daniel sought the restoration for which Solomon pleaded (1 Kgs 8:46–53; Dan. 9:16–19).

---

[2] Though translated slightly differently, the same Hebrew verbs are used in these two texts, differing only in stem. In 1 Kgs 8:47, the first verb is in the qal stem, the second in the hiphil, and the third in the qal. In Dan. 9:5, the first two verbs are in the qal stem and the third is hiphil. Steinmann (2008: 437, n. 10) observes that the stem changes do not substantially affect the meaning of the verbs.

Plot, place and characterization are all significant here: the plot is one of exile and restoration. The place concerns the city of Jerusalem and the temple. The characterization in view is the God who keeps covenant and steadfast love. The Lord responded to Solomon's prayer with a promise to answer it (1 Kgs 9:3), so Daniel confidently appealed to the Lord on the basis of his character to bring the plot to pass and restore the people to their place.

Daniel's prayer emphasizes the righteousness of Yahweh (Dan. 9:7, 14, 16) and the shame of the people (9:7–8) because they have neither obeyed the Torah (9:5, 10–13) nor hearkened to the prophets (9:6, 10). The curses of the covenant have been poured out on Israel (9:11). Daniel prays that the Lord will also show mercy 'for his own sake' (9:9, 17, 19). The sense in which mercy will be done for God's own sake is that when he shows mercy he shows something unique about himself: only God can be perfectly just *and* show mercy, not punishing those who deserve punishment.

The mercy Daniel sought was the promised new exodus, and one of the ways Daniel requested that promised new exodus was by referring to Yahweh's 'mighty hand', which he stretched forth at the original exodus from Egypt. The exodus from Egypt became the template for the prophesied new act of salvation by which Yahweh would bring his people back from exile. This note is sounded in Solomon's prayer at the dedication of the temple (1 Kgs 8:42, 51, 53), and the prophets pick up on it and promise that the new salvation will eclipse the old (e.g. Jer. 16:14–15; 23:7–8). Daniel's final words before turning directly to the requests he is making recall the exodus from Egypt: 'And now, O Lord our God, who brought your people out of the land of Egypt with a mighty hand, and have made a name for yourself, as at this day, we have sinned, we have done wickedly' (Dan. 9:15). Even as he confesses sin Daniel is thinking of the exodus, and just before he starts asking for a new exodus he references the old, and he does so with a virtual quotation of Jeremiah 32:20–21.[3]

Daniel asks for God to turn away his wrath from Jerusalem (Dan. 9:16), for him to hear Daniel's prayer and – Aaronic blessing style – make his face to shine upon it (9:17; cf. Num. 6:24–26), for God to forgive, pay attention, act without delay, and all for the sake of his own name (Dan. 9:18–19). The Old Testament repeatedly portrays Yahweh answering prayers made on the basis of his own concern

---

[3] So Steinmann (2008: 440), and see his discussion (436–442) on the pervasive influence of Jeremiah in this passage.

for his own glory (see Hamilton 2010b: 352–353), and this instance is no different.

The revelation

Daniel knew the unfolding Old Testament storyline from his study of earlier Scripture, which had likewise taught him God's character, which had in turn assured him of God's commitment to put his people back in the place he had promised to them. In keeping with the character of God, the purpose of his plotline, and the promises and prayers of earlier Scripture about the holy place, God sent Gabriel to reveal the events of coming days. The most striking feature of this revelation is that though Gabriel uses different language and imagery than the other revelations of the book, he tells the same story as he talks Daniel through the same period of time forecasted by the book's other visions. Point for point as we progress through Daniel 9:20–27, we see kaleidoscopic refractions of other passages in the book of Daniel.

Daniel had introduced his prayer in 9:1–4a; then rehearsed the words he prayed in 9:4b–19. At 9:20, Daniel turns to what happened next. Resuming the action from 9:3, where he was seeking God 'by prayer and pleas for mercy with fasting and sackcloth and ashes', he explains in 9:20, 'While I was speaking and praying, confessing my sin and the sin of my people Israel, and presenting my plea before the LORD my God for the holy hill of my God . . .' Daniel was praying, and God answered his petitions with revelation. This recalls the way that Daniel had been seeking mercy when Nebuchadnezzar's dream and its interpretation were revealed to him in 2:18 (cf. 9:3), and the pattern occurs again in chapter 10, where Daniel was mourning and fasting for three weeks in 10:2–3 before experiencing the revelation of chapters 11–12. When he relates in 9:20 that he was presenting his plea 'for the holy hill of my God', the holy hill is the temple mount, and the plea is for restoration and rebuilding (cf. 9:25). This is not unlike Daniel's prayer in 6:10, when 'he went to his house where he had windows in his upper chamber open towards Jerusalem'. Daniel had windows opened towards Jerusalem to act out what Solomon described about how the exiles would 'pray to you towards their land, which you gave to their fathers, the city that you have chosen, and the house that I have built for your name' (1 Kgs 8:48).

There is uncertainty as to the best translation for the second half of Daniel 9:21, but the first half of the verse continues to link this passage to others in the book. Daniel refers in 9:21a to 'the man Gabriel, whom I had seen in the vision at the first'. Since Daniel's first vision was related in chapter 7, this statement would seem to point to Gabriel being the 'one of those who stood there' (7:16), with whom Daniel spoke in chapter 7. The formation rendered 'at the first' in 9:21 is also used in 8:1, and there too it seems to refer back to the Daniel 7 vision. In Daniel 8:16, Gabriel is instructed to explain to Daniel what he had seen in the Daniel 8 vision as well. The heavenly beings with whom Daniel interacts in Daniel 10 – 12 are not named, but there are other points of contact between Daniel 9 and Daniel 10 – 12. The naming of Gabriel in 8:16 and 9:21 links the visions of chapters 8 and 9, and the references to what Daniel saw 'at the first' in 8:1 and 9:21 link the visions of chapters 8 and 9 to the one in chapter 7.

The strong connections between these visions has me convinced that they should be interpreted in the light of one another, which is also a decisive consideration on how Daniel 9:21b should be interpreted. The uncertainty arises from the fact that the Hebrew phrase in question (מֻעָף בִּיעָף, *mu'āp bî'āp*) could mean 'being flown in flight' (ESV: 'swift flight', derived from the verb עוּף, *'ûp*, 'to fly') or 'being wearied in weariness' (NASB: 'in *my* extreme weariness', derived from the verb, יעף, *yā'ēp*, 'be weary'). The decision made on this question then influences the understanding of the next phrase (נֹגֵעַ אֵלָי, *nōgēa' 'ēlay*), which could mean 'he came to me in swift flight' (ESV) or 'being wearied in weariness he touched me' (my tr.; cf. AV). The most natural way to take these phrases would result in a rendering along the lines of Steinmann's 'the man Gabriel . . . touched me in [my] complete exhaustion' (2008: 443–444). To the considerations of morphology and usage that led Steinmann to his rendering, I would add that this translation reflects a meaning that matches what happens to Daniel elsewhere in the book.

Prior to the explanation of the Daniel 7 vision, we read in Daniel 7:15, 'As for me, Daniel, my spirit within me was anxious, and the visions of my head alarmed me.' Following Daniel's description of his condition, he approaches 'one of those who stood there' (7:16), who explains the vision to him (7:17–28), in response to which Daniel says, 'my thoughts greatly alarmed me, and my colour changed, but I kept the matter in heart' (7:28). Similarly, having seen the Daniel 8 vision, we read in 8:17, 'So he [Gabriel, v. 16] came near where I stood. And when he came, I was frightened and fell on my face. But he said to me . . .' Once Gabriel has addressed Daniel, we read in 8:18, 'And when he had spoken to me, I fell into a deep sleep with my face to the ground. But he touched me and made me stand up.' The verb rendered 'he touched me' is the same verb (נגע, *nāga'*) used in 9:21. Once Gabriel has explained the vision, Daniel concludes the account with the words 'And I, Daniel, was overcome and lay sick for some days. Then I rose and went about the king's business, but I was appalled by the vision and did not understand it' (8:27). In both Daniel 7 and 8, then, Daniel sees a vision, describes his anxiety and fright, has the vision explained, and then concludes the account with another statement of how he was physically affected by the vision. Daniel had a similar reaction to Nebuchadnezzar's account of his dream in 4:19 (MT 4:16), 'Then Daniel . . . was dismayed for a while, and his thoughts alarmed him.'

The introduction to the Daniel 10 – 12 vision is similar. Daniel relates that when he saw the 'man clothed in linen' (Dan. 10:5–6), 'no strength was left in me. My radiant appearance was fearfully changed, and I retained no strength . . . and as I heard the sound of his words, I fell on my face in deep sleep with my face to the ground' (10:8–9). Then a hand 'touched' (נגע, *nāga'*) him and set him on his hands and knees (10:10). Daniel stood (10:11), but once the angel had spoken to him (10:12–14) he relates, 'I turned my face towards the ground and was mute' (10:15). At that point, Daniel writes, 'one in the likeness of the children of man touched my lips' (10:16), again using the same verb we find in 9:21 (נגע, *nāga'*).

From these observations it becomes clear that for Daniel to describe himself in 9:21 as 'being wearied in weariness', at which point the angel Gabriel 'touched' him, would match the descriptions of what happens in Daniel 7, 8 and 10 – 12, even if the same vocables are not employed in each instance. Important, too, is the fact that Gabriel, referred to as a 'man', is never described elsewhere in Daniel or the rest of the Bible as either having wings or flying (Steinmann 2008: 444).

It may seem of little consequence whether Gabriel was *flying swiftly to* Daniel or Daniel was *touched* by Gabriel when he was *wearied in weariness*, but the interpretative principle this example demonstrates is an important one: even though the language and imagery may vary, these visions communicate overlapping messages that are largely synonymous. Similar features that relay similar meanings mark the visions, and as we proceed through the Daniel 9 vision, this principle will guide my interpretations of more momentous matters.

The similarity between the Daniel 9 vision and the others in the book continues with the mention of *understanding* in 9:22, where Daniel states, 'He made me understand, speaking with me and saying,

"O Daniel, I have now come out to give you insight and understanding."' Daniel 1:4 states that Nebuchadnezzar wanted 'youths . . . skilful in all wisdom, endowed with knowledge, understanding learning'. Then Daniel 1:17 states of Daniel and his three friends, 'God gave them learning and skill in all literature and wisdom, and Daniel had understanding in all visions and dreams' (cf. also Dan. 1:20). Once Nebuchadnezzar's dream was revealed to him, Daniel extolled God as the one who

> gives wisdom to the wise
> and knowledge to those who have understanding.
> (Dan. 2:21)

Regarding the interpretation of the Daniel 4 dream, the queen says of Daniel in 5:11, 'In the days of your father, light and understanding and wisdom like the wisdom of the gods were found in him' (cf. 5:14). After seeing the Daniel 7 vision, Daniel tells how he approached a member of the heavenly entourage and 'asked him the truth concerning all this. So he told me and made known to me the interpretation of the things' (7:16). After the Daniel 8 vision, in 8:17, Daniel says that Gabriel 'said to me, "Understand, O son of man . . ."' At the end of the vision, however, Daniel 'did not understand' (8:27; similarly, 12:8). The angel declares to Daniel in 10:14 that he 'came to make you understand', and in 10:21, 'I will tell you what is inscribed in the book of truth' (cf. 11:2), and in 11:33 he says, 'the wise among the people shall make many understand'. Later he tells Daniel, 'none of the wicked shall understand, but those who are wise shall understand' (12:10).

The upshot of all this is twofold: first, in all these visions God is giving understanding and wisdom to Daniel. Secondly, those who would endure the persecution are to be made wise by the revelations given to Daniel, and this is seen particularly in 11:33 and 12:10. Just as Daniel and his friends were equipped to endure, so it shall be with those their story makes wise.

When Gabriel tells Daniel in 9:23, 'At the beginning of your pleas for mercy a word went out, and I have come to tell it to you, for you are greatly loved,' this statement anticipates both the references to Daniel as 'greatly loved' in 10:11, 19 and the way the angel was opposed for twenty-one days before coming to Daniel (10:13), who had been fasting for three weeks (10:2–3). The similarities in these passages suggest that they are similar visions to be interpreted in interlocking fashion, as will be seen as we continue through the rest of Daniel 9.

Interestingly, the final words of Daniel 9:23 are, 'Therefore consider the word and understand the vision.' What is intriguing about this statement is the difference between what follows – Gabriel *telling* Daniel what will take place – and the way that Daniel actually *saw* visions that were then explained by Gabriel in chapters 7 and 8. Daniel *saw* the beasts in Daniel 7, and then the angelic figure explained what he had seen. The same with chapter 8: Daniel *saw* the ram and the goat, and then Gabriel explained them. In chapter 9, by contrast, Daniel does not *see* but has the events of the seventy weeks narrated by Gabriel. After the narration, Daniel 10:1 states that in the third year of Cyrus 'a word was revealed to Daniel . . . And the word was true . . . And he understood the word and had understanding of the vision.' Daniel then has a vision of 'a man clothed in linen' (10:5, 7–8), and the heavenly being narrates for Daniel 'what is inscribed in the book of truth' (10:21) through the rest of chapters 11 and 12. The wording of Daniel 9:23 indicates that a revelatory word (דבר, *dābār*) is tantamount to beholding a vision (מראה, *mar'eh*).[4] The overlap between word and vision can also be seen in Amos 1:1, 'The words [דברי, *dibrê*] of Amos . . . which he saw [חזה, *ḥāzâ*].'

In what follows we will take three trips through Daniel 9:24–27, and the aim is for each cycle to take us deeper into the text, as we seek to extend our understanding of it by looking at it from three different angles. On our first trip through this text we will focus on the periodization of the seventy weeks, asking how the temporal markers within these statements divide up what Gabriel says to Daniel. Our interest is in how the seventy weeks are divided into separate units or blocks of time. From there, the second trip through the passage will examine the points of contact between what Gabriel says to Daniel in 9:24–27 and other statements in Daniel. The aim here is to allow other statements in the book of Daniel to shed their interpretative light on the statements in 9:24–27. Having examined the blocks of time in 9:24–27 and their points of contact with other passages in Daniel, our third trip through the passage will seek to explain its statements by expositing what Gabriel describes taking place in history to fulfil Scripture.

---

[4] Goldingay and Collins both indicate that the word and the vision are equivalent (Collins 1993: 352; Goldingay 1989: 228).

The periodization of Daniel 9:24–27

The vision itself (Dan. 9:23) consists of Gabriel's narration of the seventy weeks (9:24–27). Gabriel announces that there will be 'seventy weeks' for Daniel's people and their 'holy city' (9:24). Then as he explains the weeks, he lays out in 9:24 what will be accomplished when they are completed, how long it will be 'from the going out of the word to restore and build Jerusalem to the coming of' Messiah in 9:25, and what will follow after that time down to 'the end' in 9:26–27. The time markers in the passage are as follows:

- 'Seventy weeks are decreed' (9:24)
- 'from the going out of the word' (9:25a)
- 'to the coming of messiah the prince, there shall be seven weeks and sixty-two weeks' (9:25b, my tr.)[5]
- 'and after the sixty-two weeks messiah shall be cut off' (9:26a, my tr.)
- 'and to the end there shall be war' (9:26b)
- 'for one week' (9:27a)
- 'for half of the week' (9:27b)
- 'until the decreed end is poured out' (9:27c)

Daniel presents Gabriel stating six things that will be accomplished in Daniel 9:24. Gabriel tells Daniel that the 'seventy weeks' are appointed for 'your people and your holy city':

1. To complete the transgression.
2. To finish sin.
3. To atone for iniquity.
4. To bring in righteousness of the ages.
5. To seal vision and prophet.
6. To anoint the holy of holies.

---

[5] This rendering is not in conflict with the Masoretic accentuation, as, in addition to separating clauses, the athnach can join pairs (cf. Steinmann 2008: 471–472). In my view the ESV confuses the issue by rendering the clauses in Dan. 9:25 as follows: 'to the coming of an anointed one, a prince, there shall be seven weeks. Then for sixty-two weeks . . .' (cf. also CEB, NRSV, RSV). This wrongly gives the impression that the Messiah comes after the first seven weeks (contra e.g. Greidanus 2012: 302–304), which would seem to demand a different Messiah then being cut off after the sixty-two weeks in 9:26. The Greek translations (OG and Th) join the seven weeks and sixty-two weeks, as do many English translations (CSB, AV, NASB, NET, NIV, NKJV, NLT).

Having announced in 9:24 what will be true at the completion of the whole of the seventy-week period, Gabriel moves to a discussion of the period of time 'from the going out of the word to restore and rebuild Jerusalem . . . to messiah the prince' in 9:25 (my tr.). Gabriel says this about the period between the word to rebuild Jerusalem and the Messiah (my tr.):

1. There will be seven weeks and sixty-two weeks.
2. [The city] will be restored and rebuilt with square and moat in a troubled time.

The 'seven weeks and sixty-two weeks' are to be taken together to refer to a sixty-nine-week period presented as two units, as can be seen from the fact that the period of time is presented as 'from the . . . word . . . to messiah' in 9:25, and then 'messiah' is cut off 'after the sixty-two weeks' in 9:26. This would seem to indicate that 9:25 points to a seven-week period in which the city is restored and rebuilt[6] with square and moat in a troubled time. Then follows a sixty-two-week period, after which Messiah will be cut off in 9:26.

Gabriel spoke of the whole of the seventy-week period in Daniel 9:24; then presented the first sixty-nine weeks in two blocks, one of seven weeks, the other of sixty-two weeks, in 9:25. Gabriel states what will happen after the second unit of the sixty-nine-week period, the sixty-two-week block, in 9:26:

1. The Messiah will be cut off and have nothing.
2. The people of the prince who is to come will destroy the city and the sanctuary.
3. Its end will come with the flood.
4. Until the end there will be war.
5. Desolations are decreed.

Gabriel finishes the revelation with what will take place in the seventieth week, and like the sixty-nine weeks the seventieth is divided into two units in 9:27:

---

[6] Dan. 9:25 states, 'from the going out of the word to restore and build Jerusalem', and then the same two verbs are used later in the verse in the phrase 'it will be restored and rebuilt with square and moat'. I have supplied the subject, 'the city', in brackets above because the verbs 'restored and rebuilt' are feminine singular, as is the Hebrew word for 'city', implying that 'city' is the unstated subject of the verbs.

1. He will make a firm covenant with the many for one week.
2. And for half of the week he will put an end to sacrifice and offering.
3. And on the wing of abominations will come one who makes desolate.
4. Until the decreed end is poured out on the desolator.

The two units of the seventieth week are the two halves of that week. What Gabriel says about these seventy weeks, then, can be depicted as in table 5.1.

Table 5.1 The seventy weeks

Seventy weeks are decreed			
1. To complete the transgression. 2. To finish sin. 3. To atone for iniquity. 4. To bring in righteousness of the ages. 5. To seal vision and prophet. 6. To anoint the holy of holies.			
Sixty-nine weeks			*Seventieth week*
'from the going out of the word . . . to Messiah the prince'	'after the sixty-two weeks'		'for one week . . . for half of the week'
Seven weeks	And sixty-two weeks	First half of the week	Second half of the week
1. [the city] will be restored and rebuilt with square and moat in a troubled time.	1. Messiah will be cut off and have nothing. 2. The city and the sanctuary will be destroyed by the people of the prince who is to come. 3. Its end will come with the flood. 4. Until the end there will be war. 5. Desolations are decreed.	1. He will make a firm covenant with the many for one week. 2. For half of the week he will put an end to sacrifice and offering. 3. On the wing of abominations will come one who makes desolate. 4. Until the decreed end is poured out on the desolator.	

In order to gain traction on the meaning of these statements, on our second pass through Daniel 9:24–27 we will consider how what is said here matches and/or adds to other statements in Daniel.

Scripture interprets Scripture: Daniel 9:24–27 in the light of other passages in Daniel

In Daniel 9:24 Gabriel announces that all things will be consummated at the completion of seventy weeks. In the context of the book of Daniel, it is only natural to understand the seventy weeks as another way of describing the period of time between Daniel's own day and the fulfilment of God's promises when he establishes the kingdom that will be neither destroyed nor left to others (cf. Dan. 2:44). This means that the seventy weeks Gabriel describes for Daniel cover the same period and culminate in the same resolution that we have seen in Daniel 2, 7, 8 and 10 – 12 (see chapter 4 above).

How can Daniel 9:24–27 depict the same resolution as Daniel 2 and 7? Those passages speak directly of a king and a kingdom, while Daniel 9:24–27 speaks only of the Messiah being cut off (Dan. 9:26). Are there indications in Daniel 9 that the Davidic promises will be realized? To appreciate what Daniel 9:24 says about the holy place, we must remember that it was King David who wanted to build the temple and King Solomon who built it. When the people were exiled, the line of Davidic kings came to an end and the temple was destroyed (cf. Pss 79:1; 89:38–45). The rebuilding of the temple and the anointing of a holy of holies (Dan. 9:24) would recall the 2 Samuel 7:13 promise of a king from David's line who would build a house for God's name and have his throne established for ever. The temple and the king are two parts of one hope, and to mention the one is to imply the other.

Daniel 2 and 7 describe the four kingdoms that will control the land of promise until God's kingdom is established, and the first sixty-nine of the seventy weeks in Daniel 9 pertain to that same period of time between Daniel's own day and the inauguration of God's kingdom. Daniel 7:12 speaks of dominion being taken from the beasts though 'their lives were prolonged for a season and a time'. This would seem to match the way that Messiah comes after the sixty-nine weeks in Daniel 9:26, and then there would appear to be a foreign power making a strong covenant and putting an end to sacrifice and offering in the seventieth week in Daniel 9:27.

Daniel 9:24 states, 'Seventy weeks are decreed . . . to finish the transgression, to put an end to sin'. This reference to the completion of transgression and the ending of sin suggests that there is a certain amount of sin that will be allowed, and that the whole amount will be completed in the seventy-week period. Once the allotted amount has been completed, sin will be ended. This idea is similar to the statement about the time of the little horn from the third kingdom in Daniel 8:23, 'at the latter end of their kingdom, when the transgressors have reached their limit, a king of bold countenance . . . shall arise'. This appears to mean that the transgressors of the third kingdom have a certain amount of iniquity they can accomplish, and that the type of the Antichrist, the little horn from the third kingdom, will arise as they fulfil their allotted portion of evil. These concepts in Daniel 8 and 9 correspond to the statement in Genesis 15:16 that 'the iniquity of the Amorites is not yet complete'. More on that below.

Daniel is in exile because of Israel's covenant-breaking sin, the very sin he confessed in 9:3–19. These 'seventy weeks are decreed . . . to atone for iniquity' (Dan. 9:24). So the iniquity that got Israel exiled will be atoned for at the end of the seventy weeks. Isaiah 40:2 speaks of iniquity being pardoned at the end of exile, and the servant in Isaiah 53 'was crushed for our iniquities' (Isa. 53:5) as Yahweh laid on him 'the iniquity of us all' (53:6) so that the servant bore the iniquity of the many (53:11). The reference to the Isaiah 53 servant as a 'root out of dry ground' (53:2) connects him to the Isaiah 11:1 'shoot from the stump of Jesse', making it probable that Daniel would have understood the cutting off of the Messiah in 9:26 as the fulfilment of Isaiah 53. More on this below, too.

The 'seventy weeks are decreed', Gabriel tells Daniel, 'to seal both vision and prophet' (Dan. 9:24). The only other references to 'sealing' in Daniel are in 12:4, where Daniel is told to 'shut up the words and seal the book, until the time of the end', and 12:9 where he is told, 'the words are shut up and sealed until the time of the end'. Since the sealing of a scroll indicates that the writing on it has been completed and it is ready to be stored or sent, as the case may be (cf. 1 Kgs 21:8; Neh. 9:38 [MT 10:1]), it would appear that the 'sealing' of vision and prophet refers both to the conclusion and the ratification of revelatory visions and prophetic disclosures. In other words, what vision and prophet reveal will be fulfilled and completed at the end of the seventy weeks.

The Torah called for the tabernacle to be anointed (Exod. 30:26; 40:9), as were the priests who served in it (Exod. 28:41; 30:30). This is the background for the statement that the 'seventy weeks are decreed . . . to anoint the holy of holies' (Dan. 9:24, my tr.). There is a natural connection between the verb used to refer to the 'anointing' of the holy of holies in Daniel 9:24 (מָשַׁח, māšaḥ) and the adjective used to describe the anointed one, 'Messiah', in Daniel 9:26 (מָשִׁיחַ, māšîaḥ).

The holy of holies is obviously in the sanctuary, which means that Messiah and holy place/sanctuary also meet the same fate after the sixty-nine weeks in Daniel 9:26 – Messiah is cut off and the holy place is destroyed with the rest of the temple. This means that if the holy of holies is to be anointed at the completion of the seventy weeks, the temple must be rebuilt. There being no temple in Daniel's day, it would appear that the temple rebuilt under the prophetic ministries of Haggai and Zechariah and the leadership of Joshua and Zerubbabel is the one to be destroyed by 'the people of the prince who is to come' in 9:26, and that torn down temple will be raised up for the anointing of the holy of holies spoken of in 9:24. The temple was destroyed in 586 BC, rebuilt in 516, destroyed in AD 70 (cf. Dan. 9:26), and at the completion of the seventy weeks Daniel 9:24 says the holy of holies will be anointed. This conclusion aligns with the depiction of a new temple in Ezekiel 40 – 48 and Revelation 21 – 22.[7]

We will consider Daniel 9:25–26a more closely in the next section. At this point I want to focus on 9:26b–27, which I here break into its independent statements:

> And the people of the prince who is to come
> shall destroy the city and the sanctuary.
> Its end shall come with a flood,
> and to the end there shall be war.
> Desolations are decreed.
> And he shall make a strong covenant with many
> for one week,
> and for half of the week he shall put an end to
> sacrifice and offering.
> And on the wing of abominations shall come one
> who makes desolate,
> until the decreed end is poured out on the desolator.

As noted above, there is a connection between the Messiah as the anointed man and the sanctuary as the anointed place. Daniel 9:26 speaks of the Messiah being cut off and the sanctuary being destroyed. Once again, my view is that what Daniel 9 describes should be understood in the light of other passages in the book of Daniel. In Daniel 8:11–13 the little horn from the third kingdom attacked both 'the

---

[7] As I discuss in my exposition of Revelation, I think that rebuilt temple is the new heaven and earth (see Hamilton 2012b: 393).

Prince of the host' and the sanctuary and sacrifice; then 8:14 speaks of the restoration of the sanctuary. Along these same lines, Daniel 11:29–31 presents that same little horn from the third kingdom, Antiochus Epiphanes, attacking the holy covenant, the temple and the sacrifices offered there, setting up 'the abomination that makes desolate'.

I have argued that the little horn from the third kingdom, Antiochus Epiphanes, typifies the little horn from the fourth kingdom. If this is correct, it would seem that 'the prince who is to come' whose people will 'destroy the city and the sanctuary' should be understood as a foreign power, probably the little horn from the fourth kingdom depicted in Daniel 7:8. This means that though the same terms for 'Messiah' and 'prince' are used in Daniel 9:25 and 9:26, 'the prince who is to come' in 9:26 is not 'messiah the prince' from 9:25 but a hostile invader. The Messiah, after all, has just been described in 9:26a as having been cut off.

This hostile invader, 'the prince who is to come' in 9:26b, would seem to be the subject of 9:27a, the 'he' who will 'make a strong covenant with many for one week'. No other figure has been introduced who could be the subject of these verbs, and therefore it is also this hostile invader who puts 'an end to sacrifice and offering' for 'half of the week'. The final lines of Daniel 9:27, on this understanding, would refer to this hostile invader as the 'one who makes desolate', or perhaps to one who arises alongside him (cf. Rev. 13:1, 11).

Some suggest that 'the prince who is to come' in Daniel 9:26 is actually the Messiah, with the Jews destroying the city and the sanctuary in the sense that they provoked the Romans to do it (e.g. Gentry and Wellum 2012: 548–563; and Steinmann 2008: 447–448, 473–474). This could then lead to the attractive understanding that the 'strong covenant with many' refers to the 'many' of Isaiah 53:11–12 and the new covenant of Jeremiah 31:31–34. For a number of reasons, however, this interpretation fails to convince. Most prominent in my view is the way this understanding would depart from the picture seen in Daniel 7, 8 and 10 – 12, a picture not of the Jews causing their temple to be destroyed with sacrifice brought to an end but of a foreign attacker cutting off sacrifice and trampling the sanctuary. Another severe difficulty for this view is that, as noted, the Messiah has just been cut off in 9:26, so it is difficult to account for how, or why, his people would then destroy city and sanctuary. The idea that Daniel meant to communicate that the Jews would provoke a foreign army to destroy the temple strains against the more natural reading of the text, the reading that matches what Daniel depicts elsewhere.[8] Rather than understanding the first lines of Daniel 9:27, then, as a fulfilment of Isaiah 53 and Jeremiah 31, they seem to point in the direction of a satanic parody of those passages.[9] God promises to justify the 'many' in Isaiah 53:11, and to enter into a 'new covenant' with his people in Jeremiah 31:31–34, and the foreign invader is depicted in Daniel 9:27 as offering a twisted perversion of what God offers, as the one who has destroyed Jerusalem and the temple makes a 'strong covenant with many for one week'. Other satanic parodies in the book of Daniel include Nebuchadnezzar's 'image', around which the officials gather (Dan. 3:3), as contrasted with those in God's image, around which the same officials gather (3:27); and the pagan king's threatened punishment (2:5; 3:29) as compared with God's (12:2). The problem with the pagan kings in Daniel is that they arrogate God's prerogatives to themselves, and this pattern of activity can be seen in the little horns from kingdoms three and four.

Like the little horn from the third kingdom, who in Daniel 8:13 brought on 'the transgression that makes desolate, and the giving over of the sanctuary and host to be trampled underfoot', this foreign invader of Daniel 9:26b–27 will bring his people who will 'destroy the city and the sanctuary' (9:26). These events are set after the sixty-nine weeks. The foreign power then enters into a strong covenant for the final, seventieth, week. The last half of that week seems to be depicted when Daniel 9:27 states, 'and for half of the week he shall put an end to sacrifice and offering'. I take this to mean that, having destroyed the temple, at the midpoint of the seventieth week the foreign power will seek to stamp out the worship of God by ending sacrifice. Then

---

[8] Schreiner (2013: 395) rightly notes that the active verbs in the passage indicate that a foreign prince and his army destroy city and sanctuary, rather than the Jews provoking them to do so, which would seem to call for reflexive verbs. I am thus not persuaded that Daniel meant to prophesy that the Jews would provoke the Romans to destroy the city and the sanctuary, and that this was fulfilled in AD 70. Would such an interpretation imply that apart from Josephus we would not know about the fulfilment of this prophecy of Daniel's?

[9] Portier-Young (2011: 272–276) has a nice table and discussion, summarizing points of contact between Isa. 53 and Daniel, which concern 'acting wisely' (שׂכל, śākal, Isa. 52:13; Dan. 1:4, 17; 7:8; 9:13, 22, 25; 11:33, 35; 12:3, 10), 'the many' (רבים, rabîm, Isa. 52:14–15; 53:11–12; Dan. 11:33–34; 12:3, 10), 'make many righteous' (hiphil forms of the verb צדק, ṣādaq, Isa. 53:11; Dan. 12:3), 'understanding' (בין, bîn, Isa. 52:15; Dan. 11:33), and reconciliation/atonement (cf. Isa. 53:4, 6, 10–12; Dan. 9:24; 11:33, 35; 12:10).

121

comes, with extreme abominations, 'one who makes desolate'. This would appear to be a figure who is himself the desolating sacrilege (9:27; cf. 8:13; 11:31; 12:11). The implication is that he will desolate 'until the decreed end is poured out on the desolator' (9:27).

Thus, like the little horn from the third kingdom who 'shall be broken – but by no human hand' (Dan. 8:25), who 'shall come to his end, with none to help him' (11:45), and like the statue crushed to chaff driven off by the wind (2:35), this abomination of desolation described in Daniel 9:27 will be nothing more than a usurping beast boasting against the Most High who will be 'killed, and its body destroyed and given over to be burned with fire' (7:11). This way of understanding Daniel 9:27 fits best with the idea found in Mark 13:14 that the abomination of desolation is a person. Among the references to desolating abominations in Daniel, Daniel 9:27 most clearly indicates that the 'one who makes desolate' is a person (cf. again, Dan. 8:13; 11:31; 12:11). I contend that the whole of Daniel 9:26b–27 describes the actions of the wicked against God's people. This would match the way that in 2 Thessalonians 2:3–8 Paul seems to blend the personal 'man of lawlessness', which he would derive from Daniel 9:27, with the figure of Antiochus Epiphanes described in Daniel 11:36–45. By putting Daniel 9:27 together with 11:36–45, Paul points in the interpretative direction we should go. John's interpretative signposts also point this way, as can be seen from his interpretation of Daniel's seventieth week in Revelation 11 – 13 (see the discussions in chapters 8 and 9 below).

Daniel 9:24–27 in history and Scripture

Now that we have seen the periodization of the seventy weeks and the points of contact between Daniel 9:24–27 and other passages in Daniel, we are prepared to attempt an explanation of these verses that seeks to connect the statements with history, interpreting them in the light of their inter-biblical points of contact with earlier Scripture (for the most part, the way later authors interpreted Daniel will be reserved for chapters 7–10 below).

A profoundly significant concourse pulses together when the possible historical referents of Daniel 9:24–27 meet its use of earlier Scripture, and these waters flow on, roiling through later Scripture. We should expect Daniel 9:24–27 to address history in a way that corresponds to and builds on the way that previous passages of Scripture have addressed history. Most significant are two related passages, one in Isaiah, and the other in Ezekiel.

The Isaiah passage shows us that Babylon was not the only foreign power for whom seventy years was appointed. Isaiah 23:15 states, 'In that day Tyre will be forgotten for seventy years, like the days of one king. At the end of seventy years, it will happen to Tyre as in the song of the prostitute . . .' Then again in 23:17, 'At the end of seventy years, the LORD will visit Tyre . . .' The seventy-year period appointed for Tyre in Isaiah 23:15 is compared to 'the days of one king', a description reminiscent of Psalm 90:10:

> The years of our life are seventy,
> or even by reason of strength eighty . . .

Isaiah 23:15 and Psalm 90:10 indicate that seventy years was a period of time associated with a typical human lifespan. People tend to live for roughly seventy years. This reality, particularly the comparison of seventy years with 'the days of one king' in Isaiah 23:15, indicates that the seventy years Jeremiah prophesied for Babylon need not be a literal seventy years, but can be seen as roughly seventy years, pointing to a typical human lifespan.

Isaiah 23:15 compares the seventy years appointed for Tyre to 'the days of one king'. If Jeremiah, a prophet clearly influenced by Isaiah, prophesied that seventy years were appointed for Babylon, it would seem reasonable to understand this also to refer to a period corresponding to 'the days of one king'. If this was a widely shared assumption among those who knew Isaiah 23:15, it would explain why Daniel, having perceived the seventy years in Daniel 9:2, immediately begins to call on the Lord to act in 9:3–19. Daniel does not call on the Lord to act once a few more years have passed and seventy years have been literally completed. Daniel seems to take the seventy years as a round number that broadly corresponds to an individual's lifespan. Just as every person does not live exactly seventy years, no more no less, Daniel seems to read the prophesied period of time as completed.[10]

If Daniel counted from the time of his own exile to Babylon in 605 BC, the first year of Darius in 539/538 BC would be *roughly* seventy years. As noted above, Daniel prays for the Lord to act and makes no reference to the exact number of years needing to scroll by, apparently because he understood the seventy years the same way that period of time is referenced in Psalm 90:10 and Isaiah 23:15 – as a round number

---

[10] This way of approaching the issue is more satisfying than strained attempts to show that seventy literal years actually did pass between Daniel's exile in 605 BC and the first year of Darius in 539/538 BC.

roughly seventy years in length, corresponding to the typical human lifespan.

Read in the light of Isaiah 23:15, Jeremiah's seventy years for Babylon were not intended to be interpreted *literally*, and thus Daniel, correctly, does not demand that they be literally completed. In keeping with this, I do not think that Daniel intended the seventy weeks to be understood literally either. To get traction on how Daniel intended the seventy weeks to be understood, we want to accustom our feet to time-reckoning on prophetic terrain. The enacted parable in Ezekiel 4 will train our toes for treading these paths, as it provides a way of thinking about time and history analogous to the seventy weeks prophesied in Daniel 9:24–27.

In Ezekiel 4, at the Lord's instruction Ezekiel makes a model of Jerusalem to which he lays siege (4:1–2), placing an iron wall between himself and the city (4:3). The Lord commands Ezekiel to lie on his side for 390 days for Israel and 40 days for Judah, each day corresponding to a year of punishment. The point does not seem to be that Israel and Judah will be punished for these literal amounts of time (and historically they were not). Rather, the point seems to be that the exile from the land corresponds to the sojourn in Egypt, the exodus from Egypt pointing forward to the new exodus that will open the way to the return from exile. Why the numbers if they are not literal? The 390 days for Israel and the 40 days for Judah add up to 430 years, a number that recalls Exodus 12:40–41, 'The time that the people of Israel lived in Egypt was 430 years. At the end of 430 years, on that very day, all the hosts of the LORD went out from the land of Egypt.'[11] The paralleling of the exile from the land with the sojourn in Egypt can also be seen in Isaiah 52:4, 'My people went down at the first into Egypt to sojourn there, and the Assyrian oppressed them for nothing,' as well as Hosea 11:5:

> They shall not return to the land of Egypt,
> but Assyria shall be their king . . .

The exile to Assyria/Babylon[12] is likened to the sojourn in Egypt, and the return from exile is likened to the exodus from Egypt in Isaiah 11:16:

---

[11] Understanding of Ezekiel's 430 days in parallel with Israel's 430-year sojourn in Egypt is another insight I owe to stimulating conversation with Peter Gentry.

[12] The OT prophets often speak of Assyria and Babylon interchangeably, as Ezra does (Ezra includes Persia in the overlap: see Ezra 4:24 and 6:22, and 4:5 and 5:13; cf. also 1:2; 3:7; 4:3; 5:13; 6:14; 7:1). The association of these cities and empires probably derives from their common founder, described in Gen. 10:10–11.

> And there will be a highway from Assyria
> for the remnant that remains of his people,
> as there was for Israel
> when they came up from the land of Egypt.

The 430 years in Ezekiel 4:5–6, then, are not intended to refer to 430 literal years. Instead, this period of time should be understood as a symbolic reference to the sojourn in Egypt, which Ezekiel prophesies will be matched by the exile to Assyria/Babylon, followed by a new exodus that corresponds to and increases the significance of (i.e. typologically fulfils) the exodus from Egypt.

The symbolic value of the 430 years in Ezekiel 4:5–6 is similar to the symbolic value of the seventy weeks in Daniel 9:24–27. The symbolic value of the seventy weeks in Daniel 9:24 seems to derive from the year of jubilee in Leviticus 25. The Lord instructed Moses regarding the sabbatical year (Lev. 25:1–7); then continued, 'You shall count seven weeks of years, seven times seven years, so that the time of the seven weeks of years shall give you forty-nine years' (25:8). Then on the Day of Atonement, the tenth day of the seventh month of the forty-ninth year, 'you shall sound the loud trumpet . . . And you shall consecrate the fiftieth year, and proclaim liberty throughout the land to all its inhabitants. It shall be a jubilee for you, when each of you shall return to his property and each of you shall return to his clan' (25:9–10). The proclamation of liberty to the captives and return to tribal inheritance and clan fellowship is reminiscent of the way that Israel was liberated from slavery in Egypt to return to the land promised to the patriarchs. These concepts also inform the prophecies of what will take place in the future (cf. Isa. 27:13; 61:1–3).

Isaiah looked beyond exile not only to proclaim 'liberty to the captives' (Isa. 61:1) but to foretell the restoration of the people after the new exodus and return from exile. Isaiah prophesied of the fulfilment of the year of jubilee, picking up on the 'loud trumpet' to be blown on the Day of Atonement in the forty-ninth year signalling the jubilee (Lev. 25:9). Isaiah prophesied, 'And in that day a great trumpet will be blown, and those who were lost in the land of Assyria and those who were driven out to the land of Egypt will come and worship the LORD on the holy mountain at Jerusalem' (Isa. 27:13).

There is similarity, then, between the liberty and inheritance received at exodus and conquest and the restoration of the same liberty and inheritance at the year of jubilee. The jubilee looks back to exodus and forward to new exodus, as can be seen when Isaiah connects the jubilee trumpet to the glorious eschatological restoration. The year of jubilee thus crystalizes a significant pattern from Israel's past, celebrated yearly in their feasts, pointing forward to the culmination of itself when God definitively restores his people.

Significant for Daniel 9:24–27 is the simple fact that the 'seventy weeks' of Daniel 9:24 amount to a tenfold jubilee of 490 years (cf. van Goudoever 1993: 61). The seventy weeks appointed for Jerusalem, at the culmination of which all things will be accomplished, come to pass in the forty-ninth year ten times over. This indicates that like the 430 years in Ezekiel 4, the seventy weeks of Daniel 9 are prophesied for Jerusalem not because there will be 490 literal years between 'the going out of the word to restore and build Jerusalem' and the consummation of all things, any more than we should expect a literal 430 years of punishment from Ezekiel 4:5–6. In both texts the value of the years is symbolic, not literal. The 430 years of Ezekiel 4:5–6 indicate that just as an appointed amount of time passed before the exodus from Egypt, an appointed period of time will pass before the new exodus fulfilment. Similarly, the seventy weeks of Daniel 9:24–27 indicate that just as liberty was proclaimed in Israel in the year of jubilee, at the ultimate tenfold jubilee the captives will go free, the land inheritance will be enjoyed and clan fellowship renewed.[13]

These parallels increase our ability to understand the connection observed above between Genesis 15:16 and the references in Daniel 8:23 to the transgressors reaching their limit and transgression being finished and sin ended in 9:24. In Genesis 15:13 Yahweh told Abraham that his offspring would 'be sojourners in a land that is not theirs and will be servants there, and they will be afflicted for four hundred years'. Yahweh then announced that he would judge the oppressing nation and bring his people out with great possessions (Gen. 15:14), explaining to Abraham that the time had not yet come for these things to be accomplished, 'for the iniquity of the Amorites is not yet complete'

---

[13] Questions multiply for those who would take the 490 years literally, involving both the date from which to count (from 538, 458 or 445 BC?) and the event that marks completion (until the birth of Jesus, until his triumphal entry, until the destruction of Jerusalem in AD 70, or until his return?). And do we factor in a 'parenthesis' that is the church age, leaving a literal seventieth week, or do we switch from a literal understanding of the first sixty-nine weeks to a symbolic understanding of the seventieth? In addition to these there would seem to be an additional question: How are Daniel's 490 years to be harmonized with Ezekiel's 430? Steinmann concludes, 'none of the proposals that view the weeks as groups of seven literal years can adequately explain Gabriel's words and the fulfillment of the prophecy' (2008: 462). Davis also concludes, 'I cannot take the "weeks" as weeks of years. . . I do not take the "weeks" literally; instead, I take them schematically' (2013: 134).

(15:16). In view of the broader parallels between the exodus and the new exodus, the similarities between Genesis 15:16 and Daniel 8:23 and 9:24 show that it was revealed to Daniel that Israel coming out of Egypt to put the Canaanites under the ban, bringing judgment on those who had filled up the measure of their sins, typified the filling up of iniquity seen in the third and fourth kingdoms in Daniel 8 and 9. When those kingdoms had filled up the measure of their sin, the one who 'changes times and seasons; / [who] removes kings and sets up kings' (Dan. 2:21) would do his work. The filled-up sin of the third kingdom typifies that of the fourth, which like the Canaanites will be put under the ban when the people of God conquer the Promised Land and God sets up his kingdom. These concepts also informed the apostle Paul, who referred to the way that Jewish enemies of the gospel hindered his attempts to proclaim the good news of Jesus the Messiah 'so as always to fill up the measure of their sins' (1 Thess. 2:16).

After the reference to finishing transgression and ending sin in Daniel 9:24, we read that there will be atonement for iniquity. Once again we can connect this to Isaiah's prophecies of the glorious eschatological restoration after the punishment of exile. When Isaiah describes the way God will comfort his people (Isa. 40:1), the tender words to be spoken to her are that 'her warfare is ended' (40:2). What warfare? The warfare that resulted in the destruction of land and temple and got them carried off to Babylon. That warfare is over and 'her iniquity is pardoned' because

> she has received from the LORD's hand
> double for all her sins.
>
> (40:2)

If we search the book of Isaiah for an explanation of how Israel will receive from the hand of the Lord double for her sins, how her iniquity will be pardoned, the answers come in Isaiah 53. Isaiah 53 is in turn connected to Isaiah 6 and 11. The exile prophesied in Isaiah 6:11–13 depicts Israel as a tree that is chopped down, but 'The holy seed is its stump.' These ideas are picked up in Isaiah 11:1, where the imagery of the tree chopped down at exile informs the restoration prophesied when 'There shall come forth a shoot from the stump of Jesse.' Israel's enemies will chop her down like a tree at the exile, but the king from the line of David is the holy seed in the stump, and that shoot from Jesse's line will grow again into a great tree. This imagery also informs Isaiah 53:2:

> For he grew up before him like a young plant,
> and like a root out of dry ground.

Moreover, Yahweh flexed his strong arm and mighty hand at the exodus from Egypt (Deut. 7:19), and as Isaiah prophesied of the new exodus he asked in Isaiah 53:1, 'to whom has the arm of the LORD been revealed?' At the new exodus, when Yahweh would once again save with a mighty hand and an outstretched arm, the shoot from Jesse's stump would be like a root out of dry ground. And this descendant of David, Isaiah said, would bear the griefs of the people, carry their sorrows, be stricken, smitten and afflicted (53:4). In this

> he was pierced for our transgressions;
> he was crushed for our iniquities;
> upon him was the chastisement that brought us peace,
> and with his wounds we are healed.
>
> (53:5, adapted ESV)

These statements explain how the people of God will receive from the hand of the Lord double for their sins – as

> by his knowledge shall the righteous one, my servant,
> make many to be accounted righteous,
> and he shall bear their iniquities.
>
> (53:11)

This is how their iniquity can be pardoned, because the servant was 'stricken for the transgression of my people' (53:8). And this, too, informs what Daniel 9:24 envisions in the words 'to atone for iniquity'.

The bringing in of everlasting righteousness referenced next in Daniel 9:24 states what Jeremiah prophesied about the new exodus when the Lord declared through him:

> I will raise up for David a righteous Branch, and he shall reign as king and deal wisely, and shall execute justice and righteousness in the land. In his days Judah will be saved, and Israel will dwell securely. And this is the name by which he will be called: 'The LORD is our righteousness.' (Jer. 23:5–6)

Ezekiel prophesied of that day of restoration, 'I will put my Spirit within you, and cause you to walk in my statutes and be careful to obey my rules' (36:27). When Daniel 9:24 mentions everlasting right-eousness, those words tap into the hope that when God restores his people he will circumcise their hearts so that they will no longer sin but love him wholeheartedly (cf. Deut. 30:4–6).

The next thing for which the seventy weeks are appointed in Daniel 9:24 is 'to seal both vision and prophet'. Documents are sealed to signify that they are ratified by a king or those in authority (cf. Neh. 9:38 [MT 10:1]; Esth. 8:8, 10). Once the deposit of revelation is committed to Daniel, he is instructed to 'seal the book, until the time of the end' (12:4). When he asks for more information (12:8), he is told, 'Go your way, Daniel, for the words are shut up and sealed until the time of the end' (12:9).

I would propose the following synthesis of the sealed scrolls in Daniel and Revelation: Daniel is given revelation that stretches from his own day to the coming of the Messiah and beyond. Once that revelation of the four kingdoms that will precede the establishment of God's kingdom has been made, the scroll is sealed. In Revelation 6, the seals on a scroll, perhaps the same 'book of truth' whose contents were revealed to Daniel (Dan. 10:21), are broken open by Jesus himself. An angel then brings that scroll to John, who eats it in Revelation 10, and prophesies of the events that will bring history to its consummation. At the great white throne judgment of Revelation 20:11–15, 'books were opened' (20:12). The four kingdoms are proph-esied to Daniel; then the scroll is sealed until more of its contents are revealed to John. The sealing of the scroll seems to point to the certainty of its disclosures. Perhaps the reference in Daniel 9:24 to the sealing of vision and prophet indicates a time when all that ever has been or will be revealed has been made known, and the certainty of what is prophesied will be signified by the sealing of vision and prophet. At that point, the glorious conditions God has brought about will obtain for ever.

The final purpose for which the seventy weeks are appointed is 'to anoint a most holy place' (Dan. 9:24). The temple was destroyed in 586 BC, and Daniel prophesied its rebuilding in 9:25. The rebuilt temple is presupposed in the statement that city and sanctuary will be destroyed in 9:26, so that the anointing of a most holy place at the conclusion of the seventy weeks points to its final restoration. Here again there is fulfilment of the pattern typified with the third kingdom, where the little horn from the third kingdom attacks the sanctuary (8:11; 11:31), which is given over to desolation for a period of time (8:13; 11:31), before being 'restored to its rightful state' (8:14).

Ezekiel likewise prophesies of a restored temple (Ezek. 40 – 48), and Haggai and Zechariah prophesy at the building of the second temple. That second temple is the one whose destruction is described in Daniel 9:26, leaving the fulfilment of the anointing of the most holy place to the consummation of all things.

We noted in our discussion of Daniel's prayer of repentance earlier in this chapter that Daniel quotes Solomon's prayer at the dedication of the temple. Among other things, Daniel was praying for God to make his face shine upon his 'sanctuary, which is desolate' (9:17). The temple whose holy of holies will be anointed at the end of the seventy weeks in Daniel 9:24 is the one that fulfils what was symbolized by the temple to begin with: the new heaven and new earth. That is to say, the temple was a microcosm, a small-scale version of the world God made, in which he would be present, known, served and worshipped. The temple was a preview of the new heaven and new earth. The holy of holies to be anointed in Daniel 9:24, then, is the holy of holies that John sees descend from heaven having the glory of God in Revelation 21:9–22:5, the new Jerusalem.

Daniel 9:24 joins with many other passages in the Old Testament to point to the day when God decisively restores his people. The patterns that have pointed forward will be repeated in climactic expression. Sinners will have done their worst, and they will be permitted to do no more. Atonement will be accomplished, righteousness introduced, prophecy fulfilled and the dwelling of God will be with man. Daniel 9:25–27 sketches in some of what will take place between Daniel's own day and the consummation of all things at the tenfold jubilee, when the appointed seventy years for Israel are complete.

In the discussion above we saw that the seventy weeks are periodized into a seven-week period, followed by a sixty-two-week period, followed by statements of what will happen after those first sixty-nine weeks, concluding with the seventieth week being halved into two units (see table 5.1 above and the accompanying discussion). We also 'intertexted' these statements, considering the ways that Daniel 9:24–27 hyperlinks with other statements in the book of Daniel and earlier Scripture. Moreover, in the immediately preceding paragraphs we have seen that when the seventy weeks are complete, the ages will reach their consummation at the tenfold jubilee. I can now propose a kind of schematic timeline on the basis of these realities that looks like this:

| seven → weeks | sixty-two → weeks | Messiah cut off → city and sanctuary destroyed | first half of → seventieth week | second half of seventieth week |

The conclusion of the seventieth week, again, will be followed by the consummation of all things. How might these periods of time align with the presentation of history recorded in and projected by the Scriptures? I would propose the following understanding of these non-literal, schematic periods of the seventy weeks.

The first seven weeks after the going out of the word to restore and build Jerusalem (Dan. 9:25) matches the period of time between the revelation of these things to Daniel and the conclusion of Malachi's prophetic ministry. During this period of time the people benefit from the Spirit-inspired leadership of Ezra and Nehemiah as well as the Spirit-inspired prophetic ministries of Haggai, Zechariah and Malachi. Once the Scripture-producing, Spirit-inspired leaders and prophets leave the scene, this first seven-week period comes to its end.

Following that seven-week period comes a sixty-two-week period that is a 'troubled time' (Dan. 9:25).[14] This troubled time is marked by the lack of prophetic guidance (cf. e.g. 1 Macc. 4:46; 9:27; 14:41), and in keeping with Proverbs 29:18, 'the people cast off restraint'. In the northern kingdom of Israel prior to the Assyrian destruction thereof in 721 BC, a series of upstarts and usurpers murdered kings and – with neither prophetic word nor the validation of prophetic anointing – seized the throne. Similarly, after the prophets went silent once the second temple was built, a series of usurpers bribed, killed and conspired to make themselves high priest of Israel (for the history of the period, see Hengel 1974; Schürer 1973; Tcherikover 1959; Wright 1992; Portier-Young 2011).

After the seven weeks and the sixty-two weeks, prophecy returns with the rise of John the Baptist and the coming of Jesus the Messiah (cf. Luke 1). Jesus was cut off and had nothing,[15] and then in AD 70,

---

[14] Steinmann's assessment is similar: 'The "seven weeks" refer to the period of the restoration of Jerusalem from the time of Cyrus' decree in 538 BC authorizing the return to Jerusalem and the rebuilding of its temple to the completion of Jerusalem's walls by Nehemiah in 445 BC. The "sixty-two weeks" represent the period from Nehemiah to the life and ministry of Jesus' (2008: 472).

[15] Contrasting 'The Guild of Biblical Scholars and Ordinary Bible Readers', Izak J. J. Spangenberg writes of the strange people who (like the present author) actually believe the Bible: 'According to some of them the Maccabean theory undermines the authority of the Bible since Jesus himself regarded the book as a prophecy (cf Mark 13,14). Some of these readers even cherish the old idea that Daniel 9,26 ("an anointed one will be cut off and not exist [anymore]") is a prophecy about the crucifixion of Jesus' (2006: 441).

the people of the prince who was to come, the Romans, in an instalment in the pattern of fourth kingdom activity, destroyed city and
sanctuary (Dan. 9:26). I put it this way because the fourth kingdom
is never identified as Rome in Daniel, whereas the first kingdom is
clearly Babylon/Nebuchadnezzar ('you are the head of gold', Dan.
2:38), and Medo-Persia and Greece are likewise named (8:20–21;
11:1–2). This seems to leave the fourth kingdom open as a type, and
the pattern receives instalments from Rome and other wicked nations
who engage in this kind of activity, awaiting fulfilment in the Antichrist. I understand Revelation 11 as a description of the church
bearing witness to the gospel (see chapter 9 below and Hamilton
2012b: 231–244), and John may have the destruction of city and
sanctuary in view when he writes of the court of the temple and the
holy city being trampled for forty-two months in Revelation 11:2.

That leaves the seventieth week in Daniel 9:27. The following briefly
states what will be presented in more detail in chapter 9 when we
consider John's interpretation of Daniel in the book of Revelation.
In contrast with the way that Babylon, Medo-Persia and Greece are
identified as the first three kingdoms in Daniel, the fourth kingdom
is not specifically named. This matches the way that John in Revelation
idcntifies the wicked world that has rejected Jesus as belonging to one
kingdom. John does this when he identifies Jerusalem with Sodom
and Egypt in Revelation 11:8. The fourth kingdom is not one kingdom
in particular but the wicked world system that has united itself against
God and his people.

The covenant for one week in Daniel 9:27 refers to the way the
nations join together against the Lord and his Messiah after the cutting
off of the Messiah. Daniel 9:27 says that 'for half of the week he shall
put an end to sacrifice and offering', and we should understand this
as a figurative reference to an end-time attempt to stamp out the
worship of God. This need not mean that literal sacrifices and offerings
will be offered in the future. Rather than describing a resumption of
the sacrificial system, Daniel simply speaks of worship in the future
using the terms that describe worship in his own day. Along with the
attempt to stamp out the worship of God, Daniel 9:27 indicates that
a person will arise as the 'one who makes desolate'. This provides the
basis for the view that the 'abomination of desolation' will be a person
(cf. Mark 13:14).

This person who is the abomination of desolation, then, will do
what the little horn from the fourth kingdom did in Daniel 7, waging
war on the saints and speaking against God. Daniel 9:27 states that

the decreed end will be poured out upon him, and at that point the seventy weeks will have reached their conclusion. Then all that was articulated in Daniel 9:24 will be realized.

The halving of the seventieth week is a key to interpreting the book of Daniel because it demonstrates that the different visions in Daniel are to be understood as interlocked presentations. Thus the halving of that seventieth week informs the reference to the saints being given into the hand of the little horn from the fourth kingdom 'for a time, times, and half a time' in Daniel 7:25 (an understanding also demonstrated in Revelation, see chapter 9 below). Similarly, the halving of the seventieth week aids Daniel's audience in their effort to understand the various three-and-a-half-year periods described in Daniel: 2,300 evenings and mornings in 8:14; 1,290 days in 12:11; and 1,335 days in 12:12. Each of these periods is roughly three-and-a-half years. In Daniel 8:14 the little horn from the third kingdom will have a reign of terror similar to and thereby typifying the one prophesied for the little horn from the fourth kingdom. And the two statements at the end of Daniel, 12:11 and 12:12, join to pronounce a blessing on the one who keeps the faith through the time when the Antichrist will do his worst.

Conclusion

Daniel began to pray when he saw that the seventy years Jeremiah prophesied had been roughly fulfilled. He was not looking for a literal completion of those seventy years but understood them along the lines of Isaiah 23:15, as 'the days of one king'. Gabriel then revealed to Daniel that the remainder of human history would comprise a symbolic tenfold jubilee, that there would be a period of rebuilding, followed by a time of trouble; then the Messiah would be cut off. After the Messiah's cutting off and the destruction of the temple, the wicked world would join against the Lord. Next to arise will be an abomination of desolation, the Antichrist, who will seek to end the worship of Yahweh. His decreed end will come at the appointed time, and everything prophesied in Daniel 9:24 will be realized in the glorious eschatological restoration.

This revelation speaks to the people of God who suffer through the times of trouble and prepares them for the climactic difficulties at the end of history. There is no postmillennial optimism in Daniel about the people of God somehow taking over the world. Rather, the people of God are told in plain terms that the world will be against them, but that the arch-persecutor will be destroyed, and then God's purposes will be consummated when the son of man receives the kingdom and they reign with him.

Chapter Six

The one like a son of man and other heavenly beings in Daniel

This chapter intends to explore the identity of the heavenly beings described in the book of Daniel. We will first consider the ways the heavenly beings in Daniel are described, seeking to discern whether Daniel intended any of these to be understood as manifestations of God himself. One of the tasks of biblical theology is to trace the progress of revelation. The authors of the Old Testament are decisively monotheistic (House 1998). At the same time, there are references to the Spirit of God (e.g. Gen. 1:2), and there are accounts like Genesis 18, in which 'three men' visit Abraham, and one of these is described as 'Yahweh' speaking with Abraham (cf. Gen. 18:1–2, 10, 16–17, 22, 33; 19:1). There are two issues that can be distinguished here: (1) What we can say about what the human authors of these Old Testament texts intended to communicate. (2) What we can say about such instances in the light of the whole Bible (cf. Schreiner 2013: 4–5). This chapter investigates what Daniel intended to communicate in an effort to clarify how he forwards the progress of revelation.

The disputes in the early centuries of the Christian church indicate that the triune nature of God and the deity of Christ were progressively revealed. Working back from the early church, the four Gospels in the New Testament show everyone surprised when Jesus did something divine, like calm a storm (cf. Mark 4:35–41). In these instances, the followers of Jesus are not presented doing what we might expect them to do if the Old Testament clearly taught that the coming Messiah would be incarnate deity. We would expect to see them announcing in response to the divine actions of Jesus that this is exactly what they anticipated because the Old Testament clearly teaches it; then quoting a passage like Isaiah 9:6 ('his name shall be called . . . Mighty God . . .'). Rather than this, we find them asking, 'Who then is this?' (Mark 4:41), as though the mighty deeds of Jesus are forcing them to a conclusion they do not expect. Thus, when we work back from the Gospels to the Old Testament, we should not expect to find Chalcedonian Christology. If the authors of the Old Testament had understood and intended to teach such concepts, we would expect to find their instruction understood by the believing remnant, preserved and passed down until Jesus appeared on the scene, at which point they would not be surprised to find the Messiah doing what only God can do.

How, then, did the Old Testament authors understand the relationship between Yahweh and his king, the Messiah?[1] A number of passages (e.g. Isa. 9:6; Jer. 23:5–6; Pss 2:7; 45:6, etc.) evidence a close association of Yahweh and the human king. The human king of Israel seems to have been thought of as the Adamic image and likeness of God par excellence. He was the one who represented the many (cf. 1 Sam. 17:8–9); he was Israel's representative and example; he was Yahweh's adopted son (Ps. 2:7); and his throne was the earthly manifestation of Yahweh's (Ps. 45:6). This way of thinking about the issues puts us in a position to contemplate the mysterious and awe-inspiring contribution made to Old Testament theology by what was revealed to Daniel.

To explore the contribution Daniel makes to the Bible's presentation of God and Christ, this chapter will analyse Daniel's references to heavenly beings. Did Daniel intend any of these figures to be identified with Israel's expected Messiah? If so, how did Daniel intend his audience to understand the relationship between Yahweh and his Messiah?

Because Christ is described in the New Testament as the image of the invisible God (Col. 1:15; cf. John 14:9; Heb. 1:3, etc.), I will use the catchphrase 'pre-incarnate Christ' to refer to possible manifestations of God himself prior to the birth of Jesus of Nazareth.[2] We will first consider each of the heavenly beings described in Daniel *other than the one like a son of man in Daniel 7:13–14*. Having examined each of the others, we will then circle back to Daniel 7 and look more closely at that passage. The rationale for this is simple, and it is based squarely upon my evangelical presuppositions and methodology: the New Testament straightforwardly identifies Jesus as the Daniel 7:13–14 son of man. If any of the other heavenly beings in Daniel can be identified with the son of man, we have reason to believe that Daniel intended those passages to describe the same figure. In the light of the rest of

---

[1] There is, of course, a massive scholarly discussion of these issues. See e.g. Bauckham 2009; Chester 2007; Hurtado 2003; and Capes et al. 2007.

[2] For related studies, see the dissertations by Juncker (2001) and Malone (2012).

the Bible, we can therefore confidently describe those figures as the pre-incarnate Christ. The decisive evidence is in the text itself, to which we turn.

Heavenly beings in Daniel

The first step is to set forth the various ways the book of Daniel denominates these heavenly beings. In Daniel we find the following:

'I see four men . . . and the appearance of the fourth is like a son of the gods' (Dan. 3:25)

הא־אנה חזה גברין ארבעה . . . ורוה די רביעיא דמה לבר־אלהין

hā' 'ănâ ḥāzēh gubrîn 'arb'â . . . wĕrēvēh dî rĕbî'āy'a dāmēh lĕbar-'ĕlāhîn

'Blessed be the God . . . who has sent his angel' (Dan. 3:28)

בריך אלההון . . . די־שלח מלאכה

bĕrîk 'ĕlāhăhôn . . . dî-šĕlaḥ mal'ăkēh

'behold, a watcher, a holy one, came down from heaven' (Dan. 4:13; cf. 17, 23 [MT 4:10; cf. 14, 20])

ואלו עיר וקדיש מן־שמיא נחת

wa'ălû 'îr wĕqadîš min-šĕmayyā' nāḥit

'there fell a voice from heaven' (Dan. 4:31 [MT 28])

קל מן־שמיא נפל

qol min-šĕmayyā' nĕpal

'the fingers of a human hand' (Dan. 5:5)

אצבען די יד־אנש

'eṣbĕ'ān dî-yad-'ĕnāš

'My God sent his angel and shut the lions' mouths' (Dan. 6:22 [MT 23])

אלהי שלח מלאכה

'ĕlāhî šĕlaḥ mal'ăkēh

'a thousand thousands served him, / and ten thousand times ten thousand stood before him' (Dan. 7:10)

אלף אלפים ישמשונה ורבו רבון קדמוהי יקומון

'elep 'alpîm yĕšamšûnēh wĕribô ribwān qādāmôhî yeqûmûn

'there came one like a son of man' (Dan. 7:13)

כבר אנש אתה הוה

kĕbar 'ĕnāš 'ātēh hăwâ

'I approached one of those who stood there' (Dan. 7:16)

קרבת על־חד מן־קאמיא

qirbēt 'al-ḥad min-qā'ămayyā'

'the host of heaven' (Dan. 8:10)

צבא השמים

ṣĕbā' haššāmāyîm

'Prince of the host' (Dan. 8:11)

שר־הצבא

śar-haṣṣābā'

'I heard a holy one speaking, and another holy one said to the one who spoke' (Dan. 8:13)

ואשמעה אחד־קדוש מדבר ויאמר אחד קדוש לפלמוני המדבר

wā'ešmĕ'â 'eḥād-qādôš mĕdabēr wayyo'mer 'eḥād-qādôš lapalmônî hamĕdabbēr

'there stood before me one having the appearance of a man. And I heard a man's voice . . . and it called, "Gabriel . . ."' (Dan. 8:15–16)

עמד לנגדי כמראה־גבר ואשמע קול־אדם . . . ויקרא ויאמר גבריאל

'ōmēd lĕnegdî kemar'ēh-gāber wā'ešma' qôl-'ādām . . . wayyiqrā' wayyōmar gabrî'ēl

'the man Gabriel, whom I had seen in the vision at the first' (Dan. 9:21)

והאיש גבריאל אשר ראיתי בחזון בתחלה

wĕha'îš gabrî'ēl 'ăšer rā'îtî beḥāzôn batĕḥillâ

(cf. the use of 'after . . . the first' [בתחלה . . . אחרי, 'aḥărê . . . batĕḥillâ] in Dan. 8:1)

'a man clothed in linen' (Dan. 10:5)

איש־אחד לבוש בדים

'îš-'eḥād lābûš baddîm

'The prince of the kingdom of Persia . . . Michael, one of the chief princes . . . kings of Persia' (Dan. 10:13)

ושר מלכות פרס . . . אחד מיכאל השרים הראשנים . . . מלכי פרס
wĕśar malkût pāras . . . 'aḥad mîkā'ēl haśśārîm hari'šōnîm . . . malkê pārās

'one in the likeness of the children of man' (Dan. 10:16)
כדמות בני אדם
kidmût bĕnê 'ādām

'How can my lord's servant talk with my lord?' (Dan. 10:17)
והיך יוכל עבד אדני זה לדבר עם־אדני זה
wĕhēk yûkal 'ebed 'ădōnî zeh lĕdabbēr 'im-'ădōnî zeh

'one having the appearance of a man' (Dan. 10:18)
כמראה אדם
kĕmarēh 'ādām

'the prince of Persia . . . the prince of Greece' (Dan. 10:20)
שר פרס . . . שר־יון
śar pārās . . . śar-yāwān

'there is none who contends by my side against these except Michael, your prince' (Dan. 10:21)
ואין אחד מתחזק עמי על־אלה כי אם־מיכאל שרכם
wĕ'ên 'eḥād mitḥazzēq 'imî 'al-'ēlleh kî 'im-mikā'ēl śarkem

'At that time shall arise Michael, the great prince who has charge of your people' (Dan. 12:1)
ובעת ההיא יעמד מיכאל השר הגדול העמד על־בני עמך
ûbā'ēt hahî' ya'ămōd mîkā'ēl haśśar hagādôl hā'ōmēd 'al-bĕnê 'amekā

'behold, two others stood, one on this bank . . . and one on that bank' (Dan. 12:5)
והנה שנים אחרים עמדים אחד הנה לשפת היאר ואחד הנה
wĕhinnēh šĕnayim 'ăḥērîm 'ōmĕdîm 'eḥād hēnnâ liśpat hayĕ'ōr wĕ'eḥād hēnnâ

'someone said to the man clothed in linen, who was above the waters of the stream' (Dan. 12:6)
ואמר לאיש לבוש הבדים אשר מימעל למימי היאר
wayyōmer lā'îš lĕbûš habbaddîm 'ăšer mimma'al lĕmêmê hayĕ'ōr

139

'I heard the man clothed in linen' (Dan. 12:7)

ואשמא את־האיש לבוש הבדים

wā'ešma' 'et-hā'îš lĕbûš habaddîm

'O my lord' (Dan. 12:8)

אדני

'ădōnî

When these descriptions of heavenly beings are isolated and examined, their anthropomorphic character stands out. These figures are called men, have the body parts of men, have voices and use the words of men, wear the clothes of men, do the actions of men and for the most part are described as being *like* sons of men. The preponderance of anthropomorphic description can be contrasted with the few instances of descriptions that are more heavenly than anthropomorphic.

Classifying the evidence Daniel provides on the heavenly beings in the book will further the effort to determine the identity of these beings. Determining the identity of these beings by means of the ways they are described will enable us to know whether we can confidently conclude that the pre-incarnate Christ appears in Daniel, and if so where.

The *anthropomorphic descriptors* are as follows.

Heavenly beings referred to as men:

- 'four men' (3:25; cf. 8:16)
- 'the man Gabriel' (9:21; cf. 10:5; 12:6)

Having the body parts of men:

- 'the fingers of a human hand' (5:5)

Having the voice of men:

- 'a voice from heaven' (4:31 [MT 28])
- 'a man's voice' (8:16)

Doing what men do:

- 'ten thousand times ten thousand stood before him' (7:10)
- 'one of those who stood there' (7:16)

- 'a holy one speaking . . .' (8:13)
- 'two others stood' (12:5)

Holding offices of men:

- 'Prince of the host' (8:11)
- 'prince of . . . Persia . . . Michael, one of the chief princes . . . kings of Persia' (10:13)
- 'my lord' (10:17)
- 'prince of Persia . . . prince of Greece' (10:20)
- 'Michael, your prince' (10:21)
- 'Michael, the great prince' (12:1)
- 'my lord' (12:8)

Clothed like men:

- 'a man clothed in linen' (10:5)
- 'the man clothed in linen' (12:6)
- 'the man clothed in linen' (12:7)

Likened to men:

- 'one having the appearance of a man' (8:15)
- 'one having the appearance of a man' (10:18)

Like a son of man:

- 'one like a son of man' (7:13)
- 'one in the likeness of the sons of man' (10:16, my tr.)

The descriptions that are *more heavenly than anthropomorphic* are as follows:

- 'like a son of the gods' (3:35)
- 'a watcher, a holy one' (4:13, 17, 23 [MT 4:10, 14, 20])
- 'his angel' (6:22 [MT 6:23])
- 'the host of heaven' (8:10; cf. 8:11–14)

We saw in chapter 5 of the present volume that Gabriel is referred to in Daniel 9:21 as the man whom Daniel saw 'in the vision at the first'. Gabriel is also named in Daniel 8:16, but prior to that the vision of Daniel 8 was introduced in 8:1 as coming 'after that which appeared to me at the first'. I take this to mean that Gabriel served as the interpreter of the Daniel 7 vision, since that vision is the first of Daniel's own visions (cf. 7:10, 16). Gabriel, then, provided the interpretations given to Daniel in 7:16–27, 8:17–26 and 9:22–27. Since Gabriel is not named in Daniel 10 – 12, and since the descriptions of the heavenly being(s) in Daniel 10 – 12 are not exact verbal matches of those found in earlier chapters, we can at least say that we have no confirmation that Gabriel is one of the heavenly beings in Daniel 10 – 12.[3] It would go slightly further to say that Gabriel is definitely *not* in Daniel 10 – 12. Since it is possible, though perhaps unlikely, that Gabriel was one of the figures with whom Daniel interacted in Daniel 10 – 12, because Daniel neither names nor overtly identifies him, we cannot confidently identify Gabriel as one of the heavenly beings in Daniel 10 – 12.[4]

This way of thinking about Gabriel impinges on the view that some have taken that the fourth man in the fire in Daniel 3 is the pre-incarnate Christ. Daniel presents Nebuchadnezzar describing the fourth man in the fire as 'like a son of the gods' (Dan. 3:25). As above, I contend that we are simply not in a position to confirm that this fourth man in the fire is indeed the pre-incarnate Christ.[5]

At various points in the New Testament Jesus is identified as the Daniel 7:13 son of man (see discussion below and chapters 9 and 10). If there were a linguistic match between the son of man in Daniel 7:13 and the fourth man in the fire in Daniel 3:25, we could confirm that the fourth man in the fire is indeed the pre-incarnate Christ. The logic would be that Daniel intended to communicate that the figure he saw in Daniel 7:13–14 was the same figure Nebuchadnezzar saw with the three men in the fire. We have no such linguistic match, and apart from that I see no indication that Daniel meant to present the one like a son of man (Dan. 7:13) as the same figure Nebuchadnezzar saw in the fire in Daniel 3.

[3] In English translation, the phrase 'one having the appearance of a man' in Dan. 10:18 matches 'one having the appearance of a man' in 8:15, but different Hebrew words for 'man' are used in these two texts (גבר, *gbr*, in 8:15; אדם, '*dm*, in 10:18). This description in 8:16, moreover, is of the one who speaks to Gabriel rather than of Gabriel himself.

[4] Similarly, Carrell: 'Thus we see no secure answer to the question of the identity of the angel' (1997: 44; cf. 43).

[5] Greidanus likewise concludes that the identification of the fourth man in the fire as the pre-incarnate Christ 'rests on a weak basis', and suggests, 'A better case can be made for seeing the angel as a type of Christ' (2012: 95). As will be evident from the way I speak of the relationship between Christ and the angels who reflect his glory, I do not think the angel is a type of Christ.

When we considered the literary structure of the book of Daniel (in chapter 3 above), we saw parallels between Daniel 3 and Daniel 6. In the light of those parallels, it is relevant that Daniel says in 6:22, 'My God sent his angel and shut the lions' mouths', because Nebuchadnezzar calls the fourth man in the fire an angel in 3:28. Daniel saw the angel in 6:22 and the one like the son of man in 7:13, and he gives no indication that the two figures should be identified with one another. Since the account of the deliverance from the fire parallels the account of the deliverance from the lions' den, it would seem that in both cases an angel was God's agent of deliverance. Like other angels in Daniel, the agent of deliverance from the fiery furnace is referred to as a man ('I see four men', Dan. 3:25). This is part of the Aramaic section of Daniel, but angelic figures are elsewhere in Daniel described with the cognate Hebrew term (גבר, *gbr*, 8:15). It seems more probable than not that Daniel intended the fourth man in the fire to be understood as an angelic figure. If he meant for the fourth man in the fire to be identified with the son of man (Dan. 7:13), he left no overt indication or literary link that would lead to that conclusion.

What of the heavenly beings in Daniel 10 – 12? How many are there, and can any be confidently identified as the pre-incarnate Christ? There are either one or two figures in Daniel 10, possibly even three. Then Michael is named, the only angelic figure named in Daniel 10 – 12: in 10:13, 10:21 and 12:1. The angelic figure speaking to Daniel from at least 10:18 forward (if not also from 10:16, possibly even from 10:9) speaks right on through 12:4, at which point in 12:5 Daniel sees 'two others', and then in 12:6 'someone said to the man clothed in linen'.

When we arrive at Daniel 12:5, there are at least four angelic figures: one on each side of the stream (Dan. 12:5), 'the man clothed in linen, who was above the waters of the stream' (12:6) and the 'someone' who spoke to him (12:6). Because of the way 'the man clothed in linen' is identified in 12:6, it would appear that the one in view is the one described as clothed in linen in 10:5–9. Since the one who spoke with Daniel in 10:16 – 12:4 is not identified as 'clothed in linen' (cf. 10:16, 18), the one speaking in 10:16 – 12:4 is distinguished from this man clothed in linen. So the one who has been speaking with Daniel would be a fifth angelic figure.

Adding to the possibility that we should distinguish 'the man clothed in linen' of Daniel 10:5–6 from the speaker of 10:16 – 12:4 are the different ways these figures are described. The 'man clothed in linen' is described in detail in Daniel 10:5–6, and then rather than refer back to this 'man' (after the manner of 12:6) in 10:10, Daniel states in 10:16, 'And behold, one in the likeness of the children of man.' It is worth observing at this point that the expression used in 10:16 (כדמות בני אדם, *kidmût běnê 'ādām*) differs from references to 'the son of man' by including the phrase 'according to the likeness' (כדמות, *kidmût*) and putting 'son' in the plural, thus 'children' (בני, *běnê*; cf. the Hebrew expression in Ps. 8:5, ובן־אדם, *ûben-'ādām* and the Aramaic of Dan. 7:13, כבר אנש, *kěbar 'ěnāš*). Then finally there is the reference in 10:18 in the phrase 'Again one having the appearance of a man' (כמראה אדם, *kěmarēh 'ādām*). If Daniel intended his audience to identify the 'man clothed in linen' with whoever touched and spoke to him in 10:16 and 18, it would have been an easy thing to refer back to the figure described in 10:5–6. Since Daniel does not do this, we have warrant for suggesting that there are at least two figures in Daniel 10, the 'man clothed in linen' and then whoever it was who touched and spoke with Daniel later in the chapter.

The 'man clothed in linen' appears to interact with Daniel to 10:14. The opening words of 10:15 close off that interaction ('When he had spoken to me according to these words'), and a new figure is introduced in 10:16, 'one in the likeness of the children of man'. The 'again' (ויסף, *wayyōsep*) at the beginning of 10:18 indicates that the same figure – the one from 10:16 – again touches, strengthens and then speaks to Daniel (though there is a slightly different expression used to describe the 'one having the appearance of a man' in 10:18). This figure speaks to Daniel to 12:4.

To summarize, then, we can propose the following: the first figure Daniel encounters is the 'man clothed in linen' (10:5–6), with whom Daniel interacts to 10:14. At that point Daniel is helped by 'one in the likeness of the children of man' (10:16, 18), who speaks to him to 12:4. Daniel then sees two more figures, one on each side of the stream; then he again encounters the 'man clothed in linen' over the stream, to whom 'someone' speaks. Daniel thus describes at least four – possibly five – heavenly beings in Daniel 10 – 12.

The pre-incarnate Christ?

Can any of the heavenly beings in Daniel 10 – 12 be identified as the pre-incarnate Christ? I cannot make that identification with confidence for the following reasons. First, as with the fourth man in the fire from Daniel 3:25, Daniel does not decisively link any of the heavenly beings in Daniel 10 – 12 to the 7:13 son of man. Though Daniel 7 is in Aramaic and chapters 10 – 12 are in Hebrew, the Aramaic expression for 'son of man' in Daniel 7:13 is closer to the Hebrew equivalent in Psalm 8:5 and other places (such as Ezek. 2:1) than it is to any similar expression in Daniel. In Daniel we find 'son of the gods' in 3:25; 'the likeness of the children of man' in 10:16; and 'one having the appearance of a man' in 10:18. It is not difficult to imagine ways that Daniel could have indicated that any one of these figures was to be equated with the 'one like a son of man' in 7:13. We have as a reference point the way that Gabriel is referred to as 'the man . . . whom I had seen in the vision at the first' in Daniel 9:21. There is no equivalent reference to the Daniel 7:13 one like a son of man when Daniel elsewhere describes heavenly beings.

Since Jesus identifies himself as the Daniel 7:13 son of man in the New Testament, had Daniel made clear that the Daniel 7:13 son of man had also appeared in any of the other visions in his book, we could confidently assert that the pre-incarnate Christ was to be found in those places. Daniel does not give grounds for such confidence.

Some suggest that the pre-incarnate Christ appears as the 'man clothed in linen' in Daniel 10:5–6. Gieschen (1998: 132–133), by contrast, argues that Gabriel appears to Daniel in 10:5–6, and Carrell writes, 'we conclude that the glorious figure in Daniel 10.5–6 is an angel' (1997: 41). Gieschen and Carrell come to this conclusion because of the way that this figure is sent to Daniel (Dan. 10:11) and receives help from Michael (10:13, 21). Carrell regards the information that this figure *was sent* to be decisive because he considers the question in terms of whether this figure is a manifestation of God. God would not be sent; therefore this figure is not a manifestation of God. Viewing this figure as a pre-incarnate Christ would resolve this difficulty, since Jesus is the one sent by the Father in the Gospels. Steinmann (2008: 500) harmonizes the help from Michael with his view that the Daniel 10:5–6 figure is the pre-incarnate Christ. Against Steinmann's conclusion, however, the decisive factor in my thinking is the line of reasoning I have set forth above and will restate here:

- Daniel saw the pre-incarnate Christ in the vision of chapter 7 when he saw the one like a son of man approach the Ancient of Days (Dan. 7:13).
- If Daniel saw the pre-incarnate Christ again in 10:5–6, he would have perceived him as the same figure he saw in 7:13.

- If he had seen the same figure in 10:5–6 that he had in 7:13, he would have given some literary indication of that reality, probably by describing the two figures in the same terms or stating (along the lines of what he does with Gabriel in 9:21) that he was again seeing the one he had seen in the earlier vision.
- Conclusion: since Daniel does not describe the figure in 10:5–6 in a way that links him with the figure in Daniel 7:13–14, he does not mean for his audience to identify the two figures with each other.

The best reasons to identify this figure with Christ would be the similarity between the description of this figure in Daniel 10:5–6 with both the one on the throne in Ezekiel 1:26 (cf. also Ezek. 8:2) and with Jesus in Revelation 1:13–16 (see the discussion in Rowland 1982: 98–101). For some, these considerations are decisive (e.g. Steinmann 2008: 497–501). Weighing against this conclusion, however, is the fact that we find other heavenly beings in Revelation who are described in terms that are reminiscent of the ways Jesus is described in the book. For instance, the face of Jesus in Revelation 1:16 'was like the sun shining in full strength', and then in Revelation 10:1 we encounter 'another mighty angel . . . and his face was like the sun . . .' (cf. also Rev. 18:1). I am not convinced that John would refer to Jesus as 'another mighty angel' (10:1),[6] so I would explain such similarities as follows: those who represent Jesus reflect his glory, aspects of their appearance corresponding to and reflecting aspects of his appearance. If that can be the case with the angel in Revelation 10:1, the same can be the case with the 'man clothed in linen' in Daniel 10:5–6. Similarly, if the one on the throne in Ezekiel 1:26 is to be identified with Yahweh and his glory (cf. Ezek. 1:28), then the similarity between the one on the throne and the angel who represents him seems to explain what we find in Daniel 10:5–6. Because of this, while it may be possible that Daniel describes the pre-incarnate Christ in Daniel 10:5–6, I am unable to find evidence in the text that decisively confirms that reality and grants confidence in that conclusion. I find it more plausible, therefore, that the man clothed in linen in Daniel 10:5–6 is an angel who reflects the glory of the Lord, who was himself seen clearly by John when he beheld Jesus, as described in Revelation 1:13–16.

---

[6] Rightly Collins and Collins: 'The letter to the Hebrews strongly and clearly rejects the idea that Christ is an angel (Hebrews 1). . . . The figure in Daniel [10:5–9] is best understood as an angel' (2008: 189, 191).

The one like a son of man

In contrast with my conclusions about Daniel 3 and 10, I would suggest that the Daniel 7 vision treats the Davidic son of man (Dan. 7:13; cf. Ps. 8:5) as a member of the heavenly court who will have the throne of his kingdom established for ever (2 Sam. 7:13), enjoying 'everlasting dominion' (Dan. 7:14; cf. Gen. 1:28). Davidic features of the text, such as the 2 Samuel 7:13 everlasting kingdom and the link between Psalm 8, where the Davidic son of man enjoys Genesis 1:28 dominion over the beasts, and the same realities in Daniel 7, prompt me to disagree with Caragounis's conclusion that Daniel 'has given up on humanity . . . and has centered his hopes upon a direct divine intervention' (1986: 80). It cannot be the case that God has abandoned the promised programme of a king from a line of David, for if God is to be faithful to the promises he made to David in 2 Samuel 7, the conquering king must be a human descendant of David. Caragounis (61–81), however, makes a number of intriguing points about the presentation of the one like a son of man in Daniel 7.[7]

The evidence points to the one like a son of man being a member of the heavenly court who is distinguished from and identified with Yahweh himself. As stated in the introduction of this chapter, I do not think this evidence necessitates the conclusion that Daniel understood and meant to communicate that the coming king from David's line would be Yahweh incarnate. Now that Christ has come and the New Testament has been written, we can look back and see that what Daniel saw and described fits perfectly with what the New Testament reveals about Jesus the Messiah. From Daniel's perspective, however, it seems safer to suggest that in ancient Israel there was a close connection between Israel's king and Israel's God, along the lines of what we see when the king is addressed as God in Psalm 45:6, or when the child will be called Mighty God in Isaiah 9:6.

Others may feel comfortable suggesting that the Old Testament authors understood that the Messiah would be God incarnate. I cannot make that assertion, because when Jesus began to do divine things and exercise divine prerogatives, the Gospels present everyone as being surprised. No one in the Gospels – not even those who believed that Jesus was the Messiah – responded to his mighty deeds by quoting one of these passages from the Old Testament as proof

---

[7] For a recent interaction with broader scholarship, see the volume edited by Larry Hurtado and Paul Owen (2011).

that the prophets foretold that the expected Messiah would be God incarnate.

That said, Daniel contributes to the progress of revelation by describing the Daniel 7:13–14 one like a son of man in undeniably divine terms. The evidence for this conclusion appears in the text in the following order under these headings: the thrones, the coming with the clouds, the description – as being *like* a son of man with the connections to Ezekiel's vision, and the way that the one like a son of man from 7:13–14 is interpreted in 7:15–27.

In Daniel 7:9:

> thrones were placed,
> and the Ancient of Days took his seat.

Taking the temporal markers in the texts at face value, when Daniel saw this vision 'In the first year of Belshazzar' (Dan. 7:1), Ezekiel's vision in 'the fifth year of the exile of King Jehoiachin' (Ezek. 1:2, 593 BC) would presumably have been available to him, as both Ezekiel and Daniel were in Babylon. Ezekiel saw only one throne (Ezek. 1:26), but only in Ezekiel and Daniel do we read of prophets seeing wheels (Ezek. 1:15–23; Dan. 7:9). The flames and wheels described by Ezekiel and Daniel invite us to interpret each vision in the light of the other. Apparently these two prophets in exile saw visions that communicated God's ability to travel; thus the chariot-style wheels (the term used to describe the wheels in Ezekiel describes chariot wheels in Exod. 14:25 and Nah. 3:2). Yahweh was not confined to the holy of holies. Other connections between Ezekiel 1 and Daniel 7 include the references to flames (Ezek. 1:4, 13, 27; Dan. 7:9–10) and the depiction of one seated on the throne. Consider the two passages side by side in table 6.1

Why would 'thrones' – more than one – be placed in the vision of Daniel 7:9–10? Assuming Daniel had access to the Davidic Psalm 110 (Jesus attributed Psalm 110 to David in Mark 12:36), his perception and interpretation of what he saw in the vision could have been influenced by the statement in Psalm 110:1:

> Sit at my right hand,
> until I make your enemies your footstool.

The fact that Jesus connected the Daniel 7:13 son of man with Psalm 110:1 strengthens this possibility: 'you will see the Son of Man seated at the right hand of Power and coming on the clouds of heaven' (Matt.

Table 6.1 Ezekiel 1:26–28 and Daniel 7:9–10

Ezekiel 1:26–28	Daniel 7:9–10

'And above the expanse over their heads there was the likeness of a throne, in appearance like sapphire; and seated above the likeness of a throne was a likeness with a human appearance [דמות כמראה אדם, *děmût kěmarēh 'ādām*]. And upwards from what had the appearance of his waist I saw as it were gleaming metal, like the appearance of fire enclosed all round. And downwards from what had the appearance of his waist I saw as it were the appearance of fire, and there was brightness around him. Like the appearance of the bow that is in the cloud on the day of rain, so was the appearance of the brightness all round. Such was the appearance of the likeness of the glory of the LORD [מראה דמות כבוד־יהוה, *marēh děmût kěbôd-yhwh*]. And when I saw it, I fell on my face, and I heard the voice of one speaking.'	As I looked,
	
	'thrones were placed,
	  and the Ancient of Days took his seat;
	his clothing was white as snow,
	  and the hair of his head like pure wool;
	his throne was fiery flames;
	  its wheels were burning fire.
	A stream of fire issued
	  and came out from before him;
	a thousand thousands served him,
	  and ten thousand times ten thousand
	    stood before him;
	the court sat in judgment,
	  and the books were opened.'

26:64). Rather than simply one throne for the Ancient of Days, Daniel saw 'thrones', and in view of what takes place in the vision, where the one like a son of man receives the kingdom (cf. Dan. 7:14), the natural conclusion is that there is a throne for the one like a son of man. The inclusion of the detail that 'thrones were placed' (Dan. 7:9) testifies to its significance. This would also suggest that Daniel understood his vision as an enactment of what David described in Psalm 110:1, connecting the Daniel 7 vision with the hope for a king from David's line and validating the way that Matthew presents Jesus interpreting these texts.

The placement of thrones in Daniel 7:9 indicates that when the one like a son of man receives his kingdom, he will be enthroned alongside Yahweh. This concept fits not only with Psalm 110:1 but with the way that Psalm 45:6 addresses the Davidic king (cf. Ps. 45:1–5) with the words 'Your throne, O God, is for ever and ever.' The king's throne is closely associated with God's throne.

The description of the one like a son of man coming 'with the clouds of heaven' in Daniel 7:13 indicates that not only is this figure taking part in a drama enacted in the heavenly court, but he travels the way Yahweh himself does. As Peter Gentry notes, 'The coming on clouds suggests an appearance or theophany of Yahweh himself. If Daniel 7:13 does not refer to an appearance of deity, it is the only

exception in about seventy instances in the OT' (2003: 73).[8] The one
like a son of man, then, participates in the heavenly scene, where he
apparently has a throne next to Yahweh, and where he travels as only
Yahweh does.

That 'thrones' are set in Daniel 7:9, with the 'son of man' of 7:13
receiving the kingdom in 7:14, connects this passage to the promises
to David reflected in Psalm 110, where David's Lord is invited to sit
at Yahweh's right hand, and in Psalm 8, where David reflects on the
dominion over the beasts given to the son of man. These points of
contact lash the Daniel 7 vision firmly to the broader Old Testament
hope for the human king from David's line. At the same time, however,
Daniel sees indications that the king is a heavenly being: the heavenly
court scene, the fact that he comes on the clouds, and the comparative
'like' in the phrase 'one like a son of man' (כבר אנש, kĕbar 'ĕnāš). A
mysterious question arises: How will the human king from David's
line also be a pre-existent member of the heavenly court? The solution
of the conundrum awaits further revelation.

At this point we can consider again Ezekiel's vision. Whereas the
'likeness as the appearance of a man' (Ezek. 1:26, my tr.) seems to
correspond to Yahweh being enthroned in Daniel 7:9, Ezekiel himself
is repeatedly addressed as 'son of man' (בן־אדם, ben-'ādām, Ezek. 2:1,
3, 6, 8, etc.). Caragounis suggests that there are aspects of Ezekiel's
role that inform the use of this phrase. Summarizing the way
Ezekiel is commissioned to preach to rebels (2:3), made their watch-
man (3:17–18), and then seems to bear their punishment when he is
bound with ropes (3:25) and parabolically enacts the siege and punishment of Israel and Judah (4:1–17 – note that Ezekiel bears the
punishment of Israel and Judah in 4:4–6), Caragounis writes, 'In all
these passages he is constantly addressed as "son of man." ' . . . The
cases cited amply show that the role which the prophet has assumed
among his people is one of representative, intercessor and substitute'
(1986: 60). The strong overtones of the Ezekiel 1 vision in Daniel
7:9–10 increase the likelihood that Daniel intended his audience to
recall Ezekiel and his role as a suffering prophet who identified with
his people when he used the phrase 'one like a son of man'. Ezekiel
was himself an instalment in the pattern of the righteous sufferer (a
pattern abundantly attested in the Psalms), and in addition Ezekiel
was a prophet like Moses. As the son of man, Ezekiel was a prophet
like Moses who was a suffering representative and substitute, all of

[8] Cf. e.g. Pss 18:10; 97:2; 104:3, etc.

which interfaces with Davidic hope and informs the reference in Daniel 9:26 to the Messiah being cut off and having nothing.

These considerations lead to a final observation about the way that Daniel deploys language to communicate what he saw in this Daniel 7 vision. Caragounis (1986: 74) observes that once Daniel has seen the vision (Dan. 7:1–14), curious lacunae stand in the interpretation (7:15–28):

> Of the vision elements which are not interpreted by name, the most conspicuous are the Ancient One and the [one like a son of man] . . . Why is [the one like a son of man] not interpreted? Or, is he perhaps interpreted, though without being named expressly, but implicitly, by way of associations made in the text?

Caragounis (1986: 75) next observes that the normal Aramaic term used in Daniel to refer to God as 'Most High' is עליא, *'illāyā'* (Dan. 3:26, 32; 4:14, 21, 22, 29, 31; 5:18, 21; 7:25). In contrast with this, in the phrase 'saints of the Most High' (7:18, 22, 25, 27), Daniel always uses the form עליונין, *'elyônîn*. Gentry (2003: 73) builds on these observations from Caragounis, noting that עליא (*'illāyā'*)

> is an Aramaic adjective, definite and singular, and may be rendered the Highest One or Most High. It refers to Yahweh, the one God of Israel and is standard in the Aramaic part of the book either as a modifier of God or as a title for God . . . By contrast, [עליונין, *'elyônîn*] is an honorific plural or plural of majesty of [עליון, *'elyôn*], the Hebrew adjective for highest plus the Aramaic plural ending.

Daniel uses the two terms side by side in 7:25, 'He shall speak words against the Most High [עליא, *'illāyā'*], / and shall wear out the saints of the Most High [עליונין, *'elyônîn*]', prompting Gentry (2003: 73) to ask:

> Why does the author use a Hebrew expression (with Aramaic ending) for the Most High in the Aramaic section and side by side with the expression standard in Aramaic? It seems a deliberate attempt to draw some distinction between a divine figure associated with the saints and yet perhaps distinguished from Yahweh in some way.

Because of the similarity of the statements in Daniel 7:14 and 7:27, we can be certain that the Most High referred to with עליונין (*'elyônîn*)

and associated with the saints in the phrase 'saints of the Most High'
is the 'one like a son of man'. Considering these two texts side by side
will bring out their similarity (see table 6.2).

Table 6.2 Daniel 7:14 and 7:27

Daniel 7:14	Daniel 7:27
'And to him was given dominion and glory and a kingdom, that all peoples, nations, and languages should serve him [לה יפלחון, *lēh yiplĕḥûn*]; his dominion is an everlasting dominion, which shall not pass away, and his kingdom one that shall not be destroyed.'	'And the kingdom and the dominion and the greatness of the kingdoms under the whole heaven shall be given to the people of the saints of the Most High; his kingdom shall be an everlasting kingdom, and all dominions shall serve and obey him [לה יפלחון וישתמעון, *lēh yiplĕḥûn wĕyištammĕ'ûn*].'

(adapted ESV)

The referent of the two third-person masculine singular pronouns at
the end of Daniel 7:27, '*his* kingdom . . . obey *him*', is the Most High
[עליונין, *'elyônîn*]. The word 'people' [עם, *'am*] is also singular and thus
could be the referent of these third-person pronouns, but for the
following reasons Most High is more probably the referent. First, 'Most
High' stands between the third singular pronouns and 'people', and
the nearer substantive is more probably the referent. Secondly, the
'people' are referred to throughout the passage with the plural 'saints'
(Dan. 7:18, 22, 25, 27), and 'saints' is closer to the pronouns than
'people'. If the pronouns referred to the 'people of the saints', they
might be plural rather than singular. Finally, the reuse of a phrase from
Daniel 7:13 in 7:27 identifies the 'one like a son of man' with the 'Most
High'. Daniel 7:14 states that peoples, nations and languages will 'serve'
the son of man, and the same Hebrew phrase is used in 7:27 (לה יפלחון,
lēh yiplĕḥûn) to state that all dominions will serve the Most High. This
is language used elsewhere in Daniel to refer to the kind of service one
renders to what one worships (cf. the use of the verb in 3:12, 14, 17–18,
28; 6:17, 21 [MT]), and it is more probable that such service would be
rendered to the Most High than to the people. Here again, Daniel used
the Hebrew adjective with the Aramaic plural ending (עליונין, *'elyônîn*)
to refer to the 'one like a son of man' as Most High, distinguishing him
from the Ancient of Days, for whom he used the normal Aramaic
expression (עליא, *'illāyā'*) when designating him as Most High.

By using these distinct forms for 'Most High' consistently, Daniel
identified both the Ancient of Days and the one like a son of man as

the Most High, even as he distinguished them from one another. In this passage, Daniel communicates that the one like a son of man will be enthroned alongside the Ancient of Days, that he comes with the clouds as Yahweh does elsewhere (e.g. Pss 18:10; 97:2; 104:3, etc.), that he receives service and worship – described with terms only elsewhere used for describing obeisance done for deity (Gentry 2003: 72–73), and that he will receive the everlasting kingdom which shall not pass away, which is exactly how God's kingdom is described. The Ancient of Days is described as Most High with one term, while the one like a son of man is described as Most High with another. And the term used to describe the one like a son of man as Most High is always used in the phrase 'saints of the Most High', apparently because the Psalm 8:5 son of man who receives dominion over the beasts, the Psalm 110:1 Lord of David who sits at Yahweh's right hand, will be king over the saints,[9] their representative who is somehow *both* identified with *and* distinguished from the Ancient of Days, even as he is *both* a descendant of David *and* a divine figure.

Conclusion

In this chapter I have argued that none of the other heavenly beings in Daniel can be confidently identified with the 'one like a son of man' in 7:13. Apart from such an identification, it is difficult to imagine Daniel intending his audience to understand that the figure he saw in that heavenly throne room scene in chapter 7 was the same figure who delivered his friends in the fiery furnace in chapter 3 or who appeared to him in chapter 10. Having examined the way that Daniel describes these other heavenly beings, the remarkable features of Daniel 7 present a figure both human and divine, identified with and distinguished from the Ancient of Days, who represents the saints as their king.

In Daniel 7, Daniel recounts his vision of the way that the Ancient of Days will be enthroned once the four kingdoms have enjoyed their appointed time and season, a vision of the way that the Davidic king will defeat the little horn from the fourth kingdom and receive the everlasting kingdom with his saints (7:21–27). The one like a son of man is called Most High by using a different expression from the one used to designate the Ancient of Days as Most High. He is clearly the

---

[9] As Schreiner puts it, 'The saints are included corporately in their leader' (2013: 393).

Davidic king, and he is clearly a participant in the heavenly scene, travelling as Yahweh does, on the clouds of heaven.

This does not demand that Daniel understood the Trinity as that doctrine progressively came to be revealed. Everyone was surprised when Jesus began to exercise divine prerogatives. What Daniel saw and described, however, fits perfectly with what would later be revealed with greater clarity. The New Testament even speaks of Jesus as begotten of the Father (1 John 5:18; cf. John 1:14, 18; 3:16, 18; 1 John 4:9; cf. John 5:26), another concept that fits well with there being an Ancient of Days and 'one like a son of man' (cf. Caragounis 1986: 78).

Chapter Seven

Interpretations of Daniel in early Jewish literature

Discussing the books of the Old Testament in *Against Apion* (1.38–41), Josephus (1926, 186: 179) wrote:

> Our books, those which are justly accredited . . . contain the record of all time. . . . from the birth of man down to the death of the lawgiver. . . . From the death of Moses until Artaxerxes, who succeeded Xerxes as king of Persia, the prophets subsequent to Moses wrote the history of the events of their own times. . . . From Artaxerxes to our own time the complete history has been written, but has not been deemed worthy of equal credit with the earlier records, because of the failure of the exact succession of the prophets.[1]

This chapter cannot be an exhaustive discussion of the use of Daniel in non-canonical Jewish literature.[2] The chapter presents a sample of the ways that Daniel was interpreted, not simply cataloguing references but pursuing insight into the hermeneutical framework within which these authors worked as they interpreted Daniel and applied it in their writings. We will see that the use of superficial details from the book of Daniel shows that Daniel (with the rest of the books of the OT)

---

[1] I am persuaded by Beckwith's (1985) treatment of this passage and discuss it in my essay 'An Evangelical View of Scripture' (2010d: 240–242).

[2] The best way to find interpretations of Daniel is to comb carefully through the texts, which is what I have done with those discussed here. This allows us to watch for patterns and other forms of interpretation that may not be noted on lists of cross-references. See DiTommaso 2005 for his massive compilation of 'apocryphal Daniel literature'. And for lists of references, see Washburn 2002: 136–139, Delamarter 2002: 32–34 and Fitzmyer 1990: 233. For the texts I have used *A New English Translation of the Septuagint* (Pietersma and Wright 2007), checking the renderings against critical texts of the Greek where available or necessary, *The Old Testament Pseudepigrapha* (Charlesworth 1983), consulting the Latin Vulgate for *4 Ezra* where necessary, and *The Dead Sea Scrolls Study Edition*, which contains both the Hebrew/Aramaic and an English translation (García Martínez and Tigchelaar 2000). Cf. also Vanderkam and Flint's brief discussion of 'Texts Featuring Daniel' in the Dead Sea Scrolls (2002: 231–232) and Beale's work *The Use of Daniel in Jewish Apocalyptic Literature* (1984).

has supplied the mental furniture used in descriptions of the schematic conceptual picture of the heavenly court and the periodization of history.[3] The set of expectations built up from the reuse of these superficial details contributed to a pattern of expectations, a typological pattern, and this pattern was applied backward on to the story of Tobit, and forward in 1 Maccabees, where it was used to interpret the historical events of the Maccabean crisis. The details and the patterns were mixed into a boiling cauldron of eschatological anticipation, brewed in the apocalyptic literature stewing with announcements of a cathartic visitation of justice on the wicked bringing about the deliverance of the righteous. To explore all this, we will consider the use of Daniel in the book of Tobit, at Qumran, in 1 Maccabees, in *4 Ezra* and in *1 Enoch*.

In their use of Daniel, the authors of these books sought to do biblical theology. That is, they attempted to apply to their own situation the interpretative perspective they discerned from the Old Testament. At many points the conclusions these authors draw, and the applications they make, are much nearer to those made by the authors of the New Testament than they are to the conclusions and applications made by biblical scholars in recent centuries. Along with what they got right, we will see places where the authors of the ancient texts considered here have departed from the interpretative perspective of the Old Testament authors, particularly Daniel.

Tobit

Among the overarching concerns of the author of Tobit were the proper burial of deceased Israelites (1:17–19; 2:4, 7–8; 4:3–4; 8:9, 11–12; 12:12–13; 14:10–13; cf. Moore 1996: 22–23) and the atoning value of alms-giving: 'Almsgiving delivers from death, and it purges away every sin' (12:8–9; cf. 4:10; 14:11). This connection between almsgiving and atonement veers away from Old Testament teaching. The audience of Tobit (14:4–5), however, was assured that God's word, spoken through the prophets, would come to pass:

for I believe the word of God about Nineue, the things Naoum spoke, that all these things will come about and happen . . . Also everything that the prophets of Israel spoke, those whom God sent,

---

[3] See Stone's (1984: 436–437) discussion of the periodization of history in apocalyptic literature.

will happen. And not one of their words will fail, but all will come true at their appointed times. . . . For I know and believe that all things that God said will be fulfilled and will come to pass, and no utterance of his words shall fail. . . . just as the prophets of Israel said concerning it.

Tobit also speaks of the Torah of Moses at several points (Tob. 1:8; 6:13; 7:11–13), and at no point does the author of Tobit claim to be inspired by the Holy Spirit or to write as a prophet. He does not class himself with the prophets, though he does present the angel Raphael ordering him, 'Write down all these things that have happened to you' (Tob. 12:20).

Tobit claims to have been a northerner who did not worship Jeroboam's golden calf but worshipped rightly in Jerusalem according to the Torah of Moses (Tob. 1:5–8). Devorah Dimant has, in my view, accurately described the use of Scripture in Tobit in terms of 'implicit compositional uses' of the biblical text, whereby the Bible provides 'the materials forming the texture of the composition. Authors employing biblical elements in this way aim at re-creating the biblical models and atmosphere, and identify themselves with the biblical authors' (2004: 419; cf. 406).[4] Thus Tobit relates how when he was exiled, like Daniel he refused to eat 'the bread of the nations' (1:11, NETS; cf. Dan. 1:8), and how 'the Most High gave me favor and good standing with Enemessaros' (Tob. 1:13; cf. Dan. 1:9). Like Daniel, Tobit's good deeds were reported to the king (Tob. 1:19a), and like Moses, Tobit fled when he realized the king sought his life (1:19b). Tobit's nephew was cupbearer like Nehemiah (1:22a), second only to the king like Joseph (1:22b). These points of contact between Tobit, Moses, Daniel, Nehemiah and, as will be seen below, Joseph and Jacob, associate Tobit with significant biblical figures who prospered outside the land of Israel. This matches Dimant's conclusion 'The Book of Tobit offers a good example of reworking biblical narrative models and motifs' (2004: 417). These connections commend the faithfulness demonstrated by the biblical figures, along with Tobit, to those who have been exiled from the land and await restoration thereto. Nickelsburg states of Tobit, 'The belief that God rewards the righteous is basic to the book' (1984: 41). The final chapter of Tobit

---

[4] In this context, to identify with the biblical authors is to consider oneself on their side over against the enemies of God and his people, but not to identify with them in the sense that one joins their ranks as a writer of Scripture.

(Tob. 14) looks forward to the same glorious eschatological restoration of Jerusalem prophesied in the Old Testament.

Like Daniel, Tobit prays confessing God's righteousness and Israel's sin (Tob. 3:1–6), and like Jonah he says it is better for him to die than live (3:6; Jon. 4:3). Sarah's experience of dying husbands is an exaggeration of the experience of Tamar, daughter-in-law twice over to Judah (Tob. 3:7–9; cf. Gen. 38:6–11), a connection strengthened by the reference to a father's head being brought down with grief to Hades (Tob. 3:10; cf. 6:15; Gen. 42:38). Just as an angel came in response to Daniel's prayers (Dan. 9:23; 10:2, 12–13), Raphael came in answer to the prayers of Tobit and Sarah, to heal Tobit and to give Sarah to Tobias (Tob. 3:16–17). Like Ezra and Nehemiah, Tobit is concerned that Tobias not marry a foreign woman (4:12; cf. Ezra 9 – 10; Neh. 13). There is no biblical analogy for the kind of healing by fish gall and demon expulsion by burned fish heart and liver seen in Tobit 6:3–9, 17; 8:2–3; 11:7.

We see a levirate marriage situation when we read that Tobias is next of kin to Sarah, as Boaz to Ruth (Tob. 6:12; cf. Ruth 3:12; 4:3–12), and the language of Tobit 7:11 reminds readers of Ruth 3:18. The meeting of Tobias and Ragouel (7:2–7) is reminiscent of Jacob's first meeting of Laban (Gen. 29:13), and the fourteen-day wedding feast is also reminiscent of Jacob's experience (Tob. 8:20; cf. Gen. 29:27). When Tobias's mother greets him, we read a redo of the reunion between Jacob and Joseph (Tob. 11:9; cf. Gen. 46:29–30). Like Daniel, Tobit speaks of the restoration – including a rebuilt temple – that will come after the desolation, which desolation will last 'until the time when the time of the appointed times will be completed' (Tob. 14:4–5; cf. Dan. 9:24–27; 12:4, 7, 9, 11).

The way that the author of Tobit uses Daniel and other Old Testament precedents indicates that he understood the patterns seen in the narratives of the Old Testament to be paradigmatic. The author of Tobit, writing after Daniel, presents Tobit as a precursor, or type, of Daniel and Nehemiah according to the pattern of Joseph. Hosea understood Jacob's experience of leaving the land and returning as paradigmatic (Hos. 12:2–13), and from these patterns and paradigms it seems that the author of Tobit has followed the methods of the biblical authors in seeking to encourage his audience at the levels of faith and practice. Nickelsburg articulates the point I seek to establish: 'For the author of Tobit, God's dealings with the suffering righteous person are paradigmatic of his dealings with Israel' (1984: 43). At the level of faith, he wants them to believe the Old Testament

(Tob. 14:4–5, quoted above), particularly on the point that the blessing of Abraham will be fulfilled (Tob. 13:12). At the level of practice, he wants them to give alms (4:10; 12:8–9; 14:11), bury the dead (see the many references above) and bless the Lord (4:19; 8:5, 15; 11:14; 12:6, 17–18, 20; 13:1, 6, 10, 13, 15, 18; 14:2, 7, 8–9, 15).

The author of Tobit uses Daniel the way he uses other Old Testament books.[5] As can be seen from this discussion, the author of Tobit laced the narrative with reminders of the language and patterns of Old Testament narratives, commending the faith and practice of those described in Scripture. The author of Tobit has rightly discerned the way Old Testament authors understand patterns to be typological, but he is wrong about the value of almsgiving and the role of fish in healing and exorcism. His interest in the burial of the dead may arise from a concern for the resurrection of the body, and his doxological purpose[6] matches that of the Old Testament (see Hamilton 2010b: 351–353).

Qumran[7]

To keep this discussion focused, my interest here is in sampling how Daniel was interpreted in the Qumran scrolls. In this vein, we saw in chapter 1 that 4Q *Florilegium* (4Q174, Frags. 1 Col. II, 3, 24, 5) quotes Daniel as Scripture: 'as is written in the book of Daniel, the prophet'. Roger Beckwith (1985: 415–416, n. 75) has pointed out that while the Qumran texts use the language of the book of Daniel, they use that language differently from the way Daniel does:

> the characteristic terminology of the Qumran biblical commentaries is that of a 'secret' (*raz*) and its 'interpretation' (*pesher*), and is drawn from Daniel . . . But whereas at Qumran the 'secret' to be interpreted is always a passage of the Old Testament, in Daniel this is never so (Dan. 2.18f., 27–30, 47; 4.9). What has happened

---

[5] See Dimant's discussion of Job in Tobit, where she also notes, 'It has often been observed that the author of this work attempts to re-create the religious ethos and atmosphere of the patriarchal narratives by evoking various motifs of the Genesis stories' (2004: 417–419).

[6] Rightly Nickelsburg: 'The book of Tobit is profoundly doxological in content and tone' (1984: 44).

[7] See Dimant's discussion of the possibility that the founding of the Qumran sect is reckoned in the light of Daniel's seventy weeks (1984: 544–547). Roger Beckwith has similarly argued that calculations of Daniel's seventy weeks factored significantly in the eschatological expectations of the Essenes, Pharisees, Zealots and early Christians (1981).

is that the Essenes have applied his language in a new and not altogether happy way.

As for the vaunted *Prayer of Nabonidus* (4Q242), there is simply not enough known about the fragmentary nine lines of this text preserved at Qumran to say anything definite about it (García Martínez and Tigchelaar 2000: 486–489). The same holds for the fragments of 'Pseudo-Daniel' (4Q243–245, García Martínez and Tigchelaar 2000: 488–493).

The so called 'Son of God Text' (4Q246), makes fascinating statements on the basis of the book of Daniel (García Martínez and Tigchelaar 2000: 492–495). The 'Son of God Text' forges an interpretative connection between the promise that the seed of David would be a son to God, God being a Father to him (2 Sam. 7:14; Ps. 2:7), and the one like a son of man in Daniel 7:13–14. This connection follows naturally from the way that the Davidic Psalm 8 (see superscription to Ps. 8) speaks of the 'son of man' (Ps. 8:4) enjoying Adamic dominion (8:6–9; cf. Gen. 1:28). Like Daniel 7, which speaks of the one like a son of man enjoying a kingdom of everlasting dominion (Dan. 7:13–14), and then speaks of the people, the saints who will receive the kingdom with him (7:27), so the 'Son of God Text' (García Martínez and Tigchelaar 2000: 495) says:

> He will be called son of God, and they will call him son of the Most High. . . . they will rule several year[s] over the earth and crush everything; a people will crush another people . . . Until the people of God arises and makes everyone rest from the sword. . . . His kingdom will be an eternal kingdom, and all his paths in truth. He will jud[ge] the earth in truth and all will make peace. The sword will cease from the earth . . . The great God is his strength . . . His rule will be an eternal rule . . .[8]

In addition to the connection made here between the rule of the Danielic son of man and the Davidic seed, the 'crushing' language might point to the seed of the woman crushing the seed of the serpent (Gen. 3:15; see further Hamilton 2006). Just as 2 Samuel 7:14 and

---

[8] Collins and Collins argue similarly, 'In Daniel 7, the eternal kingdom is explicitly given both to the "one like a son of man" and to the people of the holy ones. In the same way, the tensions in 4Q246 can be resolved if the "son of God" is understood as a messianic king, so that the kingdom is given simultaneously both to him and to the people' (2008: 72).

Daniel 7:13 are brought together, imagery from other texts such as Isaiah 11, where the Davidic Messiah judges truly (Isa. 11:3–4; cf. 9:7) and war ceases from the earth (11:9, 13; cf. 2:4), informs the statements that 'He will judge the earth in truth' and 'The sword will cease from the earth' (4Q246, Col. II, 5–6). The 'eternal rule' matches the promise that there will be no end of his kingdom found in 2 Samuel 7, Psalm 2, Isaiah 9, Daniel 7, and many other texts.

We noted in chapter 1 that 11Q *Rule of Melchizedek* (11Q13, Col. II, 18) quotes Daniel as Scripture, interpreting the anointed one predicted in Daniel 9:25 as the fulfilment of Isaiah 52:7. There is more to be seen in 11Q *Rule of Melchizedek*, not least the 'last days' interpretation of the year of jubilee prescribed in Leviticus 25 and Deuteronomy 15 (Col. II, 2–4). The text (Col. II, 5; Tigchelaar 2000: 206–209) claims that Melchizedek

will make them return. And liberty will be proclaimed for them, to free them from [the debt of] all their iniquities. And this [wil]l [happen] in the first week of the jubilee which follows the ni[ne] jubilees. And the d[ay of aton]ement is the e[nd of] the tenth [ju]bilee in which atonement shall be made for all the sons of [light] . . .

Like the seventy sevens in Daniel 9:24–27, which add up to a ten-jubilee period of 490 years, this passage speaks of a tenth jubilee. Moreover, the 'return' spoken of in this Qumran text probably picks up on the expected return from exile,[9] with the proclamation of liberty to the captives calling Isaiah 61 to mind, and atonement is made when the saviour figure, styled here as Melchizedek, comes to free his people from 'their iniquities' on the 'day of atonement' at the 'tenth jubilee' (see the discussions of this passage in VanderKam and Flint 2002: 224–225, 272–273; and Collins and Collins 2008: 79–85).

Consider the biblical texts the author of this Qumran text has brought together: the anointed of the Lord from Isaiah 61 (11Q13, Col. II, 6), reference to 'the songs of David' with quotations about God judging rebellious gods and their wicked followers from Psalms 7 and 82 (Col. II, 10–11), another servant song from Isaiah 52:7 (Col.

---

[9] The verb ישיבהם, *yšybhm*, which appears to be the hiphil 3 masc. sing. of שוב, *šûb*, with a 3 masc. pl. suffix, rendered '[Melchizedek] will make them return', could connote 'turning back' in the sense of '[Melchizedek] will cause them to repent'. This could still point to the new exodus and return from exile, for the texts indicate that the people will be restored when they return to Yahweh (e.g. Lev. 26:40; Deut. 4:29; 30:2).

II, 15), and 'the anointed of the spir[it] as Dan[iel] said' from Daniel 9:25 (Col. II, 18). These texts are heavily Davidic, with Isaiah 61 speaking of the Spirit-anointed Messiah and the anointed of Daniel 9:25 being spoken of in the same terms. This seems to indicate that the reference to 'Melchizedek' in this passage should be understood along the lines of the Davidic Psalm 110. In that case, 11Q *Rule of Melchizedek* bears witness to a hope for a Davidic and Melchizedekian figure who will be anointed by the Spirit, make atonement for his people (the sons of light, i.e., the seed of the woman), thereby freeing them from their sins, proclaiming liberty to the captives, enabling the return from exile, and all these magnificent things take place at the tenth jubilee. The liberation of the sons of light comes through the defeat of 'Belial and the spirits of his lot' who show partiality to the wicked (Col. II, 11–12; Ps. 82:2), and the mention of Belial calls to mind the way that the wicked are sometimes referred to as 'sons of Belial', that is, seed of the serpent, in the Old Testament (e.g. Deut. 13:13 [MT 13:14]; Judg. 19:22; 1 Sam. 2:12; 1 Kgs 21:10; 2 Chr. 13:7).

The salvation through judgment Melchizedek will accomplish will be accompanied by the fulfilment of the exclamation 'How beautiful on the mountains are the feet of the one who proclaims good news [מבשר, *mbśr*] announcing peace, proclaiming good news [מבשר, *mbśr*] of good things, announcing salvation' (Col. II, 15–16, my tr.). The Hebrew participle מבשר, *mbśr*, which I have rendered 'proclaiming good news', is the term the Greek translator of Isaiah 52:7 rendered with the participle εὐαγγελιζομενος, *euangelizomenos*, the noun form of which is brought into English with the word 'gospel'.

In 4Q246, the 'Son of God' text and in 11Q *Rule of Melchizedek* (11Q13), we see hopes built on the Old Testament, including Daniel. These hopes involve the triumph of God's people over their enemies, led by a Davidic 'Son of God' who also seems to be described in Melchizedekian terms *à la* Psalm 110. When he triumphs, God's people will be freed from their sins, returned and restored, dwell in peace, and the feet of the one who proclaims the victory will be beautiful. All this is projected to take place at the tenth jubilee (cf. Isa. 27:13; Dan. 9:24–27).

1 Maccabees

Against the position that chapters 7–12 of Daniel 'date from the period of the persecutions and Judas' wars' and that the authors of 1 and 2 Maccabees were 'near contemporaries' (Goldstein 1976: 42,

44), I contend that the author of 1 Maccabees understood and presented his story as at least part of the fulfilment of what Daniel prophesied. Rather than treating the book of Daniel as the product of a near contemporary, the author of 1 Maccabees treated Daniel as he did other Scripture.[10]

1 Maccabees reads as though its author sought to capture the cadence of earlier biblical narratives,[11] especially Samuel (similarly, Goldstein 1976: 21). The author could be more explicit about it than he is, but in various ways he tells the tale of 1 Maccabees such that his audience – continuing down to the present – is able to align what he presents with events predicted in Daniel. How could he be more explicit? The author does not start with Babylon and move overtly through the four-kingdom sequence. He starts with Alexander, the third kingdom predicted in Daniel, and he does not identify the *diadochoi*, the four powers that replaced Alexander (cf. Dan. 7:6; 8:8; 11:3–4), but goes directly to the little horn from the third kingdom, the 'sinful root, Antiochus Epiphanes' (1 Macc. 1:10; cf. Dan. 8:9). Nor, though Rome is mentioned in the narrative (cf. 1 Macc. 1:10; 7:1; 8:17, 24, etc.), does the author of 1 Maccabees either identify the fourth kingdom with Rome or otherwise deal with Daniel's fourth beast.[12] He does, however, connect the actions of Antiochus Epiphanes to the prophecies of Daniel, and particularly Daniel 8 and 11.

The author of 1 Maccabees signals that he understands the actions of Antiochus Epiphanes to fulfil the prophecies of Daniel when he writes in 1 Maccabees 1:54, 'And on the fifteenth day of Chaseleu in the one hundred and forty-fifth year, he constructed an abomination of desolation on the altar . . .' The Greek phrase rendered 'abomination of desolation' in 1 Maccabees 1:54 matches the Greek translation

---

[10] On the way that 1 Macc. 4:46, 9:27 and 14:41 distinguish the book of Maccabees from the Scriptures, I have argued, 'These statements all declare that at the time the narrated events took place, there were no prophets who were inspired by the Holy Spirit and able to give authoritative decisions from God. Since 1 Maccabees does not go on to narrate the resolution of the problem of the lack of a prophet, we can conclude that the author of the book did not regard himself as possessing that status' (Hamilton 2010d: 244). Goldstein is correct on the point that 'the impact of Daniel 7–12 on our two authors [of 1 and 2 Maccabees] was profound' (1976: 44).

[11] Mattathias is likened to Phineas in 1 Macc. 2:26, and there is an allusion to Jonathan's triumph over the Philistines (1 Sam. 14:6) in 1 Macc. 3:18. God's deliverance of Israel at the Red Sea is recalled at 1 Macc. 4:9. And the rebuilt altar and wall in 1 Macc. 4:47, 60 recall the narratives of Ezra (rebuilt altar in Ezra 3) and Nehemiah (rebuilt wall).

[12] Cf. the references to Persians and Medes in 1 Macc. 1:1, 6:56 and 14:2.

of Daniel 11:31 (OG) and 12:11 (Th).[13] In this way the author of 1 Maccabees firmly links his narrative to Daniel's prophecies.

Once the author of 1 Maccabees has claimed that Antiochus Epiphanes enacted the abomination of desolation Daniel prophesied, it is not hard to align Antiochus' invasion of Egypt narrated in 1 Maccabees 1:16–19 with the same thing prophesied in Daniel 11:25–28. Daniel prophesies another less successful foray into Egypt (Dan. 11:29), prompting a wrathful rampage through the holy land (11:30–31). The author of 1 Maccabees passes over that second campaign in Egypt, moving straight into Antiochus' defiling activities in the land (1 Macc. 1:20–28). Daniel 11:28–31 and 1 Maccabees 1:16–20 are not irreconcilable, but 1 Maccabees 1:20 lacks the detail of the Daniel passage. It is easy to imagine the author of 1 Maccabees assuming that his audience has the fuller account from Daniel.

The author of 1 Maccabees presents Antiochus as fulfilling what Daniel prophesied after the pattern of Nebuchadnezzar in 1 Maccabees 1:20–24. Antiochus plunders the temple of altar, lampstand, utensils and vessels (1 Macc. 1:21–23). Nebuchadnezzar plundered the vessels of the house of God in Daniel 1:2, and Daniel prophesied that the 'contemptible person' from the third kingdom (Dan. 11:21) would attack temple and covenant and take away the regular burnt offering (Dan. 8:12–13; 11:28, 30–31).

By noting the relevant dates, the author of 1 Maccabees enables his audience to see that the period of time during which Antiochus Epiphanes pursued his course of action was roughly three-and-a-half years, corresponding to the period of time predicted at several points in Daniel.[14] He set up the 'abomination of desolation' in 1 Maccabees 1:54 'in the one hundred and forty-fifth year' (167 BC), and he died 'in the one hundred forty-ninth year' (163 BC).

In addition to the 'abomination of desolation' of Daniel 11:31 in 1 Maccabees 1:54, the author of 1 Maccabees also notes that when Antiochus was forcing the Jews to conform to his idolatrous ways on

---

[13] There are two translations of Daniel in Greek, the 'Old Greek' (OG) and 'Theodotion' (Th). The Old Greek at Dan. 12:11 includes an article that Theodotion lacks (1 Macc. 1:54 also leaves it out). The phrase in Dan. 9:27 differs only in that 'desolations' is plural, and Dan. 8:13 has 'sin of desolation' in both Greek versions. The Greek translators of Daniel and the author of 1 Maccabees probably understood all of these phrases as synonymous, referring either to the same desolating sacrilege, or to instances of the same kind of wickedness.

[14] On Dan. 8:14, Goldstein sees the 2,300 evenings and mornings fulfilled when 'News of the death of Antiochus IV reaches Jerusalem, 1150 days after the desecration of 15 Kislev, 167' (1976: 166). Goldstein does not cite a text for this from 1 Maccabees.

pain of death (1 Macc. 1:41–50), 'many of the people joined them, everyone who abandoned the law' (1:52). This matches Daniel 11:32, 'He shall seduce with flattery those who violate the covenant.' Similarly, Daniel 11:32 goes on to say, 'the people who know their God shall stand firm and take action', and the author of 1 Maccabees presents Mattathias and his sons doing just that as they pursue their fight for freedom (1 Macc. 1:62–63; 2:1 – 4:61).

As the Maccabees stand firm and take action, 1 Maccabees 1:62–63 states that 'many in Israel remained strong and fortified themselves not to eat common things. And they preferred to die so as not to be contaminated by food and not to defile the holy covenant.' This faithfulness recalls the steadfastness of Daniel and his friends, who chose not to defile themselves by eating the king's food (Dan. 1:8, 11–15).

The clearest overt instance of the book of Daniel being treated on a level with other Scripture comes in 1 Maccabees 2:59–60, where Daniel and his friends are listed in a litany of Scripture's heroes. Having recounted the faithfulness of Abraham, Joseph, Phineas, Joshua, Caleb, David and Elijah, the author of 1 Maccabees invokes the narratives of Daniel 3 and 6 when he writes, 'Hananias, Azarias and Misael, because of their faith, were saved from fire. Daniel, by his simplicity, was rescued from the mouth of lions' (1 Macc. 2:59–60).

Another instance of the author of 1 Maccabees interpreting his material in the light of Daniel can be seen in 1 Maccabees 9:27, where, after the death of Judas, the author says, 'And there was a great affliction in Israel, such as had not been since the day that a prophet was not seen among them.' The Greek phrase rendered 'great affliction' here is the same one employed at Matthew 24:21, which follows hard on the heels of a reference to Daniel's abomination of desolation in Matthew 24:15. The statement made by the author of 1 Maccabees seems to derive from the concepts in Daniel 12:1, 'And there shall be a time of trouble, such as never has been since there was a nation till that time.'

The author of 1 Maccabees told his tale using the terms, concepts and expectations he learned from the Scriptures, especially the book of Daniel. He did this, like the authors of the sectarian tractates at Qumran, because he saw himself and those with him as the seed of the woman, the faithful who were living out fulfilments of what Scripture prophesied. The author of Tobit cast his characters as scriptural types. The authors at Qumran sought to bring Scripture together as they attempted to explain how things would be fulfilled: they certainly conceived of themselves as the sons of light who would triumph over darkness. And the author of 1 Maccabees saw the freedom fighters as the faithful and their enemies as the seed of the serpent who would do their worst before being undone.

4 Ezra

Before looking at how *4 Ezra* interpreted Daniel, to gain a feel for the kind of book we are examining we need to make some observations on the forged character of the document, the 'secret revelation' it claims to make, and the orientation towards works-righteousness in the book's theology. *4 Ezra* is not in the canon because these aspects of the book demonstrate that whatever the author may claim about being a Spirit-inspired prophet (*4 Ezra* 14:22), we can see that the book is not in fact inspired precisely because its author does things the Bible itself condemns (bear false witness, make unbiblical claims, and teach works-righteousness).

The document known as *4 Ezra* begins 'in the thirtieth year after the destruction of our city' (*4 Ezra* 3:1).[15] The actual destruction in view appears to be that of Jerusalem in AD 70, but the thinly veiled pseudepigraphical fiction claims that the Jewish author is not writing in AD 100 but in 556 BC, thirty years after the 586 BC destruction of Jerusalem (see Metzger 1983, 1: 520). The biblical Ezra returned to Jerusalem in 458 BC (Ezra 7:7–9), a difficulty *4 Ezra* seeks to overcome by identifying the purported author of *4 Ezra* with 'Salathiel' (*4 Ezra* 3:1), also known as 'Shealtiel', father of Zerubbabel, who was one of the leaders of the return to the land around 539 BC (Ezra 3:2).[16] The author of *4 Ezra* bears false witness.[17]

Perhaps reflecting a tradition that saw Ezra as responsible for the final form of the Old Testament canon, *4 Ezra* 14:40–44 claims that Ezra dictated ninety-four books to five men across forty days. The

[15] I am using Metzger's translation with its chapter and verse enumerations (see Metzger 1983, 1: 517–559). Metzger notes that in later Latin manuscripts, what is now numbered as *4 Ezra* 1 – 2 was referred to as II Esdras, while *4 Ezra* 15 – 16 came under the heading V Esdras (see also Myers 1974: 107–108). The material relevant for this discussion is in *4 Ezra* 3 – 14. In my copy of the AV that contains the Apocrypha, this document is titled II Esdras.

[16] *4 Ezra* 1:1–3 presents the genealogy of the biblical Ezra, largely matching the genealogy found in Ezra 7:1–5.

[17] Bart Ehrman has demonstrated that in the period in which *4 Ezra* was composed, forgery was scandalous (2011; 2012).

'apocryphal' or 'hidden' character of the non-canonical writings is explained in *4 Ezra* 14:45–46:

> And when the forty days were ended, the Most High spoke to me, saying, 'Make public the twenty-four books that you wrote first and let the worthy and the unworthy read them; but keep the seventy that were written last, in order to give them to the wise among your people.'[18]

The twenty-four books to be made public are the books of the Old Testament canon, which *4 Ezra* 14:21 says had been burned,[19] while the hidden books contain special, esoteric knowledge reserved for 'the wise'. Whereas in Daniel 11:33 'the wise among the people shall make many understand', in *4 Ezra*'s adoption of 'the wise' there is an unbiblical reservation of privileged information to them. In contrast to this impulse to claim access to secret information, the biblical authors everywhere proclaim the word of God for the benefit of all and sundry without discrimination.

In addition to bearing false witness and unbiblically claiming that the right kind of people get more revelation from God, the author of *4 Ezra* claims that an angel declared to him, 'you have a treasure of works laid up with the Most High; but it will not be shown to you until the last times' (*4 Ezra* 7:77). Later Ezra (8:32–36) prays:

> For if you have desired to have pity on us, who have no works of righteousness, then you will be called merciful. For the righteous, who have many works laid up with you, shall receive their reward in consequence of their deeds . . . you are merciful to those who have no store of good works.

---

[18] Cf. the similar statements about hidden, privileged information in *4 Ezra* 8:62, 'I have not shown this to all men, but only to you and a few like you'; 12:36–38, 'And you alone were worthy to learn this secret of the Most High. Therefore write all these things that you have seen in a book, and put it in a hidden place; and you shall teach them to the wise among your people, whose hearts you know are able to comprehend and keep these secrets'; 14:5–6 (spoken to Moses): 'Then I commanded him saying, "These words you shall publish openly, and these you shall keep secret."' Note how Ezra is presented in *4 Ezra* as a new Moses, since both Moses and Ezra were commanded to publish some books and keep others secret.

[19] Beckwith notes, 'the story that Ezra rewrote by divine inspiration the twenty four books of the public canon, after the Law had been burned at the destruction of Jerusalem by the Babylonians, implies that none of the inspired books of the canon is of later date than Ezra' (1985: 371). For the enumeration of the books, see Beckwith 1985: 235–273.

Then later in 13:23 we read, 'He who brings the peril at that time will himself protect those who fall into peril, who have works and have faith in the Almighty.' This is a very different understanding of justification than the by-grace-through-faith justification to be found in the Old and New Testaments (see Vickers 2013).

The influence of Daniel on *4 Ezra*, though, can be seen in superficial, structural and hermeneutical-theological moves the author makes. The superficial similarities include the pervasive reference to God as 'the Most High', the interactions between the human prophet and the angelic interpreter, three weeks of prayer and fasting followed by angelic revelation (*4 Ezra* 6:35; cf. Dan. 10:2–3), references to sealing and opening books (*4 Ezra* 6:20; 7:104; 10:23), the shining of the righteous (*4 Ezra* 7:97) and many other details.[20]

The structural influence of Daniel on *4 Ezra* can be seen in the way that just as Daniel has revelations (e.g. Dan. 7:1–15) followed by interpretations (e.g. 7:16–28), so *4 Ezra* presents revelations (e.g. *4 Ezra* 11:1 – 12:2) followed by interpretations (e.g. 12:10–39). This instance in *4 Ezra* 12 is even explicitly identified with Daniel in *4 Ezra* 12:10–11, 'He said to me, "This is the interpretation of this vision which you have seen: The eagle which you saw coming up from the sea is the fourth kingdom which appeared in a vision to your brother Daniel."' Many more examples could be cited,[21] but our real interest is in the way that *4 Ezra* interprets Daniel in the service of his theology, to which we turn.

An exhaustive discussion would be tedious and unnecessary, so here we will focus our attention on the indications of a 'temporary messianic kingdom and the end of the world' in *4 Ezra* 7,[22] the interpretation of Daniel's fourth kingdom in *4 Ezra* 11 – 12, and the one who comes on the clouds of heaven in *4 Ezra* 13.

---

[20] In response to a vision, Ezra shudders, troubled, and faints (5:14), a response similar to Daniel's (Dan. 7:28; 8:27; 10:8), and then like Daniel he is strengthened by 'the angel who had come and talked with me' (*4 Ezra* 5:15; cf. 5:21; Dan. 8:18; 10:10–12). Like the magicians in Daniel, Ezra asks, 'who is able to know these things except he whose dwelling is not with men?' (5:38; cf. Dan. 2:11). In 6:7 Ezra asks about 'the dividing of the times' and 'the end of the first age and the beginning of the age that follows', statements reminiscent of Dan. 2:21 and the many references to the end in Daniel. Then Ezra is told, 'the word concerns the end' (6:15).

[21] For instance, just as Gabriel is sent to Daniel in response to his prayer, Uriel is sent to Ezra in response to his (*4 Ezra* 3:4 – 4:1). Some of the more superficial examples noted above also contribute to similarity between the two books in structural features: for instance, just as in Daniel (cf. Dan. 12:6–12) the angel interacts with Ezra about how 'the age is hastening to its end' (4:26), in response to which Ezra asks, 'How long and when will these things be?' (4:33).

[22] The phrase is Metzger's subtitle over *4 Ezra* 7:26–44 (1983, 1: 537).

The temporary messianic kingdom

In *4 Ezra* 6:59, Ezra asks, 'If the world has indeed been created for us, why do we not possess our world as an inheritance? How long will this be so?' The angel who has been interacting with Ezra is sent to him again (*4 Ezra* 7:1–2), and that angel opens with admonitions that Ezra is 'not a better judge than God' (7:19; cf. 7:3–25). The angel then gives Ezra a revelation in *4 Ezra* 7:26–44 that is clearly dependent on Daniel. That dependence is displayed by the words of verse 43: 'For it will last for about a week of years.'[23] This reference to 'a week of years' comes directly from Daniel 9:24–27, where seventy weeks of years were divided into three units: seven weeks, sixty-two weeks and one week. Daniel 9:25 speaks of an anointed one coming after seven weeks, and there is uncertainty about whether the sixty-two years that follow also precede the coming of the Messiah, or if the Messiah comes after the seven weeks and then the sixty-two weeks follow (see the argument in chapter 5 above that the Messiah comes, and is cut off, after the seven weeks and sixty-two weeks). This passage in *4 Ezra* presents us with an ancient Jewish interpretation of Daniel 9:24–27.

4 Ezra 7:26–44 is not interpreting Daniel alone, however, but reading Daniel in concert with other Old Testament prophets. Thus *4 Ezra* 7:26 describes the appearance of 'the city' and 'the land', and some Latin and Syriac translations render 'bride' for 'city' (cf. Rev. 21:9–10). This idea of the city that is the bride appearing in glory grows out of many passages in the prophets that personify Jerusalem as, on the one hand, the adulterous wife of Yahweh who will be punished for her infidelity (e.g. Hos. 2:2; Isa. 52:2), and on the other as the city that will be exalted in the future and betrothed anew to her covenant Lord (Isa. 2:1–5; 4:2–6; Hos. 2:16–23; Jer. 31:31–34).[24] The author of *4 Ezra* read Daniel 9 to speak of that future restoration of land, city and people.

It appears that *4 Ezra* 7:27 has in view the Messianic Woes:[25] 'And everyone who has been delivered from the evils that I have foretold

---

[23] Metzger notes that *4 Ezra* 7:36–105 has been restored from Codex Ambianensis (1983, 1: 518, 538 n. j), thus these verses are not included in my copy of the AV containing the Apocrypha. Myers renders it, 'The time period will be, as it were, a week of years' (1974: 210).

[24] Commenting on *4 Ezra* 5:26, Michael E. Stone writes, 'The chief biblical source used here by our author is an allegorical interpretation of Song 2:14 and 5:2' (1990: 130).

[25] So also, independently, Stone (1990: 214). For the references I have found to this theme across the canon, see table 6.2, 'The Messianic Woes in the Old and New Testaments', in Hamilton 2010b: 493.

shall see my wonders.' These 'evils' are probably the persecutions depicted in the descriptions of the little horns from Daniel's third and fourth kingdoms (cf. Dan. 7:25; 8:24; 9:27; 11:31; 12:7). After the evils, the Messiah comes, as *4 Ezra* 7:28 says, 'For my son the Messiah shall be revealed with those who are with him, and those who remain shall rejoice four hundred years.' A Syriac manuscript puts the time period at 'thirty years', while an Arabic one has 'one thousand years' (Metzger 1983, 1: 537, n. f). Myers writes that the *4 Ezra* form of messianic expectation anticipates 'an interregnum between the present period and the final judgment and partakes of a conception somewhat analogous to Jewish thought expressed in the II Isaiah [*sic*] – the period of restoration' (1974: 253).[26]

The Messianic woes are completed (*4 Ezra* 7:27), city and land are restored and God's people delivered at the coming of the Messiah, who then reigns for a period of time prior to the final judgment and the new creation (7:26, 28). The new creation is set up by the death of all the living in *4 Ezra* 7:29, after which the world is returned to its pre-creation state in 7:30, 'for seven days, as it was at the first beginnings'. The new creation is awakened (7:31), the dead are raised (7:32) and the day of judgment arrives (7:33). All this is what 'will last for about a week of years' (7:44).

It appears, then, that the author of *4 Ezra* expects the Messiah to come *after* the seven weeks and sixty-two weeks in Daniel 9:25. The author of *4 Ezra* (writing thirty years after the AD 70 destruction of Jerusalem) seems to expect the final week to encompass the period of time during which the Messiah reigns in the restored Jerusalem, prior to the final judgment and the new creation.

Daniel's fourth kingdom

Ezra sees a vision of an eagle with twelve wings and three heads (*4 Ezra* 11:1; cf. 1–35), followed by a roaring lion who comes from the forest to declare to the last of the eagle's heads, 'Listen and I will speak to you. The Most High says to you, "Are you not the one that remains of the four beasts which I had made to reign in my world so that the end of my times might come through them?"' (11:38–39). These four beasts are identified as the four kingdoms prophesied by Daniel in *4 Ezra* 12:11. Daniel extolled God as the one who 'changes times and

---

[26] Bauckham writes of the millennium in Revelation, 'Thus John has taken from the Jewish apocalyptic tradition the notion of a temporary messianic reign on earth before the last judgment and the new creation (cf. 2 Bar. 40:3; *4 Ezra* 7:28–29; b.Sanh. 99a) . . .' (1993: 108).

seasons' (Dan. 2:21), and in Daniel the pride of the wicked kings resulted in God humbling them (Dan. 4:30; 5:20, 22–23). We see the influence of Daniel's account of God humbling proud rulers of the earth and his ability to change the times in *4 Ezra* when the lion announces, 'And so your insolence has come up before the Most High, and your pride to the Mighty One. And the Most High has looked upon his times, and behold, they are ended, and his ages are completed!' (11:43–44). Just as Daniel 7:11 says the beast's body was burned, so *4 Ezra* 12:3 says, 'And I looked, and behold, they also disappeared, and the whole body of the eagle was burned, and the earth was exceedingly terrified.'

As noted above, the vision in Daniel 7 is followed by an interpretation, and so it is in *4 Ezra* 11 – 12. Ezra is told that the eagle 'is the fourth kingdom which appeared in a vision to your brother Daniel. But it was not explained to him as I now explain or have explained it to you' (12:11–12). So Ezra claims to give more particular information regarding Daniel's fourth beast.

At this point we should observe that if it is correct that *4 Ezra* comes after Rome's destruction of Jerusalem in AD 70, then the author of *4 Ezra* appears to think that Daniel's fourth beast will arise *in the future* and *has not been exhausted* by what Rome did to Jerusalem in AD 70. The author of *4 Ezra* presents Ezra declaring to his post AD 70 audience, 'Behold, the days are coming when a kingdom shall arise on earth, and it shall be more terrifying than all the kingdoms that have been before it' (12:13). The eagle's wings and heads are interpreted (12:14–30), and then the lion arises (12:31). Of the lion, *4 Ezra* announces, 'this is the Messiah whom the Most High has kept until the end of days, who will arise from the posterity of David, and will come and speak to them' (12:32). The Messiah brings judgment and destroys his enemies (12:33), and thereby he mercifully delivers the remnant of his people, and, apparently elaborating on the 400-year reign of the Messiah announced in *4 Ezra* 7:28, *4 Ezra* 12:34 says that the Messiah 'will make them joyful [cf. 7:28] until the end comes, the day of judgment, of which I spoke to you at the beginning' (see the discussion in Stone 1990: 215–217).

What can we conclude from *4 Ezra*'s interpretation of Daniel's fourth kingdom? It seems that *4 Ezra* expects Daniel's fourth beast to be destroyed and judged by the lion from the forest, the Messiah. If he is writing thirty years after Rome's destruction of Jerusalem in AD 70, it would not appear that the author of *4 Ezra* thinks that Rome has exhausted the meaning of Daniel's fourth beast but expects future manifestations of the messianic woes that will be brought to an end by the Messiah's appearance to judge his enemies and thereby save his remnant. The author of *4 Ezra* then expects the Messiah to reign for a long period of time, longer than the typical three score and ten (cf. Ps. 90:10), and then all humans die, the old order comes to an end, with the new creation preceded by another seven-day period, the resurrection taking place, and 'Then the pit of torment shall appear, and opposite it shall be the place of rest; and the furnace of Hell shall be disclosed, and opposite it the Paradise of delight' (7:36; cf. 29–44). The reward of the righteous and the recompense of the wicked matches Daniel 12:2–3.

With the clouds of heaven

4 Ezra 13 has yet another vision influenced by Daniel. The 'four winds of heaven were stirring up the great sea' in Daniel 7:2, and in *4 Ezra* 13:1 'a wind arose from the sea and stirred up all its waves'. Then, as the one like a son of man came 'with the clouds of heaven' in Daniel 7:13, in *4 Ezra* 13:3 a 'man flew with the clouds of heaven'. In Revelation 1:13–14 the Daniel 7:13 son of man is described with hair like that of the Daniel 7:9 Ancient of Days, thereby identifying Jesus with the Ancient of Days. Something similar is at work in *4 Ezra* 13:3, where we also find the Daniel 7:13 figure who comes 'with the clouds of heaven' being described in terms of the Daniel 7:9–10 Ancient of Days. In Daniel 7:10 we read of the Ancient of Days:

> A stream of fire issued
> and came out from before him.

Similarly, *4 Ezra* 13:10 says of the man who comes with the clouds of heaven, 'he sent forth from his mouth as it were a stream of fire, and from his lips a flaming breath'. Just as Jesus is given Ancient of Days characteristics in Revelation 1, so in *4 Ezra* 13 the man who comes on the clouds of heaven is given Ancient of Days characteristics.

Another aspect of Danielic influence in *4 Ezra* 13 can be seen when the Daniel 2:34–35 stone, cut out with no human hand that crushes the statue and becomes a great mountain, is identified with the kingdom of the one who comes on the clouds of heaven. *4 Ezra* says of the one who comes on the clouds of heaven (13:3), 'And I looked, and behold, he carved out for himself a great mountain, and flew upon it' (13:6). The interpretation of the vision makes the Daniel 2 connection clearer, as *4 Ezra* 13:36 states, 'And Zion will come and be made manifest to all people, prepared and built, as you saw the mountain carved without hands.' The one who comes on the clouds of heaven is also identified with the 2 Samuel 7:14 seed of David when in the interpretation the Most High declares, 'then my son will be revealed' (*4 Ezra* 13:32).

To summarize, the author of *4 Ezra* 13 has identified the 2 Samuel 7 and Psalm 2 seed of David / son of God with the Daniel 7 son of man who comes with the clouds of heaven. Moreover, as John does in Revelation 1, he has described the one who comes with the clouds of heaven with imagery used in Daniel 7 of the Ancient of Days, and he has identified the kingdom of the one coming with the clouds of heaven in Daniel 7 with the kingdom that crushes all others in Daniel 2.

1 Enoch

Nickelsburg writes, '*1 Enoch* is a collection of apocalyptic traditions and writings of diverse genre and date, composed during the last three centuries B.C.E. and accumulated in stages' (1984: 90). Stone is more specific: 'The *First Book of Enoch* or *Ethiopic Enoch* is in fact a compilation of five books, each of which appears with its own title and usually its own conclusion' (1984: 396). The influence of the book of Daniel on *1 Enoch* is concentrated in the second of these five books, chapters 37–71, known as *The Similitudes*.[27] Beckwith (1985: 362) has explained that the Essenes, or proto-Essenes, who probably produced *1 Enoch*

> were not really meaning to add to Old Testament prophecy, any more than to Old Testament law . . . what their pseudonymous legal writings offered was an interpretation . . . what their pseudonymous apocalyptic writings offered was again an interpretation – supplemented perhaps, but only from natural sources, like arithmetic and astrology, not from supernatural.

---

[27] Stone disputes the idea that *The Similitudes* are either necessarily late or written/redacted by a Christian: 'it is difficult to conceive of a late, Christian work largely devoted to the prediction of the coming of a super-human Son of Man, existent in the thought of God before creation, which does not make the slightest hint at his (from Enoch's point of view) future incarnation, earthly life and preaching, or crucifixion and their cosmic implications. Further, in chapter 71, admittedly an appendix to *The Similitudes*, the Son of Man is specifically identified as Enoch. This is rather unlikely as an appendix to a Christian composition, which itself would undoubtedly be Christian' (1984: 399; so also Collins and Collins 2008: 87). On the absence of *The Similitudes* from the findings at Qumran, Stone writes, 'It just does not follow that the absence of a book from those manuscripts which survived at Qumran implies more than just that about their existence' (1984: 399, n. 86).

Beckwith points out what should be obvious about the authors who falsely presented their work under the names of ancient worthies to cobble up authority: 'A more straightforward explanation of their adoption of prophetic pseudonyms would be that they were conscious of *not* being inspired (or not in the same way as the prophets), but that it suited their purpose – whatever it was – to give the impression that they were' (1985: 359).

Daniel points to a day when 'the saints of the Most High shall receive the kingdom' (Dan. 7:18), when the dead will be raised and 'those who are wise shall shine like the brightness of the sky above; and those who turn many to righteousness, like the stars for ever and ever' (Dan. 12:2–3). These statements seem to stand behind the author of *1 Enoch* 38 as he describes the appearance of 'the congregation of the righteous' (*1 Enoch* 38:1; cf. Ps. 1:6) gathered at the coming of 'the Righteous One' (38:2), a title probably derived from Isaiah 53:11, when 'it will not be the mighty and exalted who possess the earth, and they will not be able to look at the face of the holy, for the light of the Lord of Spirits will have appeared on the face of the holy, righteous, and chosen' (*1 Enoch* 38:4). The author of *1 Enoch* 38 expects the fulfilment of these statements in Daniel 7 and 12 to coincide with the fulfilment of texts such as Isaiah 53 and Psalm 1.

Daniel 7:9–10 describes the Ancient of Days enthroned in the heavenly court, and then 7:13–14 describes the 'one like a son of man' being presented before him and receiving everlasting dominion. This scene is re-presented in *1 Enoch* 46:1–2, 'There I saw one who had a head of days, and his head was like white wool [cf. Dan. 7:9; *1 Enoch* 71:10]. And with him was another, whose face was like the appearance of a man . . . And I asked the angel . . . about that son of man . . .' Once again other passages are seen as fulfilled by the coming of the son of man. In this case, the declaration that God will 'break the teeth of the wicked' in Psalm 3:7, itself a refraction of Genesis 3:15, finds fulfilment when *1 Enoch* 46:4 declares, 'And this son of man whom you have seen . . . he will crush the teeth of the sinners.'

A similar instance of the influence of Daniel 7:9–13 in combination with other passages comes in *1 Enoch* 62:2, where we read of the Chosen One, who seems to be identified with the 'son of man' in 62:7, 'And the Lord of Spirits seated him upon the throne of his glory, and the spirit of righteousness was poured upon him. And the word of his mouth will slay all the sinners . . .' (62:2). Here the Chosen One is enthroned with the Lord of Spirits, calling to mind Daniel 7 and Psalm 110, and then the outpouring of the 'spirit of righteousness' and the slaying of the enemies by 'the word of his mouth' (62:2) envision the fulfilment of Isaiah 11:1–4, where the 'shoot from the stump of Jesse' has the Spirit resting upon him, strikes the earth with the rod of his mouth, and judges in righteousness (cf. *1 Enoch* 70:1–2). The influence of Daniel 7:9–10, which describes the Ancient of Days taking his seat on his throne with 'a thousand thousands' serving him and 'ten thousand times ten thousand' standing before him, can be seen in the descriptions in *1 Enoch* 40:1, 60:1 and 71:8, which speak of 'thousands of thousands and ten thousand times ten' standing before the 'Lord of Spirits' and 'the Most High'. Another aspect of Daniel's vision influences *1 Enoch* 47:3, where Enoch claims, 'I saw the Head of Days as he took his seat on the throne of his glory.' This passage also speaks of the blood of the martyrs and their prayers being heard (47:1) and of the books being opened before the enthroned Lord (47:4). Danielic influence is probable, from Daniel 11:32–33, which speaks of those who will die for the faith, and from 12:9, which says 'the words are shut up and sealed until the time of the end'. *1 Enoch* purports to describe the end when the martyrs are vindicated and the books are opened (cf. Rev. 6:9–11; 8:1–4).

Daniel 5:27 declares that Belshazzar has been 'weighed in the balances and found wanting', and this statement probably informs *1 Enoch* 41:1, where 'the deeds of humanity are weighed in the balance'. *1 Enoch* 52:2 describes a 'mountain of iron, and a mountain of copper, and a mountain of silver, and a mountain of gold, and a mountain of soft metal, and a mountain of lead', and 52:6 says, 'these will be before the Chosen One like wax before the fire, and like the water that comes down from above upon these mountains, and they will be weak before his feet'. The materials and their destruction before the Chosen One are reminiscent of Daniel 2:31–45, where the dreamed-of statue is made of materials similar to those enumerated by Enoch, and then crushed by the little stone, which becomes a great mountain that fills the earth, symbolizing God's everlasting kingdom destroying and supplanting all other kingdoms. In Daniel 8 a goat (identified as the king of Greece in 8:12) first tramples a ram in 8:7 (the ram is identified as 'the kings of Media and Persia' in 8:20); then the little horn from the goat tramples 'some of the host and some of the stars' in 8:10 and 13, and the host appears to be the people of the Lord (cf. Dan. 8:25). This scenario appears to be depicted in *1 Enoch* 56:5–6, where we read of an attack 'against the Parthians and Medes', and then 'They will go up and trample the land of his chosen ones.'

The vision of the end in *1 Enoch* can be synthesized easily with what we see in *4 Ezra* and in the Qumran scrolls, and all derive from the Old Testament. The wicked will increase their wickedness and visit the messianic woes during the time appointed for them, and then the Messiah will come and slay them, thereby delivering his people, and thereby achieving the kingdom promised to the son of man presented before the Ancient of Days in Daniel 7. Nickelsburg and VanderKam (2004: 4) write of the son of man / chosen one in *1 Enoch*:

> The Chosen One combines the titles, attributes, and functions of the one like a son of man in Daniel 7:13–14, the Servant of the Lord in Second Isaiah [*sic*], the Davidic Messiah, and pre-existent heavenly Wisdom (Proverbs 8). . . . The Chosen One is the agent of God's judgment and as such is depicted with imagery that the early chapters of 1 Enoch ascribe to God.

Conclusion

The author of Tobit employs features from Daniel in his typological depiction of his hero's adventures. The authors of Qumran sectarian material understood Daniel to be prophesying the same eschatological triumph the other Old Testament prophets predicted. The author of 1 Maccabees understood Daniel historically, and he saw a correspondence between the persecution of Antiochus Epiphanes and the pattern of events Daniel described, attested by the way he described the crisis in Danielic terms. The author of *4 Ezra* evidently did not understand what Daniel depicted to be completely fulfilled in either the Maccabean crisis or the AD 70 destruction of Jerusalem, as he presented the final beast from Daniel's fourth kingdom as yet to arrive in the future, to be defeated by the Messiah. Like the author of Tobit, the author of *The Similitudes* in *1 Enoch* used features of Daniel to speak in typological terms; like the authors of the Qumran material, he interpreted Daniel to be prophesying the same eschatological triumph other Old Testament prophets heralded; and like the author of *4 Ezra*, he understood Daniel's prophecies to reveal the future triumph of Israel's Messiah, resulting in the establishment of God's kingdom.

These early Jewish authors read Daniel in ways that are similar to the interpretation of Daniel to be found in the writings of the New Testament. The authors of the books of the New Testament herald Jesus as the Daniel 7 Son of Man, and they also understood Daniel typologically, prophetically, historically and predictively, pointing forward to a climactic instalment in a pattern of events that involves an Antichrist figure visiting awful persecution to fulfil the messianic woes, who would be slain by the Davidic Messiah whose judgment and defeat of his enemies would liberate his people and establish God's everlasting kingdom. To the interpretation of Daniel in the New Testament we now give our attention.

Chapter Eight

Interpretations of Daniel in the New Testament (except Revelation)

Mnemosyne, goddess of memory, which word was the meaning of her name, mothered the Muses in Greek mythology. This mythological explanation reflects the way in which what humans remember is a source for what they say. When we consider the authors of the New Testament, of all they had in memory, their knowledge of the Old Testament was most foundational, shaping and determinative. This was in accordance with what the authors of the Old Testament intended to provide for those who came after them: a world-building, world-defining, world-shaping set of stories, laws, explanations, poems, proverbs and prophecies.

Erich Auerbach (1953: 14–15) captured this when he wrote:

> The Bible's claim to truth is not only far more urgent than Homer's, it is tyrannical – it excludes all other claims. The world of the Scripture stories is not satisfied with claiming to be a historically true reality – it insists that it is the only real world, is destined for autocracy. All other scenes, issues, and ordinances have no right to appear independently of it, and it is promised that all of them, the history of all mankind, will be given their due place within its frame, will be subordinated to it. The Scripture stories do not, like Homer's, court our favor, they do not flatter us that they may please us and enchant us – they seek to subject us, and if we refuse to be subjected we are rebels.

The biblical authors were not rebels. Their thought world was constructed from truths and teachings based on the words and phrases set down in Scripture. This chapter explores the interpretation of Daniel reflected in acknowledged New Testament quotations of Daniel.

I will use the texts listed in Appendix IV in the Nestle-Aland *Novum Testamentum Graece*, twenty-seventh edition, which has become

Appendix III in the twenty-eighth edition, 'Loci Citati Vel Allegati' (locations of citations or allusions), as the basis for this study. The benefit of using this list is that in these instances we need not first prove that Daniel has been quoted. This chapter cannot be an exhaustive discussion of the influence of Daniel in the New Testament. That would require a contextual and biblical-theological discussion of each passage, which is simply beyond the scope of this project. In this project on the theology of Daniel, we are particularly interested in how the authors of the New Testament have interpreted Daniel. It is axiomatic here that their interpretation of Daniel is in keeping with what Daniel intended to communicate.

Before plunging into the New Testament, perhaps it would be helpful to review what has been argued to this point.

A summary of what we have seen

Chapter 2 arrived at a synthesis of Daniel's contribution to salvation history in his forecast of the future: 'In the latter days, transgression will be fulfilled as a little horn makes great boasts and persecutes God's people until the appointed time of the end, when the little horn will be unexpectedly broken, at which point the son of man will receive everlasting dominion in a kingdom the saints will possess for ever.'

Chapter 3 showed that the literary structure of Daniel enables a one-sentence summary of the message of Daniel: 'Daniel encourages the faithful by showing them that though Israel was exiled from the land of promise, they will be restored to the realm of life at the resurrection of the dead, when the four kingdoms have been followed by the kingdom of God, so the people of God can trust him and persevere through persecution until God humbles proud human kings, gives everlasting dominion to the son of man, and the saints reign with him.'

Chapter 4 examined the four-kingdom schema in Daniel 2, 7, 8 and 10 – 12, with the first kingdom identified as Babylon, the second as Medo-Persia, the third as Greece, and the fourth being unnamed but having characteristics that correspond to Rome. Thus it is possible to see that the four-kingdom sequence has been fulfilled by the time Jesus arrives on the scene, with the fourth kingdom embodied in but not exhausted by Rome.

Similar statements can be made about the seventy weeks of Daniel 9, studied in chapter 5. Daniel 9:24–27 states that after sixty-nine weeks the Messiah will be cut off and have nothing. Whether one sees those weeks as literal sets of seven-year periods, sabbatical cycles or a symbolic evocation of a tenfold jubilee, the cutting off of the Messiah is fulfilled in the crucifixion of Jesus of Nazareth. The authors of the New Testament state that the restoration summarized in Daniel 9:24 will be brought to pass when Jesus returns at the completion of the seventieth week.

Chapter 6 focused on the nature and identity of the heavenly beings in Daniel. The presentation of the one like a son of man in Daniel 7 is unique: this figure is *both* a human king from David's line, as seen from the allusions to earlier Davidic texts throughout Daniel 7, *and* he is a pre-existent heavenly being who is a member of the heavenly court, as seen from his participation in the scene Daniel beholds. Even more surprising, the one like a son of man is both identified with and distinguished from the Ancient of Days: both are called Most High in different ways. The normal Aramaic expression for Most High is used for the Ancient of Days, and an Aramaized Hebrew form for Most High is used for the one like a son of man. The authors of the New Testament present Jesus as the son of man precisely as Daniel describes him. According to the teaching of Testaments Old and New, Jesus alone among mortals could fit the Daniel 7 prophecy.

As we looked at early Jewish literature in chapter 7, we saw that Daniel was understood typologically in Tobit, eschatologically at Qumran, historically in 1 Maccabees, with an expectation of yet future fulfilment (after AD 70) in *4 Ezra*, and in *1 Enoch* the son of man is a Davidic king and deliverer, an agent of Yahweh's judgment and salvation.

The authors of the New Testament proclaim the one who brings all this together in fulfilment of Daniel's visions. Daniel provided them with language, expressions that filtered through their statements, even when they were not directly engaging with his message. Daniel also contributed to broader biblical themes that the authors of the New Testament engage with, and, most importantly, the New Testament presents the fulfilment of Daniel's prophecies in the son of man, Jesus of Nazareth, who is both Davidic and divine, distinct from and identified with the Ancient of Days, the little stone who crushes the kingdoms resulting in his reign everywhere and always.

Stock language, thematic similarity and fulfilment

The New Testament authors wrote in Greek, and often their phrases come directly from Greek translations of the Old Testament. Sometimes the reuse of these terms or phrases simply reflects the currency of stock terms and phrases,[1] though we should always be open to the possibility that we are confronted with something more than the mere reuse of well-known words. The influence of the Authorized (King James) Bible on the English literary tradition testifies to the way that authors steeped in the Bible's language and themes can use simple phrases to move more freight than could be shipped by unhitched words. For instance, if an author comments that someone 'sought to make a name for himself', though a precise statement from Genesis 11 has not been quoted, and though no one is building a tower, the pride and self-exaltation of Babel are invoked – just as the author intended.

At some points New Testament authors reuse language from the Old Testament because of thematic similarity between what they are discussing and the Old Testament passage they invoke.[2] There are other places where New Testament authors refer to incidents from the Old Testament,[3] or reuse language to indicate the realization of

---

[1] Cf. the 'Introduction' to the *Commentary on the New Testament Use of the Old Testament* (Beale and Carson 2007: xxiv–xxv), and for this see the similar language from Dan. 1:2 in John 3:35; Dan. 2:5 in Acts 8:20; Dan. 2:8 in Acts 10:34; Dan. 2:8 in Eph. 5:16; Dan. 3:5, 10, 15 in Luke 15:25; Dan. 6:25 in 1 Pet. 1:2; Dan. 6:26 (MT 27) in 1 Pet. 1:23; Dan. 7:9 in Matt. 28:3; cf. Mark 9:3; Dan. 8:4, 9 (OG) in Acts 8:26; Dan. 8:16 in Luke 1:19 (Gabriel); Dan. 9:3 in Matt. 11:21 and Luke 10:13; Dan. 9:6 in Jas 5:10 and Rev. 10:7; Dan. 9:16 (OG) in Rom. 3:21; Dan. 9:18–19 in Luke 18:13; Dan. 9:21 in Luke 1:10, 19 and Acts 3:1; Dan. 12:3 in Phil. 2:15.

[2] Cf. the reference to 'the deep things' in 1 Cor. 2:10, using language from Dan. 2:22. The giving of the mystery in Mark 4:11 is reminiscent of Dan. 2:27, 47. The Lord sent his angel in Acts 12:11 as he had done in Dan. 3:28 and 6:23. In 1 Cor. 14:25 Paul seems to envision a response like Nebuchadnezzar's in Dan. 2:47, while the willingness of the three Hebrew young men to be cast into the fiery furnace in Dan. 3:19 may inform 1 Cor. 13:3. Nebuchadnezzar claims to have built Babylon in 'the power of [his] might', but God is the one who really has the power of might (Eph. 1:19). Rom. 9:28 may be literally rendered, 'The Lord will execute the word upon the earth, completing and cutting short', and the terms I have rendered 'completing and cutting short' are the same terms used in the Old Greek translation of Dan. 5:28 (LXX 5:26–27) in the phrase 'your kingdom has departed, having been cut short and completed' (the same two terms are also used in the Greek translation of Isa. 28:22). When Paul says he was 'rescued from the lion's mouth' in 2 Tim. 4:17, he may have Dan. 6:20, 27 in mind. In Matt. 19:28 Jesus speaks of the throne on which he will reign, and the thrones of his followers, in ways reminiscent of Dan. 7:9–14, 22, 27 (cf. Luke 22:30; 1 Cor. 6:2), Matt. 25:31 also speaks of the Son of Man coming in glory to sit on his throne. Just as Daniel 'kept the matter in [his] heart' (Dan. 7:28), 'Mary treasured up all these things, pondering them in her heart' (Luke 2:19; cf. 1:66; 2:51). Cf. also Dan. 10:6 in Matt. 28:3; Dan. 10:7 (Th) in Luke 1:22 and Acts 9:7; Dan. 10:9 in Matt. 17:6; Dan. 10:12 in Luke 1:13; Dan. 10:13, 21 in Jude 9; Dan. 10:16 in Luke 1:64; Dan. 12:1 in Jude 9; Dan. 12:2 in Matt. 25:46, 27:52, John 5:29 and Acts 24:15.

[3] For instance, the reference to those who 'quenched the power of fire' in Heb. 11:34 probably refers to the three Hebrew young men in the fiery furnace (Dan. 3:23–25).

what the Old Testament predicted.[4] The body of this discussion will be given to those places where language from the Old Testament indicates that the New Testament authors are engaging in a biblical-theological discussion based largely on Daniel. That is to say, this chapter is devoted to those places where New Testament authors offer an interpretation of the book of Daniel.[5] A thick reading of the New Testament's reuse of phrases and concepts from the Old Testament deepens and enriches our appreciation of what is written, giving insight into the meaning of the texts the authors of the New Testament interpret from the Old.

New Testament quotations of Daniel

The King and his kingdom: Daniel 3:6 in Matthew 13:42, 50[6]

In Daniel 3:6, Nebuchadnezzar threatened to throw those who would not worship the golden image he had set up into 'a burning fiery furnace'. The phrase used by the Old Greek translation of Daniel, 'into the furnace of fire', appears verbatim in Matthew 13:42 and 13:50.[7] Matthew also uses the same verb for 'cast', but in a slightly different formation. In this text, Matthew (Matt. 13:41 43; 13:50 is

---

[4] Such as when language very similar to the OG of Dan. 7:14, 'and authority was given to him, even over all the nations of the earth', is used in Matt. 28:18, 'all authority in heaven and on earth has been given to me'. Cf. also Dan. 7:14 in Luke 1:33 and Heb. 12:28, with Dan. 7:18 and Luke 12:32. Daniel often speaks of the arrival of the time when the saints will receive the kingdom (e.g. Dan. 7:22, 27), and in the NT this time is inaugurated with the coming of Jesus (Mark 1:15) and will be consummated at his return (Luke 21:8). Dan. 9:26 says, 'to the end there shall be war. Desolations are decreed,' and Luke 21:22 presents Jesus declaring, 'these are days of vengeance, to fulfil all that is written'. Cf. also Dan. 12:3 in Matt. 13:43; Dan. 12:7 in Luke 21:24; Dan. 12:12 in Matt. 10:22 and Mark 13:13.

[5] This chapter treats the whole of the NT except what John does in Revelation, which the next chapter attempts. As noted above, I have used Appendix IV in the Nestle-Aland *Novum Testamentum Graece* (27th ed.), which has become Appendix III in the twenty-eighth edition, 'Loci Citati Vel Allegati' (locations of citations or allusions). The references in the preceding footnotes classify many texts in those lists not discussed in the body of this chapter (excluding references from Revelation). Material from the additions to Daniel found in the Greek translations has been excluded from this discussion. See also Pennington's (2009) helpful study of Daniel's influence on Matthew, Gladd's (2008) work on the Danielic 'mystery' in 1 Corinthians, Caragounis (1977) on the same in Ephesians, and Chase's (2013) biblical-theological discussion of resurrection hope building to and growing from Dan. 12:2.

[6] With allusions to Dan. 2:34–35 in Matt. 13:31–32, Dan. 4:12 in Matt. 13:32, Dan. 7:13 in Matt. 13:41, and Dan. 12:3 in Matt. 13:43.

[7] Theodotion has the same phrase as the OG but adds one word at the end, bringing the text formally closer to the original Aramaic.

very similar) presents Jesus warning that those who do not respond to his message of the kingdom will be penalized:

> The Son of Man will send his angels, and they will gather out of his kingdom all causes of sin and all law-breakers, and throw them into the fiery furnace. In that place there will be weeping and gnashing of teeth. Then the righteous will shine like the sun in the kingdom of their Father.

The phrase from Daniel 3:6 is not the only way Matthew 13:41–43 reflects Danielic language and imagery:

- Matthew presents Jesus speaking of himself as the Daniel 7:13 son of man (Matt. 13:41).
- The kingdom Jesus claims (Matt. 13:41) is the one prophesied in Daniel.
- Those who respond rightly to his message of the kingdom will experience the Daniel 12:2–3 resurrection to shining glory (Matt. 13:43).

How is the phrase from Daniel 3:6 functioning in Matthew 13:42?

The immediately preceding context sheds light on that question. A few verses earlier, Matthew 13:31–32 portrayed Jesus describing the kingdom of heaven with the parable of the mustard seed. Like the small stone that became a great mountain and filled the earth in Daniel 2:34–34, Jesus describes how the small mustard seed grows 'larger than all the garden plants and becomes a tree, so that the birds of the air come and make nests in its branches' (Matt. 13:32).

Likening a kingdom to a tree in which the birds make nests calls to mind Nebuchadnezzar's dream of a kingdom symbolized by a tree 'and the birds of the heavens lived in its branches' (Dan. 4:12; cf. 4:21; see also Mark 4:32 and Luke 13:19). Why would Jesus use imagery that depicted Nebuchadnezzar's kingdom to describe the kingdom he brings? Perhaps the answer is to be found in the way that the human king and his kingdom are a shadow and anticipation of the true king. The appropriation of these elements from Daniel subtly indicates that *what Nebuchadnezzar was as king* will have its fulfilment in King Jesus.

How does this shed light on the quotation of Daniel 3:6 in Matthew 13:42 and 50?

Matthew depicts Jesus using the language of Daniel 3:6 to describe the wicked being cast into the furnace of fire, which is what

Nebuchadnezzar did to the three Hebrew young men who refused to commit idolatry. What Jesus describes is a reversal of human wickedness that sets things right:

- Nebuchadnezzar commanded people to commit idolatry. Jesus commands people to render true worship.
- Nebuchadnezzar cast the righteous into a fiery furnace. Jesus will cast the wicked there.
- Nebuchadnezzar was unable to punish the righteous, and his own soldiers suffered because of his rash foolishness. Jesus will succeed in visiting justice against the wicked; his angels are in no danger; nor will Jesus be foolish or rash.

Jesus will succeed in righteousness where Nebuchadnezzar failed in wickedness.

The reuse of these phrases and images from Daniel indicates that Jesus is the substance of which human kingship is the shadow, that everything anticipated by human rulers will find its holy realization in King Jesus. Jesus will bring a just judgment, punishing the wicked and vindicating the righteous, fulfilling the prophesied resurrection of the just and the unjust in Daniel 12:2–3. In Matthew 13, Jesus is depicted making statements that reflect a profound synthesis of themes and statements from Daniel 2, 3, 4, 7 and 12: the kingdoms of the world will be crushed. The attempt of wicked rulers to persecute the righteous will be overturned. The wicked will be punished, the righteous raised from the dead, and Christ will reign as King for ever, from the rising of the sun to the place of its setting.

The Olivet Discourse: Daniel 7:13 in Matthew 24:30 and Mark 13:26[8]

Matthew and Mark both present accounts of the Olivet Discourse, and both reference Daniel 7:13:

> behold, with the clouds of heaven
> there came one like a son of man.

Neither Matthew nor Mark present exact quotations of a Greek translation of Daniel 7:13 – each presents a slight rephrasing (cf. also Luke 21:27). Daniel 7:13 is indisputably in view, however, for no other

---

[8] With allusions to Dan. 12:11 in Matt. 24:15, and Dan. 12:1 in Matt. 24:21–22.

Old Testament passage speaks of a son of man coming on the clouds of heaven. Moreover, the influence of Daniel on both Matthew 24 and Mark 13 goes well beyond this one statement. Matthew 24 and Mark 13 run largely parallel, but because of significant inclusions from each (lacking in the other), both will be brought to bear in this discussion.

The Olivet Discourse in Matthew 24 and Mark 13 is almost a commentary on what Daniel indicates about the consummation of the ages. At several points Matthew and Mark present Jesus making reference to the end:

• 'the end is not yet' (Matt. 24:6; Mark 13:7)
• 'the one who endures to the end' (Matt. 24:13; Mark 13:13)
• 'then the end will come' (Matt. 24:14)

These statements in Matthew do not use the very terms found in the following verses in the Greek translations of Daniel, but the synonymous concern for the end can be seen in English translation:

• 'the end is yet to be at the time appointed' (Dan. 11:27)
• 'At the time appointed' (Dan. 11:29)
• 'until the time of the end, for it still awaits the appointed time' (Dan. 11:35)
• 'At the time of the end' (Dan. 11:40)

In addition to the references to the end, both Matthew and Mark use the phrase rendered 'This must take place' (Matt. 24:6; Mark 13:7; cf. also Luke 21:9; Matt. 26:54), which matches the Greek translations of Daniel 2:28–29 and 2:45 (Th) exactly (δει γενεσθαι, *dei genesthai*). This phrase occurs in the Greek translations of the Old Testament only in these places in Daniel. The references to the end, which are synonymous with the focus of Daniel 11 – 12, and the phrase (rendered into English from the Greek) 'what must take place' from Daniel 2, point to a synthetic understanding of what is prophesied in Daniel 2 and 11 – 12.

Matthew and Mark present Jesus interpreting Daniel, and it seems the 'wars and rumours of wars' of which Jesus speaks in Matthew 24:6 and Mark 13:7 is a phrase used to summarize the kinds of conflicts described in Daniel 11. Matthew and Mark present Jesus explaining how the rise of the abomination of desolation (Matt. 24:15; Mark 13:14) functions as a signal to flee (Matt. 24:16–20; Mark 13:15–18), because at that point 'the great tribulation' will take place (Matt. 24:21–26; cf. Mark 13:19–20); then, after the days are shortened, the Son of Man comes like lightning (Matt. 24:27; Mark 13:24–27).[9]

As noted, Matthew and Mark present Jesus speaking of the abomination of desolation. It is clear that what Jesus says here flows out of Daniel, because Daniel contains the only Old Testament references to an abomination of desolation. The phrase both Matthew and Mark use for 'the abomination of desolation' is an exact match of the Old Greek translation of Daniel 12:11 (cf. similar phrases in Dan. 8:13; 9:27; 11:31).

Matthew has, 'So when you see the abomination of desolation spoken of by the prophet Daniel, standing in the holy place (let the reader understand) . . .' (Matt. 24:15). After the phrase 'abomination of desolation', Mark (13:14) includes the phrase 'standing where he ought not to be'. The masculine 'he', pointing to a man as the abomination of desolation, is based on Mark's presentation of Jesus modifying the grammatically neuter 'abomination' with a masculine participle. Moo writes, 'The fact that Mark uses a masculine participle after the neuter *bdelygma* ("abomination") shows that he is thinking of a person' (1996: 246, n. 4).

Both Matthew and Mark present Jesus operating on the basis of several Danielic prophecies: the conflicts outlined in Daniel 11 (wars and rumours of wars) will precede the end (the end is not yet). The references to 'what must take place' recall Nebuchadnezzar's Daniel 2 dream. At some point a man will arise as the abomination of desolation. It would appear that the little horn from the third kingdom typified this person (Dan. 8:13; 11:31), and the one who fulfils these statements as *the* abomination of desolation seems to be the little horn from the fourth kingdom (Dan. 2:33, 42–43; 7:8, 25; 9:27; 12:11). Jesus indicates that once he has arisen (Mark 13:14), it will be time for the faithful to understand from Daniel ('let the reader understand') that the time to flee has arrived.

Matthew portrays Jesus saying, 'For then there will be great tribulation, such as has not been from the beginning of the world until now, no, and never will be. And if those days had not been cut short, no human being would be saved. But for the sake of the elect those days will be cut short' (Matt. 24:21–22). This 'great tribulation' (cf.

---

[9] See Blomberg's discussion on the visible nature of this 'public return at the end of human history as we know it' (2007: 87). On Matt. 24:34, 'this generation will not pass away' (cf. Mark 13:30), see the important study by Lövestam (1995). I have also addressed this question in blog posts (2011a; 2011b).

Mark 13:19, 'such tribulation') very probably refers to the 'time of trouble' announced in Daniel 12:1. The construction of the two statements is parallel (my layout):

- Daniel 12:1,
  'And there shall be a time of trouble,
  such as never has been since there was a nation till that time.
  But at that time your people shall be delivered, everyone whose name shall be found written in the book.'

- Matthew 24:21–22,
  'For then there will be a great tribulation,
  such as has not been from the beginning of the world until now,
  no, and never will be.
  And if those days had not been cut short, no human being would be saved.
  But for the sake of the elect those days will be cut short' (cf. Mark 13:19–20).

This would appear to be an important synthesis that Matthew and Mark present Jesus forging: the culminating typological fulfilment of the abomination of desolation depicted in Daniel 8, 9, 11 and 12 is here placed *prior to* the 'time of trouble' from Daniel 12:1. In fact, with the abomination of desolation functioning as the signal to flee, the logic of both Matthew 24 and Mark 13 points to the conclusion that this abomination of desolation will initiate the circumstances that lead to the great tribulation.

Those will be days of 'false christs and false prophets' who 'perform signs and wonders' (Matt. 24:24; Mark 13:22). Jesus warns his followers not to be deceived by these fakers (Matt. 24:23, 25–26; Mark 13:21–23), because 'Immediately after the tribulation of those days' (Matt. 24:29; cf. Mark 13:24, 'after that tribulation') the son of man will come on the clouds of heaven (Matt. 24:30; Mark 13:26) in fulfilment of Daniel 7:13. At that point Jesus 'will send out his angels with a loud trumpet call, and they will gather his elect' (Matt. 24:31; cf. Mark 13:27).

In both Matthew and Mark, Jesus warns his followers to flee from the tribulation and tells them not to be deceived by those who pretend to be him or represent him, apparently as the tribulation happens. There is no indication that those who belong to Jesus will be raptured prior to the tribulation, but at his coming the 'loud trumpet' will be sounded and his elect gathered (Matt. 24:31; cf. 1 Thess. 4:16).[10] In Daniel we see a sequence of human kings whose actions typify the rise of a final king who will speak against God, persecute God's people and seek to 'change the times and the law' (Dan. 7:25). Matthew and Mark present Jesus identifying this human king as 'the abomination of desolation', saying that his rise will be preceded by 'wars and rumours of wars' and nation rising against nation, while his appearance will be followed by a great tribulation, after which the son of man comes on the clouds of heaven to the relief of those whose names are in the book of life (Dan. 12:1), to whom Jesus refers as 'the elect' (Matt. 24:22; cf. the persecution, and then the deliverance, of the saints in Dan. 7:25–27).

As we continue in this chapter and the next, we will see that the way that Matthew and Mark present Jesus interpreting Daniel in the Olivet Discourse matches the way that Paul (2 Thess. 2) and John (e.g. Rev. 13) interpret Daniel. These New Testament interpretations of Daniel confirm our interpretative conclusions, support the idea that Jesus taught his followers to read the Old Testament (cf. Ellis 1993), and bring clarity to what we who follow Jesus should expect regarding the flow of events leading to the consummation of history.

The son of man, priest and king: Daniel 7:13 in Matthew 26:64 and Mark 14:62

The use of Daniel 7:13 in Matthew 26:64 and Mark 14:62 does not explore the chronological relationship between events of the end, but it does engage with the profound biblical-theological theme of the royal priest whose ultimate manifestation is Jesus. Adam in the garden was a royal figure with priestly overtones (Alexander 2008: 76). Melchizedek was king and priest in Salem (Gen. 14:18). The priest-kings Adam and Melchizedek prepare the way for a nation of king-priests: God announced that the nation of Israel was his son (Exod. 4:22), and brought Israel out of Egypt to be a kingdom of priests (19:6). The anointing oil flowed over both kings and priests: though the only people Moses was instructed to anoint in the Torah were the priests (Exod. 28:41; 29:7; 30:30, etc.), God instructed Samuel to anoint David king over Israel, giving the anointed king a kind of

---

[10] See Moo 1996 for a wider discussion of the issues surrounding the question of the rapture.

priestly overtone. As king, David wore a linen ephod not unlike that of the priests (2 Sam. 6:14), and in Psalm 110 he spoke of his Lord being made a priest for ever, according to the order of Melchizedek. In the discussion of Daniel 7 in the previous chapter, I suggested that there are indications that Daniel may have interpreted the setting up of the thrones in Daniel 7:9 along the lines of Psalm 110:1.

These themes are significant because Jesus, 'the son of David, the son of Abraham' (Matt. 1:1), was hauled before the high priest of Israel, who asked if he was claiming to be king: 'the high priest said to him, "I adjure you by the living God, tell us if you are the Christ, the son of God"' (Matt. 26:63; cf. Mark 14:61). The 'son of God' language here has passages like 2 Samuel 7:14 and Psalm 2:7 in the foreground, but in the near background is the reality that Adam (Luke 3:38) and Israel (Exod. 4:22) were also 'son of God'. The high priest asked Jesus if he claimed to be that long-awaited anointed king of Israel who descended from and fulfilled everything to which Adam and David pointed as the one who would relate to God the Father as the divine son. In his reply to this question, Jesus made a profound biblical-theological connection.

Jesus identified the son of man from Daniel 7:13 with the Davidic king, and at the same time he asserted that the Davidic king is David's Psalm 110 Lord: 'Jesus said to him, "You have said so. But I tell you, from now on you will see the Son of Man seated at the right hand of Power and coming on the clouds of heaven"' (Matt. 26:64; cf. Mark 14:62). The reference to the Son of Man coming on the clouds of heaven is clearly drawn from Daniel 7:13, and the fact that he is seated at the right hand of Power brings in Psalm 110:1. Jesus declared to the wicked high priest of Israel that he was indeed the Christ, the Son of God, and at the same time Jesus asserted himself to be the Son of Man who would come on the clouds of heaven to receive everlasting dominion (Dan. 7:13) as the Melchizedekian high priest (Ps. 110:4). Naturally, the rebel holding the role would not appreciate Jesus declaring himself the true high priest king of Israel.

The interpretation of Daniel 7 in the previous chapter shows that when Daniel 7 is read against earlier Scripture, the interpretation Matthew presented Jesus as providing in his answer to the high priest arises naturally from the text of Daniel 7 itself.[11]

---

[11] Rightly Seyoon Kim: 'With "the Son of Man" then Jesus intended to reveal himself to be the divine figure who was the inclusive representative (or the head) of the eschatological people of God, i.e., the Son of God who was the head of the sons of God' (1985: 36).

The stone-sealed pit: Daniel 6:17 (MT 18) in Matthew 27:66

Scratching the surface of the historical correspondences between Daniel and Jesus, and the escalation in significance as we move from the former to the latter, here I simply draw attention to certain correspondences between and increases in significance from Daniel to Jesus (see further chapter 10 below).

Daniel, who was righteous, was accused by those jealous of him on a trumped-up charge (Dan. 6:4–13). The king recognized the injustice of Daniel's condemnation and sought to deliver him (6:14). Nevertheless, Daniel was condemned, given over to certain death; then placed in a pit with a stone laid on the opening and sealed by the king (6:15–17). At daybreak those who lamented the way Daniel was treated came and found that his God had delivered him (6:19–23).

Jesus was also declared innocent (Matt. 27:24; cf. Luke 23:4, 14–15, 22, 41) but accused by those jealous of him (Matt. 27:18) on trumped up charges (26:59–61; 27:13–14). Pilate recognized the injustice and sought to release Jesus (27:15–19). Nevertheless, Jesus was condemned to death (27:26), and after they crucified him he was put in a new tomb, with a stone rolled over the entrance (27:60), which was later sealed (27:66). At daybreak on the first day of the week those who lamented the way Jesus was treated came and found that God had raised him from the dead (28:1–10).

These points of historical correspondence, and the obvious escalation from Daniel to Jesus, constitute grounds for considering Daniel as a type of Christ. As will be pursued in chapter 10, Daniel himself was also an instalment in an existing pattern, one that began with Joseph and culminated at the new exodus accomplished by the Nazarene.[12]

Proclaiming himself God: Daniel 11:36 in 2 Thessalonians 2:4 (cf. Jude 16)

Paul used Daniel, as exposited by Jesus, to calm and instruct the Thessalonians in the second chapter of his second letter to them. Paul

---

[12] If we seek to maintain authorial intent at the human level when dealing with themes such as this, we can posit that Daniel saw similarities between the way he was treated and the way that Joseph before him was innocent, persecuted, put in a pit, threatened with death and then vindicated and exalted for the deliverance of his people. Understanding the significance of the correspondences between himself and Joseph, Daniel then recounted his own experience, expecting a future typological fulfilment of some sort.

gave them two reasons not to be deceived into thinking that 'the day of the Lord has come' (2 Thess. 2:2). He writes (2 Thess. 2:3–4):

> Let no one deceive you in any way. For that day will not come, unless the rebellion comes first, and the man of lawlessness is revealed, the son of destruction, who opposes and exalts himself against every so-called god or object of worship, so that he takes his seat in the temple of God, proclaiming himself to be God.

We have seen from Matthew and Mark that Jesus taught, on the basis of Daniel, that the Abomination of Desolation would arise and initiate the great tribulation, the days of which would be cut short by the return of the Son of Man (Matt. 24:15–31; Mark 13:14–27). Paul now applies that teaching to the Thessalonians, whom someone had apparently tried to convince that the day of the Lord had already come (2 Thess. 2:1–2). Paul's reference to 'the coming of our Lord Jesus Christ and our being gathered together to him' matches the references in Matthew and Mark to the coming of the Son of Man on the clouds of heaven and his gathering of the elect (Matt. 24:30–31; Mark 13:26–27). These ideas are based in turn on Daniel, where in chapter 7 the little horn from the fourth beast persecutes God's people until he is suddenly destroyed, the son of man receives the kingdom, and his saints rule with him (Dan. 7:8, 11–14, 18, 23–27).

Paul explains that Jesus will not return and gather his elect before 'the rebellion' (2 Thess. 2:3), which is probably a reference to the conditions of the great tribulation (Matt. 24:21; Mark 13:19). Paul probably calls it 'the rebellion' because of the following statements in Daniel, each of which uses the Hebrew noun פֶּשַׁע (*peša'*), rendered as 'transgression' (e.g. ESV, NKJV) or 'rebellion' (HCSB, TNIV [TNIV cited here]):

- Daniel 8:12, 'Because of rebellion'
- Daniel 8:13, 'the rebellion that causes desolation'
- Daniel 8:23, 'when rebels have become completely wicked' (participial form of the cognate verb)
- Daniel 9:24, 'to finish transgression'

These texts that refer to 'rebellion/transgression' and 'rebels' in Daniel are accompanied by the references to 'the abomination that makes desolate' (Dan. 11:31; 12:11 and cf. the similar phrases in 8:13 and 9:27). Paul probably chose the term ἀποστασια (*apostasia*, see BDAG, s.v. 'defiance of established system or authority'), a term that carries connotations of abandoning one's religious traditions (cf. Acts 21:21; 1 Macc. 2:15), because of the religious claims he expected the figure who will be the Abomination of Desolation to make. Informed by Daniel, Paul references such claims in 2 Thessalonians 2:4, when he explains that this is the one 'who opposes and exalts himself against every so-called god or object of worship, so that he takes his seat in the temple of God, proclaiming himself to be God'. Clearly, anyone who follows this 'man of lawlessness', this 'son of destruction' (2 Thess. 2:3), will have apostatized from all prior religious commitments to recognize this 'lawless one' (2:8) as God. Referring to this figure as the 'son of destruction' associates him with the 'abomination of *desolation*', destruction and desolation being related concepts. Referring to him as the 'man of lawlessness' aligns him with the 'rebellion/transgression' he initiates as he seizes power, and it also associates him with the one who 'shall think to change the times and the law' (Dan. 7:25).

The self-exaltation of this man, whereby he boasts over gods and objects of worship, takes his seat in the temple and proclaims himself God (2 Thess. 2:4), is easy to connect with the actions of the little horns from the third and fourth beasts in Daniel. Note that Paul combines elements from Daniel 7 (little horn, fourth kingdom), Daniel 8 (little horn, third kingdom) and Daniel 11 as he describes the man of lawlessness. The little horns in Daniel speak 'great things' (Dan. 7:8), 'words against the Most High' (7:25), are characterized by a 'bold countenance' (8:23), do violence to the temple (8:13; 9:26), and Daniel describes Antiochus Epiphanes in terms paraphrased by Paul (Dan. 11:36–37; cf. 2 Thess. 2:3–4):

> He shall exalt himself and magnify himself above every god, and shall speak astonishing things against the God of gods. He shall prosper till the indignation is accomplished; for what is decreed shall be done. He shall pay no attention to the gods of his fathers, or to the one beloved by women. He shall not pay attention to any other god, for he shall magnify himself above all.

Paul reminds the Thessalonians that he taught them these things in person (2 Thess. 2:5), refers to 'what is restraining him now so that he may be revealed in his time' (2:6–7),[13] and then interprets the

---

[13] Beale (2003: 213–217) provides a nice summary of the identifications of the restrainer.

demise of the little horn from the fourth beast in the light of the comments of Jesus about the cutting short of the tribulation and the coming of the son of man on the clouds of heaven. In 2 Thessalonians 2:8, Paul makes explicit what was implicit in Daniel and the Olivet Discourse when he writes, 'And then the lawless one [cf. 2:3] will be revealed, whom the Lord Jesus will kill with the breath of his mouth and bring to nothing by the appearance of his coming.'

On this reading, Paul identifies the 'man of lawlessness' as the 'abomination of desolation', who in fulfilment of the actions typified by the little horn from Daniel's third kingdom arises as the little horn from Daniel's fourth kingdom, whose end is brought about by the return of Christ himself. What Paul says in 2 Thessalonians 2 readily comports with and expands upon what Matthew and Mark presented Jesus as saying in the Olivet Discourse. Further, in the next chapter we will see from John's interpretation of these realities in Revelation that all these passages can be seen to point to a schematic presentation of the end that has the same elements in the same order. As there so here, the schematic representation of the events of the end interprets and explains what Daniel intended to communicate.

Summary

In this section we have seen that Matthew presented Jesus as making use of language and imagery from Daniel to communicate what a king is, what his kingdom provides, how his enemies will suffer and how his faithful will be rewarded. We have also seen that Matthew and Mark present Jesus as teaching his followers to understand how the events of the end prophesied by Daniel will play out. Further, this teaching of Jesus lines up very well with what Paul wrote to the Thessalonians (2 Thess. 2). Matthew and Mark also present Jesus as expanding on the connection between the priest and king in the Old Testament as he identified the Daniel 7 son of man with the Psalm 110 Melchizedekian high priest. With this, we also noted ways in which Daniel's experience in the stone-sealed pit typified the death and resurrection of Jesus.[14]

---

[14] In this chapter and the next, as noted, I have followed the texts cited in NA27/28, which do not include references to Dan. 7:13 every time the phrase 'son of man' appears in the NT, excluding, for instance, John 3:13. For the son of man in the Gospel of John, see the essay by Reynolds (2011).

Thematic fulfilments of Daniel

In addition to the quotations of the book of Daniel in the New Testament, there are also clear ways in which the broader issues in Daniel, the book's themes, find their fulfilment in what the New Testament describes. Some of these have to do with the outworking of salvation history, others with who Jesus is and what he accomplishes, and still others with how the people of God are to respond to what God reveals.

The outworking of salvation history

We have seen that Daniel prophesied a schematic sequence of four kingdoms, with three of those kingdoms specified and the fourth left unnamed. Those kingdoms match up well with what takes place between Daniel's own day and the coming of Jesus: Babylon; then Medo-Persia; then Greece; then Rome. Rome fits but does not exhaust what Daniel says about the fourth kingdom.

In a way similar to the four-kingdom schema, Daniel 9:25–26 speaks of sixty-nine of the prophesied seventy weeks passing, with the Messiah cut off after the sixty-ninth week. As we saw when we examined the seventy weeks in chapter 5 above, the sixty-nine weeks describe the period between Daniel's day and the coming of Jesus. Broad thematic teaching like this stands behind the New Testament's assertions that Jesus came at the right time:

- 'The time is fulfilled, and the kingdom of God is at hand' (Mark 1:15)
- 'But when the fullness of time had come, God sent forth his Son' (Gal. 4:4)
- 'as a plan for the fullness of time' (Eph. 1:10)
- 'grace, which he gave us in Christ Jesus before the ages began, and which now has been manifested through the appearing of our Saviour Christ Jesus' (2 Tim. 1:9–10)
- 'eternal life, which God, who never lies, promised before the ages began and at the proper time manifested in his word' (Titus 1:2–3)
- 'For the grace of God has appeared, bringing salvation for all people' (Titus 2:11)

Not only do the New Testament authors assert that Jesus came at the right time, but they also say that he was crucified at the right time:

- 'The hour has come for the Son of Man to be glorified' (John 12:23)
- 'Jesus, delivered up according to the definite plan and foreknowledge of God' (Acts 2:23)
- 'at the right time Christ died for the ungodly' (Rom. 5:6)
- 'Christ Jesus, who gave himself as a ransom for all, which is the testimony given at the proper time' (1 Tim. 2:5–6)

This kind of broader thematic fulfilment of Daniel's teaching on God's plan for redemptive history also stands behind references that Jesus will return at the right time:

- 'until the appearing of our Lord Jesus Christ, which he will display at the proper time' (1 Tim. 6:14–15)
- 'waiting for our blessed hope, the appearing of the glory of our great God and Saviour Jesus Christ' (Titus 2:13)

I am obviously not claiming that in these instances the New Testament authors are quoting Daniel directly. Rather, undergirding these New Testament assertions at a deep level is an understanding that God acts in accordance with a plan, aspects of which he revealed in Daniel.

The identity, suffering, and reign of Jesus

At several points the angel Gabriel interacted with Daniel (Dan. 7, 8, 9), and Luke recounts that Gabriel also visited Mary (Luke 1:26–38). When we examined Daniel 7 in chapter 6 above, we found that the one like a son of man is identified with and distinguished from the Ancient of Days, as both are referred to as Most High, with different terms used for each. Daniel 7 indicates that when the son of man 'was given dominion' (Dan. 7:14), he was also to be enthroned next to the Ancient of Days (7:9) in keeping with Psalm 110:1. The dominion given to the son of man in Daniel 7:14

> is an everlasting dominion,
>   which shall not pass away,
> and his kingdom one
>   that shall not be destroyed.

More is revealed about the relationship between the Ancient of Days and the Son of Man when Gabriel announces the following to Mary in Luke 1:31–33:

And behold, you will conceive in your womb and bear a son, and you shall call his name Jesus. He will be great and will be called the Son of the Most High. And the Lord God will give to him the throne of his father David, and he will reign over the house of Jacob for ever, and of his kingdom there will be no end.

Here the one like a son of man from Daniel 7:13 is identified as 'the Son of the Most High', a phrase that synthesizes everything revealed in Daniel 7 and makes explicit the relationship between the Ancient of Days who is the Most High and the one like a son of man (who is also referred to as Most High in Daniel 7, using a distinct term from that used for the Ancient of Days; see chapter 6 above). Moreover, the same angel who interpreted the vision to Daniel now declares to Mary that the Son of the Most High will reign as the scion of David. As in Daniel 7:14, where the dominion would be everlasting, so in Luke 1:33 there will be no end of his kingdom. As in Daniel 7:18, 22, 25 and 27, where the one like a son of man is identified with his people in the phrase 'saints of the Most High', so in Luke 1:33 the people are mentioned in the reference to 'the house of Jacob'. Luke portrays Gabriel as making profound assertions that have deep roots in Daniel 7 soil.

In other examples of New Testament statements founded on but not directly quoting Daniel, Daniel 9:26 speaks of the Messiah being cut off and having nothing. With passages such as Isaiah 53, Zechariah 12:10, 13:7 and the whole motif of the righteous sufferer running through the Psalms, Daniel 9:26 serves as part of the basis for what Jesus says in Luke 24:26, 'Was it not necessary that the Christ should suffer these things and enter into his glory?' Jesus was crucified in fulfilment of Daniel 9:26. Jesus was also given 'all authority in heaven and on earth' (Matt. 28:18) in keeping with the dominion promised to the son of man (Dan. 7:14). His kingdom is for ever.

When we looked at the Daniel 9 prayer in chapter 5 above, we found that prayer to be plugged into the wider Old Testament hope for a new exodus and return from exile, replete with a rebuilding of the temple. These are precisely the terms in which the New Testament interprets what God accomplished in Christ. The death of Jesus is the redemptive death of a new Passover lamb (1 Cor. 5:7; 1 Pet. 1:19), and his people are being built into the new temple of the Spirit (1 Cor. 3:16; 1 Pet. 2:4–5), as they journey towards a new and better land of promise, the new heaven and new earth (1 Cor. 10:1–13; 1 Pet. 1:13; 2:9–12).

Response to revelation

One function of apocalyptic literature is to encourage a beleaguered minority to persevere through difficulty. Texts such as Daniel, parts of Isaiah, Zechariah and others teach that God's people should persevere because God has appointed a day when the oppressive brutality of the worldly powers will be judged, while the faithful martyrs of the Lord will be raised from the dead and rewarded.

The book of Daniel is foundational for the idea in the New Testament that there is an appointed amount of suffering which God's people must endure. Daniel 7:25 speaks of the wearing out of the saints, and 12:7 of the 'shattering of the power of the holy people'. The persecution spoken of in these texts will be completed before God judges the Antichrist and vindicates his faithful. Passages like these gave rise to an expectation of the so-called messianic woes, an appointed amount of suffering through which God's people must pass before kingdom come.

We see references to the messianic woes when Paul tells the churches in Acts 14:22, 'through many tribulations we must enter the kingdom of God'; when he tells the Colossians he is 'filling up what is lacking in Christ's afflictions' (Col. 1:24); when he reminds the Thessalonians, 'you yourselves know that we are destined for this. For when we were with you, we kept telling you beforehand that we were to suffer affliction' (1 Thess. 3:3–4); when Peter tells Christians to 'do good and suffer . . . For to this you have been called' (1 Pet. 2:20–21), and at many points in Revelation (on which see the next chapter, and Hamilton 2014b; see also Hamilton 2010b: 493, esp. table 6.2, 'The Messianic Woes in the Old and New Testaments').

How, then, should God's people respond? In faith, believing that though they suffer, even to the point of death, they should persevere and hold fast the confession. They should do this because they serve the God who declares the future before it takes place, because God has revealed his plan – which includes their suffering, because they serve the God who rescues from lions (cf. 2 Tim. 4:17; Dan. 6:22), and because they serve the God who raises the dead (2 Cor. 1:9; 4:14, etc.; Dan. 12:2).[15] Though antichrists and the Antichrist rage against them, which tells them it is the last hour, in accordance with Daniel's teaching (1 John 2:18, 22; 4:3; 2 John 7), believers should continue to confess Jesus, loving God and one another.

---

[15] See Chase's (2013) excellent study for a biblical theology of resurrection.

Conclusion

The authors of the New Testament interpreted Daniel as *having been* and *going to be* fulfilled. Who Jesus is and what he accomplished fulfilled much that Daniel prophesied, and the New Testament authors promise that some aspects of Daniel's prophecy, such as the consummation of all things in Daniel 9:24 and the resurrection of the dead in Daniel 12:2, await fulfilment at Christ's return (e.g. 1 Cor. 15:20–28; 1 Thess. 4:13–18; Rev. 20 – 22).[16] The authors of the New Testament show their interpretation of Daniel not only in their direct quotation of his words but also in their presentation of the fulfilment of his themes.

We now turn to the book of Revelation, where we will see John's apocalyptic presentation of the same end-time schema prophesied by Daniel, interpreted by Jesus and exposited by the other authors of the New Testament.

[16] On 1 Cor. 15:20–28, see my essay 'That God May Be All in All: The Trinity in 1 Corinthians 15:20–28' (Hamilton 2015). On the new heaven and new earth as cosmic temple, see Beale 2004.

Chapter Nine

Interpretations of Daniel in the Apocalypse

How does John's use of Daniel in the book of Revelation inform our understanding of the book of Daniel? To ask it another way: What interpretative conclusions give rise to the way that John has reused Daniel's language, imitated Daniel's structure, claimed fulfilment of Daniel's prophecies and revealed more about the issues Daniel addressed?

The purpose of this chapter is not to examine the use of the Old Testament in Revelation (for which, see Beale and McDonough 2007; and Beale 1998), or even the use of Daniel in particular in Revelation (for which, see Beale 1984). These pursuits serve the exposition of the book of Revelation (for my attempt at that daunting endeavour, see Hamilton 2012b). In keeping with the purpose of this book, this chapter focuses on understanding of the book of Daniel.

As we look at John's reuse of Danielic language, his imitation of Daniel's structural patterns, his implicit and explicit claims of the fulfilment of Daniel's prophecies, and the information he adds to what Daniel wrote, our main question is this: How does the way John used Daniel sharpen and confirm our understanding of the meaning of Daniel?

John's reuse of Daniel's language

At points John's reuse of Daniel's language simply points to the fact that John followed Daniel in the writing of apocalyptic literature. At other points the reuse of Danielic language joins with broader issues to point to the repetition of patterns from Daniel being re-enacted for John's audience. John's reuse of Daniel's language does not always give insight into how he has interpreted Daniel, but reviewing it will establish the influence of Daniel and add weight to the claim that Daniel and John are using the same terms to talk about the same things.

Language that flavors apocalyptic literature

One of the characteristics of apocalyptic literature is the insistence on absolute divine sovereignty being worked out in a predestined plan. We saw above that a phrase used to refer to 'what must take place' (δει γενεσθαι, *dei genesthai*) occurs in the Old Testament only in Daniel 2:28–29 and 2:45 (Th), and it occurs only in apocalyptic passages in the New Testament, whether in the Olivet Discourse (Matt. 24:6; 26:54; Mark 13:7; cf. Luke 21:9) or in Revelation (Rev. 1:1; 4:1; 22:6; cf. 1:19). John's use of this phrase apparently stems from Daniel and was probably filtered through his own knowledge of the teaching of Jesus. John's reuse of Daniel's phrase communicates the necessary outworking of God's plan.

Other instances of John using phrases drawn from or influenced by Daniel can be seen in Table 9:1.

Table 9.1 John's reuse of Daniel's language

Dan. 2:18, 'God of heaven'	Rev. 11:13; 16:11, 'God of heaven'
Dan. 2:32–33, 'gold . . . silver . . . bronze . . . iron . . . clay'	Rev. 9:20, 'idols of gold and silver and bronze and stone and wood'
Dan. 2:47, 'God of gods and Lord of kings'	Rev. 17:14, 'Lord of lords and King of kings'
Dan. 3:4, 'peoples, nations, and languages'	Rev. 10:11, 'peoples and nations and languages and kings'
Dan. 4:34; 12:7, 'who lives for ever'	Rev. 4:9, 'who lives for ever'
Dan. 8:10, 'some of the host and some of the stars it threw down to the ground and trampled on them'	Rev. 8:10, 'a great star fell from heaven' Rev. 12:4, 'His tail swept down a third of the stars of heaven and cast them to the earth'
Dan. 12:1, 'a time of trouble, such as never has been since there was a nation till that time'	Rev. 16:18, 'a great earthquake such as there had never been since man was on the earth'
Dan. 12:1, 'everyone whose name shall be found written in the book'	Rev. 3:5, 'I will never blot his name out of the book'; cf. 13:8; 20:12
Dan. 12:10, 'the wicked shall act wickedly'	Rev. 22:11, 'Let the evildoer still do evil'

These instances of John's reuse of Daniel's language and imagery show commonalities between the two books in terms of language, concept and authorial perspective. In some instances, the reuse of language goes beyond evidencing commonalities to highlight the recurrence of patterns.

Language that points to instalments in a pattern

When Daniel seeks permission to avoid being defiled by unclean food in Babylon, he requests that the steward, 'test your servants for ten days' (Dan. 1:12), which is done; then Daniel and his three friends are found healthier than those who ate the king's food (1:14–15). The ten days of testing contribute to a theme in the book of Daniel that involves Daniel and his friends first being tested; then being exalted. John seems to use this theme in Revelation 2:10, when he records how Jesus told the church in Smyrna, 'for ten days you will have tribulation', and then promised rewards to those who conquer (Rev. 2:10–11). The phrase 'ten days' is the point of connection here. The church in Smyrna was probably faced with more than ten literal days of testing, making it probable that the reference is to a stylized period meant to recall Daniel.

Daniel is subtly invoked by the reference to ten days of testing, but it is difficult to see how the stylized period of testing the church in Smyrna faces *fulfils* the ten-day test of Daniel and his friends. The church in Smyrna faces a test that will last a comparatively short time, as will other churches in the seven letters of Revelation 2 – 3 (cf. Rev. 3:10), as will other churches until Christ returns (cf. the refrain 'what the Spirit says to the churches' in 2:7, 11, 17, 29; 3:6, 13, 22; and Acts 14:22). Rather than look for a fulfilment of some kind, a better approach is to conclude that in Daniel there is a pattern of testing followed by exaltation for those who remain faithful, and when Jesus spoke those words to John in Revelation 2:10, he was indicating that the suffering of the church in Smyrna was to be understood as an instalment in that pattern.

The pattern of suffering followed by exaltation is seen in many places in the Old and New Testaments, supremely in Christ (Luke 24:25), and it is easy for followers of Jesus to apply it to their own experience (1 Pet. 2:20–22). When John presents Jesus as engaging with that pattern by using the phrase from Daniel 1:12 in Revelation 2:10, confirmation is provided for the idea that Daniel was written such that the historical experience of Daniel serves as a kind of exemplar, showing Daniel's audience how they should respond to the persecutions predicted in the apocalyptic sections of the book of Daniel.

A similar instalment in a pattern in Revelation that bears a resemblance to Daniel, while probably not pointing to fulfilment per se, is found in the similarity of angelic action in Daniel 12:7 and Revelation 10:5–6. In Daniel 12:7, 'the man clothed in linen, who was above the waters of the stream; he raised his right hand and his left hand towards heaven and swore by him who lives for ever . . .' The analogue for this in Revelation describes an angel 'standing on the sea and on the land [who] raised his right hand to heaven and swore by him who lives for ever and ever' (Rev. 10:5–6). Revelation 10, where John eats the scroll, strongly corresponds to Ezekiel 2 – 3, where Ezekiel eats the scroll. The similarities function to communicate that John is a prophet like Ezekiel and Daniel. Once again, there seem to be indications here that the events of the book of Daniel should be considered for the contribution they make to broader patterns, but any fulfilment that might be in view is elusive. Along these lines, too, are the similarities between the instructions to 'seal up the vision' in Daniel 8:26 and Revelation 10:4. Curiously, in Daniel 8:26, Daniel is told to 'seal up the vision, for it refers to many days from now'. In Revelation 10:4, by contrast, the voice from heaven says, 'Seal up what the seven thunders have said, and do not write it down,' and the reason for this comes in 10:6, 'there would be no more delay'. The sealing, then, is for different reasons. In Daniel, it is because the vision is for the future; in Revelation, because there will be no more delay, so what the thunders said was not to be written down. The patterns of action at least tell us that these are the kinds of things to expect in apocalyptic literature.

The instruction to seal the vision in Daniel 8:26 is repeated in Daniel 12:4, reiterated in 12:9, and in these latter two texts the book is sealed 'until the time of the end'. This lays the groundwork for Revelation 5, where the Lamb takes the sealed scroll from the one seated on the throne (cf. Dan. 7:9–14), opens its seals in Revelation 6 – 8; and this would appear to be the open scroll John eats in Revelation 10, with the result that he prophesies about the end of history through the rest of the book.

Other patterns that don't seem to point to typological fulfilment but that do indicate that Daniel, like other Old Testament authors, intended his work to depict sequences of events that are typical of the way things go (this understanding of Daniel being validated by John's instalments in the patterns) include the following:

- Michael is engaged in heavenly conflict in Daniel 10:13, 21 and Revelation 12:7.
- Daniel saw the thrones set and the books opened for judgment in Daniel 7:10, with myriads present in the heavenly court, and

John saw a similar scene in Revelation 20:12 (cf. also Dan. 7:10 and Rev. 5:11).

- At several points Daniel encountered a heavenly being and experienced sensory overload, whether that meant he was alarmed (Dan. 7:28), collapsed into sleep (8:18; 10:8–9), lay sick (8:27) or was exhausted (9:21). On several of these occasions the angel touched and strengthened Daniel (8:18; 10:10–11). Matching this pattern, John collapsed before Jesus, who touched and strengthened him (Rev. 1:17).

- The description of the man clothed in linen in Daniel 10:5–6 does not indicate that the pre-incarnate Christ appeared to Daniel there, but it does show that those who stand before God reflect the characteristics of the one they serve. This conclusion is supported by the similar description of the angel in Revelation 15:5–6. That Jesus is described in similar terms in Revelation 1:13–16 establishes that angels like the ones in Daniel 10:5–6 and Revelation 15:5–6 reflect the glory of the one they serve.

We should not think of the repetition of these things in John's Revelation as mere literary imitation. Rather, John's knowledge of Daniel shaped the way he perceived and communicated what he saw. The patterns of events in the book of Daniel left an impress on John's thinking, as the whole structure of Daniel's book seems to have done.

John's imitation of Daniel's structure

The book of Daniel should be understood as a chiasm:

1, Exile to the unclean realm of the dead
  2, Four kingdoms followed by the kingdom of God
    3, Deliverance of the trusting from the fiery furnace
      4, Humbling of proud King Nebuchadnezzar
      5, Humbling of proud King Belshazzar
    6, Deliverance of the trusting from the lions' den
  7 – 9, Four kingdoms followed by the kingdom of God
10 – 12, Return from exile and resurrection from the dead

The book of Revelation also has a chiastic structure (Hamilton 2012b: 165):

1:1–8, Letter opening: revelation of Jesus and the things that
must soon take place
1:9 – 3:22, Letters to the seven churches: the church in the
world
4:1 – 6:17, Throne room vision, Christ conquers and opens
the scroll
7:1 – 9:21, The sealing of the saints and the trumpets
announcing plagues
10:1–11, The angel and John (true prophet)
11:1–14, The church: two witnesses prophesy for
1,260 Days; then opposition from the beast
11:15–19, Seventh trumpet: 'The kingdom of
the world has become the kingdom of our
Lord and of his Christ, and he shall reign
for ever and ever.'
12:1 – 13:10, The church: the woman nourished
for 1,260 Days; then opposition from the
dragon and the second beast
13:11–18, The deceiving beast (false prophet)
14:1 – 19:10, The redemption of the saints and the
bowls of wrath
19:11 – 20:15, Return of Christ, he conquers, sets up his
thousand-year kingdom, and opens the scrolls
21:1 – 22:7, New heavens and new earth: the church in glory
22:8–21, Letter closing: Jesus is coming soon

The conclusion that these two books are structured chiastically was
reached by means of independent study of each book on its own.
That is to say, my conclusion about the structure of the one book
did not affect my conclusion about the structure of the other. Why
make such a statement? Because comparison of each in the light of
the other reveals a broad correspondence between the centre of the
chiasms and the concentric rings emanating from the centre.

At the centre of the chiasm of the book of Daniel stands the humbling
of the two proud kings of Babylon, Nebuchadnezzar and Belshazzar
(Dan. 4 – 5). At the centre of the chiasm of the book of Revelation, as
though in answer to what Daniel depicted, stands the announcement
that the kingdom of the world has become the kingdom of our Lord
and of his Christ, who shall reign for ever (Rev. 11:15–19).

The innermost framing rings around the midpoints of these chiastic
structures also match. In Daniel 3 and 6 we have the persecution and

preservation of Daniel and his three friends through fiery furnace and lion's den. Similarly, in Revelation 11:1–14 and 12:1 – 13:10 Danielic beasts attack the people of God (Rev. 11:7; 13:1), while God protects his own through satanic persecution, as they refuse to worship the beast (13:8). Even if they are martyred, God will raise them from the dead (11:11). The next framing circles out from the centre points of the chiasms again match one another, each having a prophetic focus. In Daniel, the prophetically revealed and interpreted four-kingdom dreams and visions of Daniel 2 and 7 – 9 balance each other. Similarly, in the book of Revelation the depiction of the true prophet John in Revelation 10:1–11 stands across from the depiction of the false prophet, the deceiving beast of Revelation 13:11–18.

The final framing sections in the book of Daniel are concerned with the exile in Daniel 1 and the return from exile and resurrection from the dead in Daniel 10 – 12. Once again this broadly matches what we find in the book of Revelation, as each matching frame in the rest of Revelation's chiastic structure can be summarized in terms of the church's current situation in history over against the church's future redemption, vindication, reward and glory.

Revelation is a longer book than Daniel, so naturally the chiastic structure of Revelation is more detailed than that of Daniel. In broad terms, however, the chiastic structure of the two books correspond:[1]

Table 9.2 The chiastic structure of Daniel and Revelation

Daniel	Revelation
Exile	The church in the world
Four kingdoms prophesied	True prophet: John,
Jews persecuted and preserved	Church persecuted and preserved
Kings of Babylon humbled	King Jesus exalted
Daniel persecuted and preserved	Church persecuted and preserved
Four kingdoms prophesied	False prophet: the second beast
Return from exile and resurrection	The church in glory

These broad correspondences between the two books mutually confirm one another, the chiasm in Revelation confirming the one in Daniel

---

[1] Beale's suggestion that the structure of Revelation has been influenced by the structure of Daniel first drew my attention to this topic (1999: 135). He cites Sims, who arrived independently at a similar conclusion (1995: 119). Cf. also Beale's discussions of 'The Possible Structural Significance of Daniel Allusions in the Apocalypse' (1984: 275–281), and 'The Significance of the Overall Structure of Daniel' (283–285).

and vice versa. The correspondence with Revelation strengthens the conclusions reached on the literary structure of Daniel in chapter 3 above. The similarity in the chiastic structures of Daniel and Revelation also supports the idea that both John and Daniel used literary structure to aid the communication of the message. The structure does not exhaust the message, but it does advance it.

John's fulfilments of Daniel's prophecies

In addition to the insight we get into the book of Daniel from the way John made use of his language, patterns and structure, we also find help from the fulfilments of Daniel's prophecies that John describes in Revelation. John claims fulfilments in Revelation that are both predictive and typological in nature.

Predictive fulfilments

In his vision, Daniel saw that

> with the clouds of heaven
> there came one like a son of man.
> (Dan. 7:13)

In Revelation John declares that what Daniel saw will be fulfilled at the return of Christ: 'Behold, he is coming with the clouds, and every eye will see him, even those who pierced him' (Rev. 1:7; cf. Matt. 24:30). Describing his vision of the risen Christ, John then writes that he saw 'in the midst of the lampstands one like a son of man' (1:13). Perhaps recognizing the way that the son of man was identified with and distinguished from the Ancient of Days in Daniel 7, John quotes the description of the Ancient of Days in Daniel 7:9 as he describes the risen Christ in Revelation 1:14 (cf. also John 1:1). Later in the book of Revelation, as he relates how he saw the Lord Jesus come for the harvest of the righteous, he writes, 'Then I looked, and behold, a white cloud, and seated on the cloud one like a son of man, with a golden crown on his head, and a sharp sickle in his hand' (14:14). These texts in Revelation show that John identified Jesus as the 'one like a son of man' whom Daniel saw, and John envisioned Jesus enacting the fulfilment of Daniel's prophecy when he returns to judge his enemies and save his people. While John does show Jesus being presented before the Ancient of Days in fulfilment of Daniel 7 in Revelation 5, in Revelation 1 the imagery of Daniel 7:13 appears in references to Jesus going somewhere other than to be presented before the Ancient of Days. This creative development affirms that the Son of Man's mode of travel is the same as Yahweh's, on the clouds of heaven (e.g. Ps. 104:3; cf. Acts 1:9–11).

Daniel 7:14 declared that the son of man would receive the kingdom and that his kingdom would never be destroyed or pass away. John depicts the fulfilment of that prophecy in Revelation 11:15, when the announcement is made at the seventh trumpet that Christ is King, 'and he shall reign for ever and ever' (cf. also e.g. Dan. 2:44; 1 Cor. 15:24).[2]

Daniel 7:18 declared, 'the saints of the Most High shall receive the kingdom and possess the kingdom for ever, for ever and ever'. John depicts the fulfilment of that prediction in Revelation 22:5, 'They will need no light of lamp or sun, for the Lord God will be their light, and they will reign for ever and ever.' Along these lines, Daniel 7:21–22 predicted, 'As I looked, this horn made war with the saints and prevailed over them, until the Ancient of Days came, and judgment was given for the saints of the Most High, and the time came when the saints possessed the kingdom' (cf. Dan. 7:27). John depicts the fulfilment of these prophecies when the beast of Revelation 13 'was allowed to make war on the saints and to conquer them' (Rev. 13:7; cf. 11:7). The specifics of the war and the conquering are given later in Revelation 13, when the second beast makes an image of the first beast; then gives it breath 'so that the image of the beast might even speak and might cause those who would not worship the image of the beast to be slain' (13:15). Then after Christ's return in Revelation 19, John writes in Revelation 20:4:

> Then I saw thrones, and seated on them were those to whom authority to judge was committed. Also I saw the souls of those who had been beheaded for the testimony of Jesus and for the word of God, and those who had not worshipped the beast or its image and had not received its mark on their foreheads or their hands [cf. 13:4, 8, 14–18]. They came to life and reigned with Christ for a thousand years.

John's use of Daniel adds to what we know about the beast's war on the saints. John reveals that the little horn from the fourth beast will

---

[2] In a forthcoming chapter I discuss 1 Cor. 15:20–28, 15:50–57, 1 Thess. 4:13–17 and Rev. 5, 11, 20 – 22, arguing that these passages are in agreement on the sequence of end-time events, namely who reigns and when, along with who is raised from the dead and when (Hamilton 2015).

exercise authority for forty-two months (Rev. 13:5, on which see further below), and John also clarifies and confirms for us the relationship between the 'saints' and the 'Most High', whom Daniel 7 described as receiving the kingdom and reigning together. John depicts this as being fulfilled when Christ reigns in the millennium, his resurrected faithful reigning with him (Rev. 20:4) on earth (5:10).

In these instances, what Daniel prophesied is fulfilled in Revelation. As such, what John records in Revelation provides an inspired interpretation of what Daniel predicted.

Typological fulfilments

Earlier in this chapter we considered places where John reused Daniel's language to draw attention to similarities in sequences of events (see above under the subheading 'Language that points to instalments in a pattern'). These instances of linguistic similarity support the conclusion that John saw patterns in Daniel that Daniel himself intended his audience to notice.

We now consider instances of linguistic similarity that point to more than mere instalments in a pattern. In these places there is a pattern – historical correspondence – but John's contribution to the pattern presents its climactic fulfilment. These instances clearly communicate escalation in, indeed the culmination of, the typological pattern.

The cue to the presence of the pattern is either linguistic similarity or a similar sequence of events. The escalation can be seen in the significance of what John depicts. If John has claimed fulfilment of a typological pattern, I contend that Daniel understood that he was communicating elements of a pattern that would indeed come to the kind of climactic expression we mean when we use the word 'fulfilment'.[3] This is not to claim that Daniel knew all the specifics of the fulfilment of the pattern. It is to claim that he noticed something significant that he pondered along the lines of 1 Peter 1:10–11, 'the prophets who prophesied about the grace that was to be yours searched and enquired carefully, enquiring what person or time the Spirit of Christ in them was indicating when he predicted the sufferings of Christ and the subsequent glories'.

As we saw in the discussion of Daniel 2:35 in chapter 4 above, Daniel (2:35) applied his knowledge of Psalm 1 to his perception of

---

[3] In 'The Virgin Will Conceive', I argue that the fulfilment formulas (using the verb πληροω, *plēroō*) in Matt. 1 – 2 reference typological fulfilment (2008a).

Nebuchadnezzar's dream, with the result that he told Nebuchadnezzar that

> the iron, the clay, the bronze, the silver, and the gold, all together were broken in pieces, *and became like the chaff* of the summer threshing floors; *and the wind carried them away*, so that not a trace of them could be found. But the stone that struck the image became a great mountain and filled the whole earth.

The symbolic statue comes to a paradigmatic end. Specifics are not to be pressed in a literalistic fashion. The point here is that worldly kingdoms that join against God and his people will meet the end of the wicked sung in Psalm 1:4, and they will leave only a colossal wreck, lone and level sands stretching far away.

John keys into this schematic conception of the fate of the wicked by picking up the language of Daniel 2:35, 'so that not a trace of them could be found', to speak of Satan banished from heaven: Michael and his angels drive the dragon and his angels from the heavenly field of battle, with the result that 'there was no longer any place for them in heaven' (Rev. 12:8; cf. Dan. 2:35 Th). The evil power in heaven meets the same fate as the evil power on earth. Later in Revelation, as John describes God's judgment of his enemies, he writes, 'From his presence earth and sky fled away, and no place was found for them' (Rev. 20:11). The point seems to be that nothing remains of the creation defiled by sin. Everything is renewed. The symbols that Daniel saw and communicated have thus received their intended typological fulfilment, because Daniel intended to depict the destruction and obliteration of worldly kingdoms.

Another instance of typological fulfilment can be seen in the persecution of Revelation 13:15–18. This instance is based not on the reuse of Daniel's words but on the repetition of Daniel's patterns. Daniel 3 tells the story of Nebuchadnezzar's image of gold and his demand that all render obeisance to it, threatening death on refusal. This historical pattern is typologically fulfilled by what John symbolically depicts in Revelation 13. John describes a fake-christ beast (Rev. 13:1–4) whom all but the elect worship (13:5–10); then a false-prophet beast arises, who makes an image of the fake-christ beast and demands that all worship the image (13:11–14). Those who refuse are slain (13:15), and those who will not take the beast's mark cannot buy or sell (13:16–18). We saw above that the historical narratives in Daniel 1 – 6 were intended to provide prototypes of what is revealed in the apocalyptic visions of Daniel 7 – 12. The influence of the Daniel 3 pattern on John's interpretation of what he saw and how he interpreted and presented his vision seems to confirm that approach to Daniel's historical narratives.

Throughout this discussion we have seen how Revelation sharpens and confirms our understanding of the book of Daniel. John has also interpreted the seventieth week of Daniel 9:27, and to John's clarification of that aspect of Daniel's prophecy we now give attention.

John's clarification of Daniel's revelations

We have seen that the little horn from the third kingdom typifies the little horn from the fourth kingdom. Describing the atrocities of the little horn from the fourth kingdom in Daniel 7:25, the angelic interpreter (Gabriel) tells Daniel that the saints

> shall be given into his hand
> for a time, times, and half a time.

Daniel indicates the meaning of the reference to 'time, times, and half a time' in 7:25 when he describes the halving of the seventieth week in 9:27, which also means that the 'prince who is to come' in Daniel 9:26 is to be understood as the little horn from the fourth kingdom (cf. 7:8, 21–22, 24–26), the one who makes a covenant for the seventieth week; then for half of the week puts away sacrifice and offering as desolation comes on the wing of abomination (9:27).[4]

My thesis here is simple: if we can determine how John interpreted Daniel's seventieth week in Revelation, we will know how Daniel intended that seventieth week to be understood. John does interpret Daniel's seventieth week in Revelation, and his inspired interpretation and development of Daniel's prophecy aids our understanding of what Daniel meant.

The Daniel 7 vision opens with the 'four winds of heaven . . . stirring up the great sea' (Dan. 7:2). Once the Lamb has opened the first six seals on the scroll in Revelation 6, Revelation 7 describes four angels 'holding back the four winds of the earth, that no wind might

---

[4] The use of the 'time, times, and half a time' formula in Dan. 12:7 should also be noted. There is no indication of a shift from Antiochus Epiphanes (little horn, third kingdom) to a fourth kingdom figure at the end of Dan. 11 or the beginning of Dan. 12, so the use of the formula from 7:25 (interpreted by 9:27) in 12:7 confirms the idea that the little horn from the third kingdom typifies the little horn from the fourth.

blow on earth or sea or against any tree' (Rev. 7:1). Daniel 7 follows the description of the winds stirring up the sea with the four beasts rising 'up out of the sea' (Dan. 7:3), but before the beast rises from the sea in Revelation (cf. Rev. 11:7; 13:1; 17:8) the servants of God will be sealed (7:3), which protects them from harm (9:4; 14:1–5).

Four beasts rise from the sea in Daniel 7, and the first is compared to a lion (Dan. 7:4), the second to a bear (7:5), the third to a leopard (7:6) and the fourth is a terror with iron teeth (7:7). We have seen that Daniel identified the first beast as Babylon (2:38), the second as Medo-Persia (8:20; 11:1–2), the third as Greece (8:21; 11:3) and the fourth is left unidentified, though it corresponds to Rome. These kingdoms are historical, as the history from Daniel to the birth of Jesus attests. They are also symbolic, as evidenced by the use of animal imagery to represent them. Daniel has presented them in typical terms: they act as beasts typically do and serve as types of the end-time Antichrist. Thus Nebuchadnezzar attacks Jerusalem and plunders the temple (1:1–2); Belshazzar uses the temple vessels for a debauched bender (5:1–4); the little horn from the third kingdom attacks sacrifice and sanctuary (8:9–14; 11:29–31); and the little horn from the fourth kingdom does the same (9:26–27; cf. 7:21–25).

In his presentation of the beast from the sea in Revelation 13, John seems to recognize that while there was a historical correspondence between the beasts in Daniel 7 and the four historical kingdoms, there is also a typological quality to them that allows him to present their essence fulfilled in the composite end-time beast. This is in keeping with the way John presents the wicked, who persecute God's people as belonging to the same city, even though they come from many cities, when he refers in Revelation 11:8 to 'the great city that symbolically is called Sodom and Egypt, where their Lord was crucified', and when he symbolically presents 'the great city that has dominion over the kings of the earth' (Rev. 17:18) as a 'prostitute' (17:1) whose name is 'Babylon the great' (17:5) even as she is seated on the seven hills of Rome (17:9). Sodom, Egypt, Jerusalem, Babylon, Rome: all unite to take their stand against the Lord and his anointed.

Similarly, the beast who symbolizes the end-time world-power is a composite of the four beasts of Daniel 7. Summoned from the sea by the dragon (Rev. 12:17 – 13:1), 'that ancient serpent, who is called the devil and Satan' (12:9; 20:2), rather than being like a lamb, the dragon's fake-christ beast, whose seemingly mortal wound dupes but does not save, 'was like a leopard; its feet were like a bear's, and its mouth was like a lion's mouth' (13:2). These are the very beasts to which the first three kingdoms were likened in Daniel 7:4–6, and yet John also clearly specifies that this Revelation 13 beast is the fourth beast of Daniel 7. He accomplishes this identification by noting that the beast was 'rising out of the sea, with ten horns and seven heads, with ten diadems on its horns and blasphemous names on its heads' (Rev. 13:1). This description ties the Revelation 13 beast to the fourth beast in Daniel 7:7, which 'had ten horns', which 'made war with the saints' (Dan. 7:21), whose ten horns are ten kings (7:24), after which shall arise one who speaks 'against the Most High' (7:25; cf. 11:36). Similarly, the Revelation 13 beast 'was given a mouth uttering haughty and blasphemous words' (13:5–6) and 'was allowed to make war on the saints and to conquer them' (13:7).

Not only does the Revelation 13 beast have the characteristics of the Daniel 7 fourth beast, but he is allotted the same period of time. The Daniel 7 fourth beast is given 'time, times, and half a time' (Dan. 7:25; 12:7), which Daniel 9:27 indicates will be half of the seventieth week. Because of the order of the phrases in Daniel 9:27 (my layout),

> And he shall make a strong covenant with many for one week,
> and for half of the week he shall put an end to sacrifice and
> offering.
> And on the wing of abominations shall come one who makes
> desolate,
> until the decreed end is poured out on the desolator,

it appears that the ending of sacrifice and offering takes place during the *second* half of that seventieth week, and that, with the ending of sacrifice, abominations are perpetrated by the wicked prince, the 'one who makes desolate' (Dan. 9:27). The conclusion that the abominations of the desolator take place in the second half of the seventieth week is confirmed by the question and answer in Daniel 12:6–7:

> How long shall it be till the end of these wonders? . . . he raised his right hand and his left hand towards heaven and swore by him who lives for ever that it would be for a time, times, and half a time, and that when the shattering of the power of the holy people comes to an end all these things would be finished.

As in Daniel 7, the Daniel 9 outrage continues for the appointed time: 'until the decreed end is poured out on the desolator' (9:27). The desolator's end is like that of the little horn from the fourth kingdom in Daniel 7, who holds sway 'until the Ancient of Days came' (7:22), 'for a time, times, and half a time' (7:25), at the end of which

> the court shall sit in judgment,
> and his dominion shall be taken away,
> to be consumed and destroyed to the end.
> (7:26)

Paul interprets this to refer to the Antichrist, the lawless one, 'whom the Lord Jesus will kill with the breath of his mouth and bring to nothing by the appearance of his coming' (2 Thess. 2:8; cf. discussion in chapter 8 above).

Similarly, in Revelation 13:5, 'the beast . . . was allowed to exercise authority for forty-two months'. Forty-two months is a way of referring to a three-and-a-half-year period ($12 \times 3 = 36$, and $36 + 6 = 42$), and half of seven years is three-and-a-half years. John appears to present the beast's forty-two-month period in which he is able to 'conquer' the saints as the second half of Daniel's seventieth week, during which the beast stamps out the worship of God, taking away sacrifice to celebrate abomination and desolation.

What about the first half of Daniel's seventieth week? In contrast with the way that the beast will have authority to make war on and conquer the saints for forty-two months in Revelation 13:5, the two witnesses (whom I take to symbolize the church; for exposition see Hamilton 2012b: 231–244) are protected to prophesy for 1,260 days (Rev. 11:1–6), and the woman (who symbolizes both Mary and the people of God; for exposition see Hamilton 2012b: 245–256) is likewise nourished in the wilderness for 1,260 days (12:6). The 1,260-day period is a three-and-a-half-year period, calculated as forty-two months of thirty days ($42 \times 30 = 1,260$). The forty-two months of the church being protected in Revelation 11:2 is the same period of time as the 1,260-day period in which the two witnesses prophesy in 11:3. Similarly, the woman is nourished in the wilderness for 1,260 days in Revelation 12:6, and that period of time is referred to as 'time, and times, and half a time' in 12:14 (cf. Dan. 7:25; 9:27; 12:7). Thus John seems to present God protecting and providing for his people through the first half of Daniel's seventieth week.

After the two witnesses finish their testimony, the beast rises, makes war on and conquers the two witnesses (Rev. 11:7). The reuse of the words of Revelation 11:7 in Revelation 13:7 links the death of the two witnesses with the beginning of the beast's forty-two months of authority (13:5). John has thus interpreted both halves of Daniel's seventieth week. During the first half, the gospel is 'proclaimed throughout the whole world as a testimony to all nations' (Matt. 24:14), 'the fullness of the Gentiles' comes in (Rom. 11:25), and then the appointed number of martyrs is fulfilled (Rev. 6:9–11). The first half of Daniel's seventieth week comprises most of church history between the ascension and return of Christ.

Through flame and flood, with fire and blood (cf. Rev. 11:5–6; 12:15), God protects the church and provides for her as she proclaims the gospel and makes disciples of all nations through the first half of Daniel's seventieth week. When the testimony is finished (11:7), the beast rises and it is given to him 'to make war on the saints and to conquer them' (13:7; cf. 11:7). The beast is allowed to overcome God's people for the second half of Daniel's seventieth week (13:5; cf. Dan. 7:25; 12:7).

John indicates, however, that the second half of Daniel's seventieth week will not last as long as the first, even as he symbolically refers to both halves of the week as three-and-a-half-year periods of time. John prophetically foreshortens the beast's three-and-a-half years by twice referring to that symbolic period of time with other, shorter, symbolic periods of time.[5]

First, in Revelation 11:7, when the beast rises, he kills the two witnesses. Their bodies are then exposed 'for three and a half days' (Rev. 11:9). Then in Revelation 11:11, 'after the three and a half days a breath of life from God entered them, and they stood up on their feet'. Once raised from the dead, dramatically enacting Ezekiel 37, 'they heard a loud voice from heaven saying to them, "Come up here!" And they went up to heaven in a cloud' (Rev. 11:12). Then falls an earthquake (11:13), the seventh trumpet sounds, and 'the kingdom of the world has become the kingdom of our Lord and of his Christ' (11:15). So it seems that John symbolically presents the church prophesying for the first half of Daniel's seventieth week, at which point the beast initiates a vicious persecution, almost totally eradicating Christianity, but rather than presenting the time between the death of the witnesses and their resurrection as three-and-a-half years, John presents it as three-and-a-half *days*. At the end of those three-and-a-half days Christ reigns as king.

---

[5] Cf. Beckwith's discussion of prophetic foreshortening as it relates to the periods of time in Daniel's seventieth week. He takes the first half of the seventieth week to go 'from the death of Jesus to the destruction of Jerusalem (historically, a period of about forty years), and the other half of that week takes us from the destruction of Jerusalem to the end of history' (Beckwith 1996: 308–309).

Similarly, in the second instance of prophetic foreshortening, Revelation 17:12 speaks of the ten horns who 'are ten kings who have not yet received royal power, but they are to receive authority as kings for one hour, together with the beast'. Here the beast's forty-two month (Rev. 13:5) period of authority is treated as 'one hour' (17:12).[6] In these two instances, John indicates that the beast's symbolic period of three-and-a-half years will be shorter, much shorter, than the church's symbolic period of three-and-a-half years. John understands Daniel's seventieth week as the whole of church history between the two comings of Christ. In the first half, the church proclaims the gospel until all the elect have heard and believed. In the second half, a time cut short for the sake of the elect, the Antichrist initiates a persecution designed to end the worship of God. That persecution will be vicious and unavoidable (Rev. 13:10). The people of God must persevere (Matt. 24:21–22):

> For then there will be a great tribulation, such as has not been from the beginning of the world until now, no, and never will be. And if those days had not been cut short, no human being would be saved. But for the sake of the elect those days will be cut short.

The beast's rule continues until Jesus returns in Revelation 19, when he captures the beast and the false prophet, consigning them to the lake of fire (Rev. 19:20), 'and the rest were slain by the sword that came from his mouth' (19:21).

The scene in Revelation 19:20–21 reveals John's understanding of the fulfilment of Daniel 7:11, which states that 'the beast was killed, and its body destroyed and given over to be burned with fire'. John states in Revelation 20:10 that the beast and false prophet, having been cast into 'the lake of fire and sulphur . . . they will be tormented day and night for ever' (Rev. 20:10).

Revelation 19 – 20 also sheds light on Daniel 7:12, 'As for the rest of the beasts, their dominion was taken away, but their lives were

---

[6] I arrived at and exposited this understanding of John's interpretation of Daniel's seventieth week as I worked through Revelation between 2009 and 2010 (which appeared in Hamilton 2012b: esp. 161–174). For a summary of other approaches, see table 21.2, 'Interpretations of Daniel's Seventieth Week', in that work on Revelation (Hamilton 2012b: 241). An article-length project afforded me the opportunity to re-evaluate my conclusions in the spring of 2013, at which point I found them confirmed (see Hamilton 2014b), and I have re-examined the relevant evidence in the work on this project, once again finding this the most convincing explanation of John's interpretation of Daniel's seventieth week.

prolonged for a season and a time.' These beasts represent the kingdoms of the world, and we have seen that John understands them *both* as historical kingdoms *and* as typological symbols (see discussion of Rev. 11:8, 13:1–2 and 17:1, 5, 9 and 18 above on Egypt, Sodom, Jerusalem, Babylon and Rome). Let us review what we have to this point:

- Daniel 7:11 speaks of the beast being killed and burned.
- Revelation 19:20 speaks of the beast captured and thrown alive into the lake of fire.
- Daniel 7:12 speaks of the rest of the beasts losing dominion but having their lives prolonged for a season and a time.

John presents the 'death' of the beast in Daniel 7:11 in terms of the physical defeat of the enemies of Christ in Revelation 19:20–21 ('the rest were slain', Rev. 19:21), and he then presents the spiritual defeat of Christ's enemies as the heavenly powers behind the human kingdoms are 'thrown alive into the lake of fire' (19:20). Revelation 19:20–21 thus appears to be John's depiction of the fulfilment of Daniel 7:11. Does John present the fulfilment of Daniel 7:12? He seems to do just that, as follows.

Revelation 20 continues the narrative from Revelation 19, as can be seen from the fact that only after the thousand years of Revelation 20 is the dragon 'thrown into the lake of fire and sulphur where the beast and the false prophet were' (Rev. 20:10; cf. 19:20). During that thousand years, the dragon is neither on earth nor in the lake of fire but in a sealed pit (20:1–3).

Daniel 7:12 speaks of dominion having been taken from the beasts, and 7:13–14 describes that dominion being given to the son of man, who reigns with his saints in 7:18, 22 and 27. In keeping with this, John depicts the fulfilment of the son of man receiving dominion and reigning with his saints as those slain during the beast's persecution (Rev. 13:15) are resurrected to reign with Christ for a thousand years in Revelation 20:4–6. It is important to point out that those whom the beast put to death for not worshipping his image in Revelation 13:15 are precisely 'those who had been beheaded for the testimony of Jesus and for the word of God, and those who had not worshipped the beast or its image and had not received its mark on their foreheads or their hands' (Rev. 20:4; cf. the mark of the beast on hand or forehead in 13:16–18). These are they who 'came to life and reigned with Christ for a thousand years' (20:4).

218

What of the beasts whose lives were prolonged without dominion in Daniel 7:12? After the thousand years, Satan is released (Rev. 20:7) and deceives 'the nations that are at the four corners of the earth, Gog and Magog, to gather them for battle' (20:8). They find no success.[7] The thousand-year reign of Christ with his saints (Rev. 20:4) fits as the time during which the 'rest of the beasts' have 'their . . . dominion taken away, but their lives were prolonged for a season and a time' (Dan. 7:12). At the end of the thousand years, 'the rest of the beasts' from Daniel 7:12 are prompted by the newly released Satan (Rev. 20:7–8) to rebel against the Lord and his Messiah, where they meet final defeat (20:9–10).

The composite quality of the Revelation 13 beast indicates that the final kingdom will combine all the vicious nature of the beastly characteristics of the wicked kingdoms of history in a culminating power of anti-Christian malice. The one who is the desolator (Dan. 9:27) is the little horn from the fourth kingdom, typified by the little horn from the third kingdom, and the Lord Jesus will kill him when he comes (2 Thess. 2:8). Jesus will then reign for a thousand years with his saints in fulfilment of Daniel 7 (Rev. 20:4–6), and the beasts whose lives were prolonged after their dominion was removed (Dan. 7:12) will join Satan's final failed putsch (Rev. 20:7–10). Then follows the great white throne judgment (Rev. 20:11–15) when 'those who sleep in the dust of the earth shall awake, some to everlasting life, and some to shame and everlasting contempt' (Dan. 12:2).

Conclusion

In this chapter and the previous one we have seen agreement on the sequence of events at the consummation of history. This agreement between the teaching of Jesus in the Olivet Discourse as presented by Matthew and Mark, Paul's teaching to the Thessalonians, and John's vision in the Apocalypse reflects a common understanding of what Daniel prophesied. The wars and rumours of wars that characterize history will continue (Dan. 11; Matt. 24:6; Rev. 6) until the rise of the one who is the Abomination of Desolation, who functions as a signal

[7] The sequence of events in Rev. 20 – 22 matches the sequence of events in Ezek. 37 – 48 as follows: resurrection of God's people (Ezek. 37:1–14; Rev. 20:4–6); Christ's reign over the land restored from war (Ezek. 37:24; 38:8, 11; Rev. 20:4–6); satanic attack by Gog of Magog (Ezek. 38:1–4, 8, 11; Rev. 20:7–8); defeat of Gog and Satan (Ezek. 38:16 – 39:24; Rev. 20:9–10); new heaven and new earth presented as a cosmic temple (Ezek. 40 – 48; Rev. 21 – 22).

for the people of God to flee (Matt. 24:15–16; Mark 13:14). He will make war on the saints and kill them (Dan. 7:21; Rev. 11:7; 13:7), as he initiates the great tribulation (Dan. 12:1; Matt. 24:21; Rev. 7:14), a time cut short (Matt. 24:22) by the coming of Christ who defeats the enemy (2 Thess. 2:8; Rev. 19; cf. Dan. 7:11, 22, 26; Matt. 24:29–30). The Son of Man then receives everlasting dominion in a kingdom with no end (Dan. 7:14; Rev. 11:15).

Chapter Ten

Typological patterns: Daniel in biblical theology

To this point we have seen a number of typological correspondences:

- The sojourn in Egypt corresponds to the exile to and sojourn in Babylon.
- The exodus from Egypt corresponds to the new exodus and return from exile.
- The filling up of Amorite iniquity followed by Israel's conquest of the land (Gen. 15:16) corresponds to the filling up of iniquity followed by a new conquest and final consummation (Dan. 8:23; 9:24).
- The pattern of suffering followed by exaltation is set forth repeatedly, in Daniel 1, 3, 5 – 7, 11 – 12.
- The little horn from the third kingdom (Antiochus Epiphanes, Dan. 8, 11) corresponds to the little horn from the fourth kingdom (Antichrist, Dan. 7, 9).
- The attacks on the sanctuary by Nebuchadnezzar (Dan. 1) and Antiochus (Dan. 8, 11) correspond to the final attack on the city and sanctuary (Dan. 9:26).
- The pattern of Nebuchadnezzar's demand to worship an image under threat of death in Daniel 3 corresponds to the same in Revelation 13.
- Daniel being sentenced to death, put in a stone-sealed pit, from which he rises, corresponds to what happened to Jesus.

This chapter will not revisit these typological patterns but suggests an interpretation of the broadly recognized correspondence between Joseph and Daniel. Wesselius (2001: 308) has written:

> The figure of Daniel has often been compared with that of Joseph: a 'son of Israel' who was forcibly taken from his country and came to live at a foreign court as a powerful and respected courtier. It has also been shown that the book of Daniel appears to derive certain elements straight from the story of Joseph in Genesis 37 – 50.

While the similarities between Joseph and Daniel (catalogued in table 10.1 on pp. 230–231 below) are often noted, the broader significance of these correspondences are seldom discussed. Why would the authors of Daniel, Nehemiah (see below) and Esther (see below) have noticed and included these similarities with Joseph? Was there an unstated assumption that informed this practice, something that would have been enough of a commonplace to be assumed by the authors of these later biblical books? Such an assumption would have to consist of a shared understanding the biblical authors were able to take for granted their audiences would recognize.

This chapter proposes an explanation of the broader typological significance of the points of contact between Joseph and Daniel. If correct, this explanation can also be applied to correspondences between Joseph and other figures, such as Nehemiah, Esther and Mordecai. If the authors of Daniel, Nehemiah and Esther meant to communicate hope to their audiences merely by drawing attention to correspondences with Joseph, those correspondences would seem to have been intended to imply future deliverance. But how did the logic work? If we can answer that question, it might also shed light on why the lifting up of Jehoiachin signals a bright future for Israel at the end of 2 Kings and Jeremiah (2 Kgs 25:27–30; Jer. 52:31–34). Like the similarities with Joseph, the lifting up of Jehoiachin is often taken as a positive sign, but how and why this should give hope is not often addressed.

What did the later biblical authors assume an allusion to Joseph would communicate that would make sense of the way they notice and include parallels with Joseph?

A promise-shaped paradigm

Joseph seems to be conceived as part of a pattern, a pattern significant before and after the accounts of Joseph in Genesis, and to call one piece of the pattern to mind was to invoke the whole. Imagine a well-known tune. In my own context, the tune to 'Amazing Grace' is so pervasive as to be recognizable to believers and unbelievers alike. Play the first two notes of the song, or sing its first two syllables, and even if the music stops at that point the song will continue in the minds of many. Play the first few measures together and the melody will be embedded, to be hummed, sung or whistled to the heart's content. What if the promise-shaped paradigm of which Joseph was a part functioned precisely this way? Mention of Joseph sold into slavery and then exalted over Egypt would be like striking the first few notes of Amazing Grace, a sweet sound that will have wayfarers whistling the rest as they await fulfilment.

For a whole song to be evoked by a few notes requires a well-known tune. For a whole narrative to be evoked likewise requires prominent placement of the significant sequence of events. An obscure, unknown song does not float on the surface of one's consciousness. For a few notes to have everyone humming a tune, the song has to have pervaded the cultural mind, and this holds also for this suggestion about the promise-shaped paradigm of which Joseph was a part.

Was the Joseph narrative that influential? The Pentateuchal narratives were intended to build the thought world and shape the cultural mindset of ancient Israel.[1] The Joseph narrative functions as the prologue to the exodus, the definitive set of events through which God saved his people, created them as a nation at Sinai, and brought them to the land of promise.

The exodus pattern was prefigured in the Genesis narratives concerning Abraham, hinted at when the story shifted to Isaac; then re-presented with variations in the accounts of Jacob. The patriarchs foreshadow the pattern, and the pattern itself is presented in the narratives that begin with Joseph and continue through the exodus to Sinai, wilderness, and on to conquest. The Joseph-to-conquest pattern was like a melody played so often that sounding its first few notes would have everyone singing the song.

What were the movements in the melody? Joseph was sold as a slave in Egypt, and then unexpectedly exalted, such that Pharaoh was only greater with respect to the throne (Gen. 41:40); his brothers and father Jacob followed Joseph into Egypt, where generations later their descendants were oppressed and enslaved, from which Yahweh delivered them at the exodus, entering into covenant with them at Sinai, and then leading them through the wilderness to the land of promise, which they conquered. This broad pattern became the paradigm Israel's prophets used to predict the future, as they promised that Yahweh would deliver them in the future as he had in the past. This was also the song of the psalmists, who retold Israel's history to shape and form the hopes of God's people for the future (Wenham 2012).

---

[1] See Wenham's summary of the work of David Carr (2005) and Paul Griffiths (1999), showing that the goal of ancient Near Eastern education was the memorization of the classic texts, and that this served the purpose of enculturation, transmitting values to future generations (2012: 42–56).

From the way that later authors reference the Torah, it appears that the Pentateuchal narratives so pervaded their thought world that when they wanted to evoke something like the Joseph-to-conquest pattern, they did not need to spell it out explicitly. They could allude to aspects of it, using the literary equivalent of a shrug of the shoulder, a raised eyebrow or an inclination of the head, and, having given the signal, they could trust that the paradigm was so well ensconced that their audiences would get the message. Thus, to suggest a correspondence between Joseph and Daniel was to activate in the imagination the whole paradigm that culminated in exodus and conquest. If Daniel was a new Joseph, following on his heels would be (after perhaps a new Egyptian oppression/enslavement) a new exodus led by a new Moses who would mediate a new covenant for the enjoyment of a new Eden conquered by a new Joshua replete with the reign of a new David.

The same paradigm would explain the correspondences between Joseph and Nehemiah, Joseph and Esther, and perhaps even Joseph and Jehoiachin. The multiple instances of a typological pattern pose no problem, as repetitions add to the impression that this is the kind of thing God does for his people. Each instalment in the pattern builds escalating anticipation. There is not just *one* exodus and *one* new exodus: there are previews of the exodus (see below on Abraham); then the exodus itself; then a number of instalments in the exodus pattern.[2] There are correspondences between the exodus from Egypt and the return from exile in Ezra 1 – 6, and the same holds for the return in Ezra 7 – 8.[3] Then the death and resurrection of Jesus is presented in exodus/Passover terms, and the pattern comes to catastasis when the exodus imagery is used again in the book of Revelation.

Sheshbazzar's return is a new exodus (Ezra 1 – 6); Ezra's return is a new exodus (Ezra 7 – 10); Jesus fulfils the pattern as the new Passover lamb of the new exodus (1 Cor. 5:7; cf. Jer. 16:14–15); and the trumpet and bowl plagues of Revelation 8 – 9 and 15 – 16 bring about the final, culminating installation in the new exodus pattern. The same dynamic would seem to be at work in the series of new Josephs we have in Daniel, Nehemiah, Esther, Mordecai, and then the pattern culminates with a final Joseph who goes to Egypt, another son of Jacob, this one husband of Mary (Matt. 1:16).

---

[2] David interprets his deliverance from Saul in Ps. 18 as his own personal exodus deliverance (see Hamilton 2014c: 82–85).

[3] For more on these themes, see my exposition of Ezra and Nehemiah (Hamilton 2014a).

To highlight correspondences between Joseph and Daniel was to fuel the flames of Israel's expectation. To invoke Joseph was to invoke the paradigm of which Joseph was a part, a paradigm that proceeded to the exodus, the Sinai covenant and the conquest of Canaan, and to invoke that procession was to point to the new exodus, the new covenant and the new conquest of the new Eden. Pointing to an Israelite figure with characteristics reminiscent of Joseph meant drawing attention to the Lord setting events in motion to bring about the fulfilment of his promises.

To demonstrate these claims, or at least to establish their plausibility, we will briefly consider the way the exodus was foreshadowed in the lives of Abraham and Isaac, with the exile and return likewise prefigured in the life of Jacob. From these narratives that precede Joseph we will turn to consider the way that Israel's history was retold with an eye to the future in Psalms 104 – 106. All of this is meant to substantiate the claim that the backstory informed biblical authors from Moses to Daniel, allowing them to rely on subtle, allusive indicators that were like power switches turning on the electric current that caused Old Testament expectation to throb and surge with life. With the power lines in place, we will set forth the parallels between Joseph and Daniel, hoping for the lights to come on, and that they will in turn illuminate our understanding of Nehemiah, Esther and Jehoiachin.

Abraham

The approach to typology I am advocating here is rooted firmly in the soil of authorial intent. The idea is that having experienced the exodus from Egypt and the Sinai covenant, Moses noticed similar events in the traditions he had received about Abraham. Understanding the significance of the parallels, Moses chose to include them; then framed and presented them to highlight the ways that Abraham's experience foreshadowed the exodus from Egypt. The parallels are as follows: as Jacob and his sons would do later (Gen. 41:54; 42:1; 46:1–3), Abram went down to Egypt because of a famine in the Promised Land (12:10). Having been in Egypt for some time, the children of Israel were oppressed and enslaved (Exod. 1:8–14), and, on Abram's arrival in Egypt, Pharaoh seized Sarai (Gen. 12:14–15). Yahweh visited plagues on Egypt to set Israel free (Exod. 7 – 12), and Yahweh visited plagues on Pharaoh to liberate Sarai (Gen. 12:17–20). Israel plundered Egypt (Exod. 11:2–3; 12:35–36), and Abram was enriched by Pharaoh (Gen. 12:16). Both Abram and Israel left Egypt for the land of promise, and both Abram and Israel experienced Yahweh initiating a covenant after saying, 'I am Yahweh who brought you out . . .' (Gen. 15:7; Exod. 20:1, adapted ESV) as he appeared in flame and smoke and thick darkness (Gen. 15:12, 17; Exod. 19:16–18). Yahweh initiated covenants between himself and both Abraham and Israel, and the covenants were inaugurated with sacrifices (Gen. 15:9–10, 17; Exod. 24:1–8). In that Genesis 15 context, so portentous of Israel's exodus from Egypt and experience at Sinai, Yahweh announced to Abram that his descendants would sojourn and serve in a land not their own, essentially predicting Israel's future oppression in and exodus from Egypt (15:13–16).

Some of these parallels are not exact matches. For instance, the oppression and enslavement of the nation differs somewhat from Pharaoh's seizure of Sarai. Nor is the order of events exactly the same, as Pharaoh gave gifts to Abram prior to the plagues, whereas the Israelites plundered Egypt before the final plague. These differences are not major, however, and they fit with the idea that *historical* correspondences are being recorded as opposed to literary parallels being contrived. That is to say, Moses and other biblical authors are not inventing similarities but noticing actual historical parallels which they take pains to include.[4]

As if to reiterate the significance of the account of Pharaoh seizing Sarah, a similar incident is recorded in Genesis 20:1–18; then again with Isaac there is an instalment in this pattern of events in Genesis 26:1–16. The fact that the Genesis 20 and 26 instances deal with Philistines rather than Egyptians unifies Israel's future enemies, who are presented doing the same thing in the same way to endanger the descent of the promised seed (cf. Exod. 1:15–22). The similarities between these accounts draw audience attention, and, as in Genesis 12, in Genesis 26 Isaac relocates because of a famine (Gen. 26:1), but he is told not to go to Egypt as Abraham did (26:2). These similarities prompt comparison and consideration, and later narratives will clarify their significance.

In chapter 7 above we noted briefly that Hosea 12:2–13 treats Jacob's journey to Laban's land (Gen. 28 – 29) as paradigmatic of the nation of Israel's exile to Babylon and return to the land. Significantly, Hosea brings Moses into his discussion of Jacob. Hosea references Jacob in 12:12:

---

[4] Contra the general approach of Wills (1990) and others.

> Jacob fled to the land of Aram;
> there Israel served for a wife,
> and for a wife he guarded sheep.

Then Hosea references Moses in 12:13:

> By a prophet the LORD brought Israel up from Egypt,
> and by a prophet he was guarded.

The juxtaposition of these two statements seems to communicate, again, the parallel between Jacob's sojourn in the east and Israel's sojourn in Babylon in Hosea 12:12. Then the reference to Moses bringing Israel out of Egypt in 12:13 recalls the exodus from Egypt in the context of Israel's exile to Babylon. As Israel was brought out of Egypt by a prophet, Israel will be brought out of exile by a prophet. I reference this here because of the connection that Hosea seems to have seen between the events of Jacob's life and the future of Israel's history.

Could it have been the case that simply by showing parallels between himself and Joseph, Daniel was presenting his understanding of himself as a new Joseph preparing the way for a new exodus? This explanation would seem at least plausible. The significance of the exodus narrative has been seen from the parallels between the exodus and Abraham's journey to and from Egypt in Genesis 12, reinforced by the similarity between the Genesis 12 narrative and those in Genesis 20 and 26. Moreover, connections between the exodus from Egypt and the new exodus and return from exile pervade the prophets. Hosea even makes such connections from the narratives of Jacob going to Laban for a wife.

Moses cannot have missed the similarity between Abraham in Genesis 12 and the exodus from Egypt, and I would argue that he chose to include the details, particularly Yahweh's words in Genesis 15:7 and Exodus 20:2, 'I am Yahweh who brought you out' (adapted ESV), to make sure that his audience would note the historical correspondence between the two events. The whole sequence of events that followed, the Joseph-to-conquest narrative, became paradigmatic for the prophets who proclaimed a new exodus and return from exile.

This sequence also informs the Psalms, not least the end of Book 4. The biblical authors do not idly retell stories from Israel's past. When the psalmists rehearse what God has done for them in the past, they do so to shape the expectation that God will act the same way in the future.

Psalms

When the book of Psalms is read not merely as a random collection of isolated poems but as a united whole, an impressionistic storyline can be discerned (see e.g. Hossfeld and Zenger 2005; 2011; and Wenham 2013: 57–79). The Psalms are presented in five books and, broadly speaking, Books 1 (Pss 1 – 41) and 2 (Pss 42 – 72) sing the life of David, with Book 3 (Pss 73 – 89) going from David to the exile. Book 4 (Pss 90 – 106) is a call to return to the Torah of Moses and seek the Lord while in exile, and Book 5 (Pss 107 – 150) hymns the triumph of the new and better David, whose victory (Ps. 110) opens the way for the new exodus and return from exile.[5]

The events of the exodus from Egypt were rehearsed in the Psalms to form a remnant in Israel that would look for God to save them in the future the way he had in the past. Gordon Wenham describes the way 'a memorized text has a peculiarly character-forming effect on the memorizer. The text becomes part of his character; he lives in it and lives it out' (2012: 53). Worshippers enculturated by the Psalms would live in the scenes sung in the book's poetry.

Book 4 of the psalter concludes with a historical review that begins at creation (Ps. 104), moves to the promise to Abraham (105:9), and then rehearses how when the Lord

> broke all supply of bread,
> he had sent a man ahead of them,
> Joseph, who was sold as a slave.
> (105:16–17)

These statements interpret Joseph's entrance into and exaltation over Egypt (105:18–22) as preparing the way for the patriarchs, who sojourned in Egypt (105:23). There the Lord multiplied the nation (105:24), which led to their oppression (105:25). Then God raised up Moses, visited the plagues and brought Israel out (105:26–38). Psalm 106 recounts how Israel rebelled and was exiled from the land (106:6–46), in response to which the psalmist calls on the Lord to save his people and gather them from the nations (106:47).

The cry at the end of Psalm 106 for God to save his people and gather them from the nations (Ps. 106:47) finds its answer in the song

---

[5] My exposition of this trajectory (for which, see further 2010b: 275–290) has been significantly influenced by Wenham's work (2012; 2013).

of the redeemed who have been gathered from east, west, north and south in Psalm 107:2–3. The psalmists invite their audiences, who sang, prayed and lived in the Psalms, to identify with and adopt the psalmists' own perspective.[6] If the psalmists expected God's salvation in the future to match the paradigm of God's salvation in the past, that paradigm included Joseph being sent ahead of his brothers into Egypt, preparing the way for them from his exalted position. After Joseph came the exodus.

The parallels between Joseph and Daniel were significant because of what they implied, which included Daniel's ability to intercede for his kinsmen from his exalted position, as well as the hoped for new exodus that would come after the new Joseph. The parallels between Joseph and Daniel deserve consideration.

Joseph and Daniel

The raw material of the correspondences between Joseph and Daniel are as shown in table 10.1.

Because of the number of and level of detail in these parallels, they cannot be regarded as accidental. Later biblical authors like Daniel were evidently familiar with the Scriptures available to them, and they apparently interpreted their own lives in the light of the Scriptures. Knowing the Joseph story, Daniel noticed the similarities and found the details worth recording.

We should not find this surprising. People generally tend to interpret the present in the light of the past. As I type these words, Barack Obama is the President of the United States of America, and, as with all politicians, he is regularly compared to those who held that office before him. Those who appreciate his agenda compare Obama to Franklin Delano Roosevelt, referring to the way that Obama carries forward the vision and accomplishments of FDR. Those who do not appreciate Obama have said he is a new Jimmy Carter, whom they view as an ineffectual failure. Politics are not my concern here; the point is that the past is regularly used to supply the categories with which we describe and interpret the present. Daniel seems to have done the same, and the Joseph narratives were particularly

---

[6] Wenham discusses several devices the psalmists employed to invite 'the worshiper to identify with the sentiments of the psalm', and these include the blessings and curses pronounced, the use of the first person, the presentation of God's point of view, and the gaps 'that the reader has to fill in from personal imagination to make sense of the passage' (2012: 59–62).

Table 10.1 Correspondences between Joseph and Daniel

Joseph	Daniel
Joseph was sold to Potiphar, the 'captain of the guard', a phrase that could be rendered literally 'chief slaughterer' (Gen. 37:36, Hebr. שר הטבחים, *śar haṭṭabāḥîm*).	When Daniel was about to be slain with the wise men of Babylon (2:13), he appealed to the 'captain of the guard', that is, the 'chief slaughterer' (Dan. 2:14, Aram. רב־טבחיא, *rab-ṭabāḥayyā'*).
Joseph was 'handsome in form and appearance' (Gen. 39:6).	Daniel and the other young men were 'of good appearance' (Dan. 1:4).
'And Joseph said to them, "Do not interpretations belong to God?"' (Gen. 40:8).	'but there is a God in heaven who reveals mysteries' (Dan. 2:28).
'Then Joseph said to him, "This is its interpretation"' (Gen. 40:12).	'This was the dream. Now we will tell the king its interpretation' (Dan. 2:36).
After Pharaoh's dream, 'his spirit was troubled, and he sent and called for all the magicians of Egypt and all its wise men. Pharaoh told them his dreams, but there was none who could interpret them to Pharaoh' (Gen. 41:8).	After Nebuchadnezzar's dream, 'his spirit was troubled . . . Then the king commanded that the magicians, the enchanters, the sorcerers, and the Chaldeans be summoned to tell the king his dreams. . . . The Chaldeans answered the king and said, "There is not a man on earth who can meet the king's demand . . . no one can show it to the king except the gods"' (Dan. 2:1–3, 10–11; cf. 4:4–7).
When it was made known that Joseph could interpret the dream, 'Pharaoh sent and called Joseph, and they quickly brought him out of the pit' (Gen. 41:14).	When Daniel announced that he could interpret the dream, 'Arioch brought in Daniel before the king in haste' (Dan. 2:25).
'I have heard it said of you that when you hear a dream you can interpret it' (Gen. 41:15).	'I have heard that you can give interpretations and solve problems' (Dan. 5:16).
'Joseph answered Pharaoh, "It is not in me; God will give Pharaoh a favourable answer"' (Gen. 41:16).	'But as for me, this mystery has been revealed to me, not because of any wisdom that I have more than all the living, but in order that the interpretation may be made known to the king' (Dan. 2:30).
'And I told it to the magicians, but there was no one who could explain it to me' (Gen. 41:24).	'Then the magicians, the enchanters, the Chaldeans, and the astrologers came in, and I told them the dream, but they could not make known to me its interpretation' (Dan. 4:7).
'God has revealed to Pharaoh what he is about to do . . . God has shown to Pharaoh what he is about to do . . . the doubling of Pharaoh's dream means that the thing is fixed by God, and God will shortly bring it about' (Gen. 41:25, 28, 32).	'there is a God . . . and he has made known to King Nebuchadnezzar what will be in the latter days . . . thoughts of what would be after this, and he who reveals mysteries made known to you what is to be' (Dan. 2:28–29).

Joseph	Daniel
'And Pharaoh said to his servants, "Can we find a man like this, in whom is the Spirit of God?"' (Gen. 41:38).	'he who was named Belteshazzar after the name of my god, and in whom is the spirit of the holy gods' (Dan. 4:8, 18; 5:11, 14).
After Joseph interpreted Pharaoh's dream, Pharaoh made Joseph second man in Egypt, gave him his signet ring, clothed him in fine linen, and put a gold chain around his neck (Gen. 41:40–42; cf. 43–44).	'Whoever reads this writing . . . shall be clothed with purple and have a chain of gold round his neck and shall be the third ruler in the kingdom' (Dan. 5:7; cf. 2:48; 5:29; 6:3).
'Joseph . . . stood before the king' (Gen. 41:46, adapted ESV).	'Daniel, Hananiah, Mishael, and Azariah . . . they stood before the king' (Dan. 1:19).

significant to his interpretation and presentation of the events of his own experience.[7]

The comparisons with Joseph are not mere curiosities. Moses had prophesied that Yahweh would restore his people after judging them (e.g. Lev. 26:33–45), the latter prophets pointed to a new and better exodus (e.g. Isa. 11:15–16), and the Psalms sing Israel's history to shape her vision of the future. In this context, the idea that Daniel presented himself as a new Joseph because he believed himself to be the forerunner of the new exodus is right at home.

Joseph advised his brothers on how to speak to Pharaoh (Gen. 46:31–34), and then oversaw the interactions between Pharaoh and his brothers and father (47:1–12). The book of Daniel does not go into these details, but, historically speaking, he was exiled in 605 BC (Dan. 1:1) and exalted over the wise men of Babylon three years later, with his three friends also receiving appointments to significant posts (2:1, 48–49). This would mean that when other Jews were deported to Babylon in 597 and 586 BC, they would enter a land where a man had been sent ahead of them, a brother Israelite able to intercede with the king on their behalf and oversee any interactions with him, just as Joseph had done with Pharaoh. Daniel was well known enough to be referenced at several points by his contemporary, Ezekiel (Ezek. 14:14, 20; 28:3).

The book of Daniel also tells us that Daniel continued until the third year of Cyrus (Dan. 10:1). This the Cyrus prophesied in Isaiah

---

[7] Cf. what Christopher T. Begg writes of Josephus: 'I wish to pursue the hunch that Josephus recognized in Daniel a Biblical precedent/warrant for his own conflicted life-course. . . . In other words, Josephus, I will suggest, not only worked over Scripture's portrayal of Daniel with his own career in view, but also recounted the latter with an eye to the former. Such a "typological" approach to Josephus's material is, of course, not original to me . . .' (1993: 540).

44:28 – 45:1, the Cyrus who issued a decree in his first year that the Jews could return to their land and take with them the temple vessels plundered by Nebuchadnezzar (Ezra 1:1–11). Neither Daniel nor Ezra comments on Daniel's role in that decree, but some scholars suggest that Cyrus and Darius are the same person (cf. Dan. 6:28; see Lucas 2002: 136–137; Steinmann 2008: 293–296), and when Darius came to power Daniel was one of the top three officials over the 120 satraps over the kingdom (Dan. 6:1–3). Again, the book of Daniel does not comment on these realities, but it seems that just when he was at the right hand of the king, the king decided that Daniel's people could return to their homeland and take the plundered temple vessels with them. This is reminiscent of the way shepherds abhorrent to the Egyptians were allotted the best pastureland in Egypt (Gen. 46:34; 47:6).

Jehoiachin, Esther and Nehemiah

Joseph was sent ahead of his brothers to prepare their way into Egypt, where they sojourned before the exodus (Ps. 105:17). When Israel was sent into exile in Babylon, a new Joseph was sent ahead of them to prepare their way, to set them up for the new exodus and return from exile. That new Joseph's name was Daniel, one of the first carried off to exile in 605 BC. Daniel was still there when Cyrus issued the decree that those who wished could return to the land and take the temple vessels with them (Ezra 1).

Meanwhile, Jeremiah was prophesying that those who surrendered to Nebuchadnezzar would have their lives as a prize of war, and those who resisted would die 'by the sword, by famine, and by pestilence' (Jer. 21:9–10). The book of Kings does not specify that Jehoiachin was obeying Jeremiah, but 'Jehoiachin the king of Judah gave himself up to the king of Babylon . . . The king of Babylon took him prisoner in the eighth year of his reign' (2 Kgs 24:12). After this episode around 597 BC, we read that Jehoiachin was exalted 'in the thirty-seventh year of' (c.560 BC) his exile (2 Kgs 25:27). Like Joseph, Jehoiachin was carried to a foreign land, imprisoned there, and then brought out of prison by the king, who gave him new clothes and an exalted seat (2 Kgs 25:27–30; Jer. 52:31–34). Once again, while nothing is said of this event in the book of Daniel, nor is Daniel mentioned in the narrative of Kings, Daniel was known at court when Evil-Merodach of Babylon, son of Nebuchadnezzar whose dreams Daniel had interpreted, freed the king of Daniel's people.

A few years later (c.480 BC) there were two figures in the Persian court, Esther and Mordecai, each of whom played a Joseph-like role, doing their part to save Israel from an attempted genocide. Like Joseph, Esther was virtually a slave in a foreign land. Like Joseph, she was 'handsome in form and appearance' (cf. Gen. 39:6 and Esth. 2:7). Like Joseph, Esther was cleaned up and presented to the king (Esth. 2:3, 9). Like Joseph, Esther found favour in the king's sight (2:17). The wording of her resolution to intercede on behalf of her people was reminiscent of Israel's words (cf. Esth. 4:16 and Gen. 43:14), probably reflecting her knowledge of the narratives. As Joseph did, Esther made requests of the king that benefited her kinsmen, even delivering the Jewish people from murderous opposition (Esth. 7:3). There are also ways in which Mordecai corresponds to Joseph: like Joseph, Mordecai was rewarded by the king with new raiment and honoured to ride in royal style with a herald before him (Esth. 6:7–11; cf. Gen. 41:42–43). Like Joseph, Esther and Mordecai were Jews in a foreign land who rose to positions of power under the king.

Later still (c.445 BC), Nehemiah was cupbearer to the king of Persia. Like Joseph, Daniel, Jehoiachin, Esther and Mordecai, Nehemiah was a Jew in a foreign land with access to the king. Like Daniel, Nehemiah was concerned for the state of the land of promise, and Nehemiah quoted Daniel's prayer of repentance (Dan. 9:4) in his own (Neh. 1:5; cf. 1:6–7). Like Joseph, Daniel and Esther, Nehemiah made requests of the king that benefited the Jews and their land. As with the opposition faced by Joseph, Daniel, Esther and Mordecai, the opposition to Nehemiah was opposition to God and his programme (e.g. Neh. 4:1–3; 6:1–14).

As with the hardening of the heart of Pharaoh and the plundering of the Egyptians for the building of the temple, God stirred up the spirit of Cyrus, and the people of Israel rebuilt the temple and the walls of Jerusalem with foreign funds (Ezra 1 – 6; 6:4; Neh. 2:7–8). As Joseph prepared the way for his brothers in Egypt, Daniel prepared their way in Babylon, along with Jehoiachin, Esther and Mordecai, and Nehemiah.

Ezra 6:14 speaks of the temple being completed by God's decree through the decrees of human kings: Cyrus, who allowed the return to the land *circa* 538 BC; Darius, who stopped the opposition to the rebuilding of the temple *circa* 516 BC; and Artaxerxes, who sent Ezra back to the land to rebuild the people (458 BC) and Nehemiah back to rebuild the walls (445 BC). In the same way that the several decrees across nearly a century can be viewed as one decree from God for the restoration of temple and land in Ezra 6:14, so also several figures played the role of new Joseph to new exodus style deliverances.

These all played their part, pointing forward to what would take place when God would deliver his people not from physical slavery or exile but from slavery to sin and exile from his presence. That deliverance was typified by these figures as well.

Fulfilment in Christ

The new exodus for which Daniel was a forerunner was anticipated but not fulfilled by the people's return to the land to rebuild city and wall. The fulfilment of the new exodus would await the one whose death and resurrection liberates people from sin and sets in motion the building of the city that has foundations, whose architect and builder is God (Heb. 11:10). That city will descend from heaven, having the proportional dimensions of the holy of holies: the new heaven and new earth (Rev. 21:1, 10, 16).

Joseph, Daniel, Jehoiachin, Esther and Mordecai, and Nehemiah all played their parts in a wider pattern that was ultimately fulfilled in Jesus, the new-exodus pattern that provides the conceptual and theological framework used by the New Testament authors to communicate how God has accomplished his 'plan for the fullness of time, to unite all things in him, things in heaven and things on earth' (Eph. 1:10).

In addition to the role these individuals played in the broader pattern that was fulfilled in Christ, we also see ways that their lives typified the one to come. Nehemiah cleansed the temple (Neh. 13:8), as Jesus would later (e.g. Matt. 21:12–17). Esther interceded for the lives of her people, and succeeded, having called for a fast when nothing would be eaten for 'three days, night or day' (Esth. 4:16), and then going before the king 'on the third day' (5:1; cf. 1 Cor. 15:4).[8] We have seen how Daniel was brought out of the stone-sealed pit of the lion's den, from which no one was expected to rise (Dan. 6), and Joseph too was brought out of the pit (Gen. 37:28).

Nehemiah anticipated the one who would cleanse the temple, Esther the one who would intercede on the third day, and both Joseph and

---

[8] Other significant third days include the one on which Abraham was to sacrifice Isaac (Gen. 22:4), the one on which Israel entered into covenant with Yahweh (Exod. 19:11), the one on which Israel crossed the Jordan (Josh. 3:2), the one on which Hezekiah was raised up to worship (2 Kgs 22:1–5), and the one of which Hosea spoke (Hos. 6:2). Cf. also Jonah's experience (Jon. 1:17), and the way Jesus referenced that (Matt. 12:40).

Daniel pointed forward to the one who would rise from the dead to give life to his people.

Conclusion

The book of Daniel contributes to the Bible's unfolding redemptive-historical storyline. Like a plug in an outlet, the book joins itself to the Bible's broader narrative, and, as the currents course through, the light of revelation shines on the way things will go until God brings about the promised consummation (see chapter 2). The literary structure of the book of Daniel (chapter 3) demonstrates that the biblical authors used wide-angle strategies to communicate (cf. chapter 9). The books of the Bible are like cathedrals, with architectural features that repay close examination. The four kingdoms prophesied by Daniel (chapter 4) are both historical and symbolic: historical in that they match the kingdoms between Daniel and the first coming of Christ, and symbolic in that they encapsulate the tendencies and characteristics of the kingdoms of the world, which will continue until the kingdom of the world becomes the kingdom of our Lord and of his Christ. Daniel's seventy-week prophecy (chapter 5) informs John, who interprets Daniel's seventieth week as the inter-advent period (chapter 9). The one like a son of man seen by Daniel (chapter 6) is identified with and distinguished from the Ancient of Days in a way that would be mysterious until Jesus came as *both* son of David *and* the incarnation of Yahweh. The interpretations of Daniel in early Jewish literature (chapter 7) attest historical, typological and eschatological interpretative strategies similar to those employed by the authors of the New Testament. The New Testament authors (chapter 8) provide a Spirit-inspired interpretation of Daniel that was learned from Jesus, and in Revelation (chapter 9) John uses Daniel's language, imitates his structure, points to the fulfilment of his prophecies and clarifies the meaning of his seventieth week. When we consider broader biblical-theological and typological structures (chapter 10), we see that Daniel seems to have seen himself as a new Joseph, forerunner of the new exodus.

God accomplished the anticipated new exodus salvation through the death and resurrection of Jesus, and he will yet once more shake the heavens and the earth as he did at Sinai. Then the kingdom that cannot be shaken (cf. Heb. 12:26–28) will fill the earth, and the knowledge of the glory of the Lord will cover the dry lands as the waters cover the sea.

Bibliography

Alexander, T. Desmond (2008), *From Eden to the New Jerusalem: Exploring God's Plan for Life on Earth*, Nottingham: Inter-Varsity Press.

Auerbach, Erich (1953), *Mimesis: The Representation of Reality in Western Literature*, Princeton: Princeton University Press.

Baldwin, Joyce G. (1978), *Daniel: An Introduction and Commentary*, TOTC, Leicester: Inter-Varsity Press; Downers Grove: InterVarsity Press.

Bauckham, Richard (1993), *The Theology of the Book of Revelation*, NTT, New York: Cambridge University Press.

—— (2007), 'The "Most High" God and the Nature of Early Jewish Monotheism', in David B. Capes, April D. DeConick, Helen K. Bond and Troy A. Miller (eds.) *Israel's God and Rebecca's Children: Christology and Community in Early Judaism and Christianity*, 39–53, 378–386, Waco: Baylor University Press.

—— (2009), *Jesus and the God of Israel: God Crucified and Other Studies on the New Testament's Christology of Divine Identity*, Grand Rapids: Eerdmans.

Beale, G. K. (1984), *The Use of Daniel in Jewish Apocalyptic Literature and in the Revelation of St. John*, Lanham: University Press of America.

—— (1994), 'Did Jesus and His Followers Preach the Right Doctrine from the Wrong Texts? An Examination of the Presuppositions of Jesus' and the Apostles' Exegetical Method', in G. K. Beale (ed.), *The Right Doctrine from the Wrong Texts? Essays on the Use of the Old Testament in the New*, Grand Rapids: Baker, 387–404.

—— (1998), *John's Use of the Old Testament in Revelation*, JSNTSup, Sheffield: Sheffield Academic Press.

—— (1999), *The Book of Revelation: A Commentary on the Greek Text*, NIGTC, Grand Rapids: Eerdmans.

—— (2003), *1–2 Thessalonians*, Downers Grove: InterVarsity Press.

—— (2004), *The Temple and the Church's Mission: A Biblical Theology of the Dwelling Place of God*, Leicester: Apollos; Downers Grove: InterVarsity Press.

—— (2008), *We Become What We Worship: A Biblical Theology of Idolatry*, Downers Grove: InterVarsity Press; Nottingham: Apollos.

—— (2012), *Handbook on the New Testament Use of the Old Testament: Exegesis and Interpretation*, Grand Rapids: Baker.

Beale, G. K., and D. A. Carson (eds.) (2007), *Commentary on the New Testament Use of the Old Testament*, Grand Rapids: Baker; Nottingham: Apollos.

Beale, G. K., and Sean M. McDonough (2007), 'Revelation', in G. K. Beale and D. A. Carson (eds.), *Commentary on the New Testament Use of the Old Testament*, Grand Rapids: Baker; Nottingham: Apollos, 1081–1161.

Beckwith, Roger T. (1981), 'Daniel 9 and the Date of Messiah's Coming in Essene, Hellenistic, Pharisaic, Zealot and Early Christian Computation', *RevQ* 10.4: 521–542.

—— (1985), *The Old Testament Canon of the New Testament Church and Its Background in Early Judaism*, Grand Rapids: Eerdmans.

—— (1996), *Calendar and Chronology, Jewish and Christian: Biblical, Intertestamental and Patristic Studies*, AGAJU, Leiden: Brill.

—— (2002), 'Early Traces of the Book of Daniel', *TynB* 53: 75–82.

Begg, Christopher T. (1993), 'Daniel and Josephus: Tracing Connections', in A. S. van der Woude (ed.), *The Book of Daniel in the Light of New Findings*, Leuven: Leuven University Press, 539–545.

Blomberg, Craig L. (2007), 'Matthew', in G. K. Beale and D. A. Carson (eds.), *Commentary on the New Testament Use of the Old Testament*, Grand Rapids: Baker; Nottingham: Apollos, 1–109.

Bray, Gerald (2012), *God Is Love: A Biblical and Systematic Theology*, Wheaton: Crossway.

Capes, David, April D., DeConick, Helen K. Bond and Troy A. Miller (eds.) (2007), *Israel's God and Rebecca's Children: Christology and Community in Early Judaism and Christianity: Essays in Honor of Larry W. Hurtado and Alan F. Segal*, Waco: Baylor University Press.

Caragounis, Chrys (1977), *The Ephesian 'Mysterion': Meaning and Content*, ConBOT, Lund: CWK Gleerup.

—— (1986), *The Son of Man: Vision and Interpretation*, Tübingen: Mohr Siebeck.

Carr, David M. (2005), *Writing on the Tablet of the Heart: Origins of Scripture and Literature*, New York: Oxford University Press.

Carrell, Peter R. (1997), *Jesus and the Angels: Angelology and the Christology of the Apocalypse of John*, New York: Cambridge University Press.

Carson, D. A., and Douglas J. Moo (2005), *An Introduction to the New Testament*, 2nd ed., Grand Rapids: Zondervan.

Charlesworth, James H. (ed.) (1983), *The Old Testament Pseudepigrapha*, 2 vols., Garden City: Doubleday.

Chase, Mitchell L. (2013), 'Resurrection Hope in Daniel 12:2: An Exercise in Biblical Theology', PhD diss., Louisville: Southern Baptist Theological Seminary.

Chester, Andrew (2007), *Messiah and Exaltation: Jewish Messianic and Visionary Traditions and New Testament Christology*, WUNT 207, Tübingen: Mohr Siebeck.

Ciampa, Roy E. (2007), 'The History of Redemption', in Scott J. Hafemann and Paul R. House (eds.), *Central Themes in Biblical Theology: Mapping Unity in Diversity*, Nottingham: Apollos; Grand Rapids: Baker, 254–308.

Collins, Adela Yarbro, and John J. Collins (2008), *King and Messiah as Son of God: Divine, Human, and Angelic Messianic Figures in Biblical and Related Literature*, Grand Rapids: Eerdmans.

Collins, John J. (1993), *Daniel: A Commentary on the Book of Daniel*, Hermeneia, Minneapolis: Fortress.

Davis, Dale Ralph (2013), *The Message of Daniel*, Nottingham: Inter-Varsity Press; Downers Grove: InterVarsity Press.

Delamarter, Steve (2002), *A Scripture Index to Charlesworth's The Old Testament Pseudepigrapha*, London: Sheffield Academic Press.

Dempster, Stephen G. (1997), 'An "Extraordinary Fact": Torah and Temple and the Contours of the Hebrew Canon: Parts 1 and 2', *TynB* 48: 23–56, 191–218.

——— (2003), *Dominion and Dynasty: A Biblical Theology of the Hebrew Bible*, NSBT, Leicester: Apollos; Downers Grove: InterVarsity Press.

deSilva, David A. (2002), *Introducing the Apocrypha: Message, Context, and Significance*, Grand Rapids: Baker.

Di Lella, Alexander A. (2001), 'The Textual History of Septuagint-Daniel and Theodotion-Daniel', in John J. Collins and Peter W. Flint (eds.), *The Book of Daniel: Composition and Reception*, VTSup, Leiden: Brill, 586–607.

Dimant, Devorah (1984), 'Qumran Sectarian Literature', in Michael E. Stone (ed.), *Jewish Writings of the Second Temple Period: Apocrypha, Pseudepigrapha, Qumran Sectarian Writings, Philo, Josephus*, CRINT, Philadelphia: Fortress, 483–550.

——— (2004), 'Use and Interpretation of Mikra in the Apocrypha and Pseudepigrapha', in Martin Jan Mulder and Harry Sysling (eds.), *Mikra: Text, Translation, Reading & Interpretation of the Hebrew Bible in Ancient Judaism & Early Christianity*, Peabody: Hendrickson, 379–419.

DiTommaso, Lorenzo (2005), *The Book of Daniel and the Apocryphal Daniel Literature*, Boston: Brill.

Dorsey, David A. (1999), *The Literary Structure of the Old Testament: A Commentary on Genesis–Malachi*, Grand Rapids: Baker.

Ehrman, Bart D. (2011), *Forged: Writing in the Name of God: Why the Bible's Authors Are Not Who We Think They Are*, New York: HarperOne.

——— (2012), *Forgery and Counter-Forgery: The Use of Literary Deceit in Early Christian Polemics*, New York: Oxford University Press.

Ellis, E. Earle (1982), 'Foreword', in Leonhard Goppelt (ed.), tr. Donald H. Madvig, *Typos: The Typological Interpretation of the Old Testament in the New*, Grand Rapids: Eerdmans, ix–xx.

——— (1993), 'Jesus' Use of the Old Testament and the Genesis of NTT', *BBR* 3: 59–75.

Fitzmyer, Joseph A. (1990), *The Dead Sea Scrolls: Major Publications and Tools for Study*, rev. ed., Atlanta: Scholars Press.

Flint, Peter W. (2001), 'The Daniel Tradition at Qumran', in John J. Collins and Peter W. Flint (eds.), *The Book of Daniel: Composition and Reception*, VTSup, Leiden: Brill, 329–367.

Freedman, David Noel (1991), *The Unity of the Hebrew Bible*, Ann Arbor: University of Michigan Press.

García Martínez, Florentino, and Eibert J. C. Tigchelaar (2000), *The Dead Sea Scrolls Study Edition*, Leiden: Brill.

Gentry, Peter J. (2003), 'The Son of Man in Daniel 7: Individual or Corporate?', in Michael A. G. Haykin (ed.), *Acorns to Oaks: The Primacy and Practice of Biblical Theology*, Toronto: Joshua, 59–75.

——— (2010), 'Daniel's Seventy Weeks and the New Exodus', *SBJT* 14.1: 26–44.

Gentry, Peter J., and Stephen J. Wellum (2012), *Kingdom Through Covenant: A Biblical-Theological Understanding of the Covenants*, Wheaton: Crossway.

Gieschen, Charles A. (1998), *Angelomorphic Christology: Antecedents and Early Evidence*, Boston: Brill.

Gilbert, Stuart (1959), *James Joyce's Ulysses*, New York: Vintage.

Gladd, Benjamin L. (2008), *Revealing the Mysterion: The Use of Mystery in Daniel and Second Temple Judaism with Its Bearing on First Corinthians*, Berlin: Walter de Gruyter.

Goldingay, John (1989), *Daniel*, WBC, Dallas: Word.

Goldstein, Jonathan A. (1976), *1 Maccabees*, AB, Garden City: Doubleday.

Goldsworthy, Graeme (2012), *Christ-Centered Biblical Theology: Hermeneutical Foundations and Principles*, Nottingham: Apollos; Downers Grove: InterVarsity Press.

Gooding, David W. (1981), 'The Literary Structure of the Book of Daniel and Its Implications', *TynB* 32: 43–80.

Goudoever, J. Van (1993), 'Time Indications in Daniel That Reflect the Usage of the Ancient Theoretical So-Called Zadokite Calendar', in A. S. van der Woude (ed.), *The Book of Daniel in the Light of New Findings*, Leuven: Leuven University Press, 531–538.

Greidanus, Sidney (2012), *Preaching Christ from Daniel: Foundations for Expository Sermons*, Grand Rapids: Eerdmans.

Griffiths, Paul J. (1999), *Religious Reading: The Place of Reading in the Practice of Religion*, New York: Oxford University Press.

Hamilton Jr., James M. (2006), 'The Skull Crushing Seed of the Woman: Inner-Biblical Interpretation of Genesis 3:15', *SBJT* 10.2: 30–54.

———— (2007), 'The Seed of the Woman and the Blessing of Abraham', *TynB* 58: 253–273.

———— (2008a), 'The Virgin Will Conceive: Typological Fulfillment in Matthew 1:18–23', in John Nolland and Dan Gurtner (eds.), *Built upon the Rock: Studies in the Gospel of Matthew*, Grand Rapids: Eerdmans, 228–247.

———— (2008b), 'Was Joseph a Type of the Messiah? Tracing the Typological Identification Between Joseph, David, and Jesus', *SBJT* 12: 52–77.

———— (2010a), 'Biblical Theology and Preaching', in Daniel L. Akin, David L. Allen and Ned L. Mathews (eds.), *Text-Driven Preaching: God's Word at the Heart of Every Sermon*, Nashville: Broadman & Holman, 193–218.

———— (2010b), *God's Glory in Salvation Through Judgment: A Biblical Theology*, Wheaton: Crossway.

———— (2010c), 'The Lord's Supper in Paul', in Thomas R. Schreiner and Matt Crawford (eds.), *The Lord's Supper*, NACSBT, Nashville: Broadman & Holman, 68–102.

———— (2010d), 'Still Sola Scriptura: An Evangelical View of Scripture', in Michael Bird and Michael W. Pahl (eds.), *The Sacred Text: Excavating the Texts, Exploring the Interpretations, and Engaging the Theologies of the Christian Scriptures*, Piscataway: Gorgias, 215–240.

———— (2011a), 'Be on Guard: The Point of Mark 13, with Some Thoughts on "This Generation"', *For His Renown* <http://jimhamilton.info/2011/06/15/be-on-guard-the-point-of-mark-13-with-some-thoughts-on-this-generation>, accessed 29 Jan. 2014.

———— (2011b), 'Jeremiah 7: Indictment of Unrepentant Israel (with Some Temple Typology)', *For His Renown* <http://jimhamilton.info/2011/11/10/jeremiah-7-indictment-of-unrepentant-israel>, accessed 29 Jan. 2014.

———— (2012a), 'A Biblical Theology of Motherhood', *JDFM* 2.2: 6–13.

———— (2012b), *Revelation: The Spirit Speaks to the Churches*, Preaching the Word, Wheaton: Crossway.

———— (2012c), 'The Typology of David's Rise to Power: Messianic Patterns in the Book of Samuel', *SBJT* 16: 4–25.

———— (2014a), *Ezra and Nehemiah*, Christ-Centered Exposition, Nashville: Broadman & Holman.

———— (2014b), 'Suffering in Revelation: The Fulfillment of the Messianic Woes', *SBJT* 17.4: 34–47.

———— (2014c), *What Is Biblical Theology?* Wheaton: Crossway.

———— (2015, forthcoming), 'That God May Be All in All: The Trinity in 1 Corinthians 15', in Bruce A. Ware and John Starke (eds.), *One God in Three Persons: Unity of Essence, Distinction of Persons, Implications for Life*, Wheaton: Crossway.

Harrington, Daniel (1999), *Invitation to the Apocrypha*, Grand Rapids: Eerdmans.

Hasel, Gerhard F. (1990), 'The Book of Daniel Confirmed by the Dead Sea Scrolls', *JATS* 1: 37–49.

Hays, Richard B. (2005), *The Conversion of the Imagination: Paul as Interpreter of Israel's Scripture*, Grand Rapids: Eerdmans.

Hengel, Martin (1974), *Judaism and Hellenism: Studies in Their Encounter in Palestine During the Early Hellenistic Period*, Philadelphia: Fortress.

The Holy Bible: English Standard Version: The ESV Study Bible (2008), Wheaton: Crossway.

Hossfeld, Frank-Lothar, and Erich Zenger (2005), *Psalms 2: A Commentary on Psalms 51–100*, Hermeneia, Minneapolis: Fortress.

────── (2011), *Psalms 3: A Commentary on Psalms 101–150*, Hermeneia, Minneapolis: Fortress.

House, Paul R. (1998), *Old Testament Theology*, Downers Grove: InterVarsity Press.

Hurtado, Larry W. (2003), *Lord Jesus Christ: Devotion to Jesus in Earliest Christianity*, Grand Rapids: Eerdmans.

Hurtado, Larry W., and Paul L. Owen (eds.) (2011), *'Who Is This Son of Man?': The Latest Scholarship on a Puzzling Expression of the Historical Jesus*, New York: T. & T. Clark.

Jerome (1958), *Jerome's Commentary on Daniel*, tr. Gleason L. Archer, Grand Rapids: Baker.

Josephus (1926), *The Life, Against Apion*, tr. H. St. J. Thackeray, LCL 186, Cambridge, Mass.: Harvard University Press.

────── (2001), *Jewish Antiquities: Books IX–XI*, tr. Ralph Marcus, LCL, Cambridge, Mass.: Harvard University Press.

Juncker, Günther (2001), 'Jesus and the Angel of the Lord: An Old Testament Paradigm for New Testament Christology', PhD diss., Deerfield: Trinity Evangelical Divinity School.

Kim, Seyoon (1985), *'The "Son of Man"' as the Son of God*, Grand Rapids: Eerdmans.

Kruger, Michael J. (2012), *Canon Revisited: Establishing the Origins and Authority of the New Testament Books*, Wheaton: Crossway.

Leithart, Peter J. (2009), *Deep Exegesis: The Mystery of Reading Scripture*, Waco: Baylor University Press.

Lenglet, Ad (1972), 'La Structure Littéraire de Daniel 2–7', *Bib* 53: 169–190.

Longenecker, Richard N. (1999), *Biblical Exegesis in the Apostolic Period*, 2nd ed., Grand Rapids: Eerdmans.

Lövestam, Evald (1995), *Jesus and 'This Generation': A New Testament Study*, tr. Moira Linnarud, ConBOT, Stockholm: Almqvist & Wiksell.

Lucas, Ernest C. (2002), *Daniel*, AOTC, Leicester: Apollos; Downers Grove: InterVarsity Press.

Lust, Johan (2001), 'Cult and Sacrifice in Daniel: The Tamid and the Abomination of Desolation', in John J. Collins and Peter W. Flint (eds.), *The Book of Daniel: Composition and Reception*, VTSup, Leiden: Brill, 671–688.

Malone, Andrew S. (2012), 'Old Testament Christophanies?', PhD diss., Ridley Melbourne: Australian College of Theology.

Metzger, B. M. (1983), 'The Fourth Book of Ezra', in James H. Charlesworth (ed.), *The Old Testament Pseudepigrapha*, 2 vols., Garden City: Doubleday, 1: 516–559.

Moo, Douglas J. (1996), 'The Case for the Posttribulation Rapture Position', in *Three Views on the Rapture*, Counterpoints, Grand Rapids: Zondervan, 169–211.

Moore, Carey A. (1977), *Daniel, Esther, and Jeremiah: The Additions*, Garden City: Doubleday.

—— (1996), *Tobit: A New Translation with Introduction and Commentary*, AB, New York: Doubleday.

Myers, Jacob M. (1974), *I and II Esdras*, AB, Garden City: Doubleday.

Nickelsburg, George W. E. (1984), 'Stories of Biblical and Early Post-Biblical Times', in Michael E. Stone (ed.), *Jewish Writings of the Second Temple Period: Apocrypha, Pseudepigrapha, Qumran Sectarian Writings, Philo, Josephus*, CRINT, Philadelphia: Fortress, 33–87.

Nickelsburg, George W. E., and James C. VanderKam (tr.) (2004), *1 Enoch: A New Translation*, Philadelphia: Fortress.

Pennington, Jonathan (2009), 'Refractions of Daniel in the Gospel of Matthew', in Craig A. Evans and H. Daniel Zacharias (eds.), *Early Christian Literature and Intertextuality*, New York: T. & T. Clark, 65–86.

Pietersma, Albert, and Benjamin G. Wright (eds.) (2007), *A New English Translation of the Septuagint and the Other Greek Translations Traditionally Included Under That Title*, Oxford: Oxford University Press.

Porter, Paul A. (1983), *Metaphors and Monsters: A Literary-Critical Study of Daniel 7 and 8*, Lund: CWK Gleerup.

Portier-Young, Anathea (2011), *Apocalypse Against Empire: Theologies of Resistance in Early Judaism*, Grand Rapids: Eerdmans.

Reynolds, Benjamin E. (2011), 'The Use of the Son of Man Idiom in the Gospel of John', in Larry W. Hurtado and Paul L. Owen (eds.), *'Who Is This Son of Man?': The Latest Scholarship on a Puzzling Expression of the Historical Jesus*, New York: T. & T. Clark, 101–129.

Ribbens, Benjamin J. (2011), 'Typology of Types: Typology in Dialogue', *JTI* 51: 81–96.

Rowland, Christopher (1982), *The Open Heaven: A Study of Apocalyptic in Judaism and Early Christianity*, New York: Crossroad.

Scheetz, Jordan M. (2011), *The Concept of Canonical Intertextuality and the Book of Daniel*, Eugene: Pickwick.

Schreiner, Thomas R. (2008), *New Testament Theology: Magnifying God in Christ*, Grand Rapids: Baker; Nottingham: Apollos.

—— (2013), *The King in His Beauty: A Biblical Theology of the Old and New Testaments*, Grand Rapids: Baker.

Schürer, Emil (1973), *The History of the Jewish People in the Age of Jesus Christ (175 B.C.–A.D. 135)*, ed. Geza Vermes, Fergus Millar and Matthew Black, 4 vols., Edinburgh: T. & T. Clark.

Seitz, Christopher (2008), 'Canon, Narrative, and the Old Testament's Literal Sense: A Response to John Goldingay, "Canon and Old Testament Theology"', *TynB* 59: 27–34.

Shelton, W. Brian (2008), *Martyrdom from Exegesis in Hippolytus: An Early Church Presbyter's Commentary on Daniel*, SCHT, Colorado Springs: Paternoster.

Silva, Moisés (1996), 'Has the Church Misread the Bible? The History of Interpretation in the Light of Current Issues', in Moisés Silva (ed.), *Foundations of Contemporary Interpretation*, Grand Rapids: Zondervan, 11–90.

Sims, James H. (1995), *A Comparative Literary Study of Daniel and Revelation: Shaping the End*, Lewiston: Mellen.

Spangenberg, Izak J. J. (2006), 'The Septuagint Translation of Daniel 9: Does It Reflect a Messianic Interpretation?', in Michael A. Knibb (ed.), *The Septuagint and Messianism*, BETL, Leuven: Peeters, 431–442.

Steinmann, Andrew E. (2008), *Daniel*, CC, St. Louis: Concordia.

Stone, Michael E. (1984), 'Apocalyptic Literature', in Michael E. Stone (ed.), *Jewish Writings of the Second Temple Period: Apocrypha, Pseudepigrapha, Qumran Sectarian Writings, Philo, Josephus*, CRINT, Philadelphia: Fortress, 383–441.

——— (1990), *Fourth Ezra: A Commentary on the Book of Fourth Ezra*, Hermeneia, Minneapolis: Fortress.

Tcherikover, Victor (1959), *Hellenistic Civilization and the Jews*, tr. S. Applebaum, Philadelphia: Jewish Publication Society of America.

Ulrich, Eugene (2001), 'The Text of Daniel in the Qumran Scrolls', in John J. Collins and Peter W. Flint (eds.), *The Book of Daniel: Composition and Reception*, VTSup, Leiden: Brill, 573–585.

VanderKam, James C., and Peter W. Flint (2002), *The Meaning of the Dead Sea Scrolls: Their Significance for Understanding the Bible, Judaism, Jesus, and Christianity*, San Francisco: HarperSanFrancisco.

Vickers, Brian (2013), *Justification by Grace Through Faith: Finding Freedom from Legalism, Lawlessness, Pride, and Despair*, Phillipsburg: P. & R.

Wacholder, Ben Zion (1975), 'Chronomessianism: The Timing of Messianic Movements and the Calendar of Sabbatical Cycles', *HUCA* 46: 201–218.

Waltke, Bruce K. (1976), 'The Date of the Book of Daniel', *BSac* 133: 319–329.

Washburn, David (2002), *A Catalog of Biblical Passages in the Dead Sea Scrolls*, Atlanta: Society of Biblical Literature.

Wenham, Gordon J. (1994), 'Sanctuary Symbolism in the Garden of Eden Story', in Richard Hess and David Toshio Tsumara (eds.), *I Studied Inscriptions from Before the Flood: Ancient Near Eastern, Literary, and Linguistic Approaches to Genesis 1–11*, Winona Lake: Eisenbrauns, 399–404.

——— (2012), *Psalms as Torah: Reading Biblical Song Ethically*, Grand Rapids: Baker.

——— (2013), *The Psalter Reclaimed: Praying and Praising with the Psalms*, Wheaton: Crossway.

Wesselius, Jan-Wim (2001), 'The Writing of Daniel', in John J. Collins and Peter W. Flint (eds.), *The Book of Daniel: Composition and Reception*, VTSup, Leiden: Brill, 291–310.

——— (2005), 'The Literary Nature of the Book of Daniel and the Linguistic Character of Its Aramaic', *Aram* 3: 241–283.

Wills, Lawrence M. (1990), *The Jew in the Court of the Foreign King: Ancient Jewish Court Legends*, HDR, Minneapolis: Fortress.

Wright, N. T. (1992), *The New Testament and the People of God* (Christian Origins and the Question of God, vol. 1), London: SPCK; Minneapolis: Fortress.

——— (2003), *The Resurrection of the Son of God* (Christian Origins and the Question of God, vol. 3), London: SPCK; Minneapolis: Fortress.

Index of authors

Index of Scripture references

Index of ancient sources